THE URBAN EXPERIENCE

CLAUDE S. FISCHER

University of California, Berkeley

Under the General Editorship of
ROBERT K. MERTON
Columbia University

HARCOURT BRACE JOVANOVICH, INC.

NEW YORK   CHICAGO   SAN FRANCISCO   ATLANTA

To Annie

ISBN: 0-15-593497-X

Library of Congress Catalog Card Number: 76-2319

Printed in the United States of America

ACKNOWLEDGMENTS: The author is grateful to The University of Chicago Press for permission to reprint several passages from "Urbanism as a Way of Life" by Louis Wirth and to Harcourt Brace Jovanovich, Inc. for permission to reprint two passages from *Chicago Poems* by Carl Sandburg.

PHOTO CREDITS: cover photo, Howard Sochurek; chapter 1, Frank Wing/ Stock, Boston; chapter 2, David A. Krathwohl/Stock, Boston; chapter 3, Klaus D. Francke/Peter Arnold Photo Archives; chapter 4, George Malave/ Stock, Boston; chapter 5, Irene Fertik; chapter 6, Arthur Tress/Photo Researchers; chapter 7, Klaus D. Francke/Peter Arnold Photo Archives; chapter 8, Marion Bernstein; chapter 9, James Carroll/Editorial Photo Archives; chapter 10, Irene Fertik

PREFACE

The purpose of this book is to summarize our knowledge of the social and psychological consequences of urban life. Does living in a densely populated community rather than in a small town or village cause any differences in a person's social relationships, psychological state, or life experience? If so, what are the differences and how can they be explained? Speculation about these questions has abounded as long as cities have existed—more than 5,000 years—and will continue to flourish as long as cities continue to exist. But it is only recently, especially in the last two decades, that the social sciences have accumulated enough facts about urban life to permit an informed stock-taking.

The Urban Experience examines many areas of urban life: Chapters 1 and 2 are devoted to the historical background of cities and the three main sociological theories of urbanism that are the foundation of the subsequent discussion; Chapters 3 and 4 consider the physical and social settings of urban life and their impact on the city dweller; Chapters 5 and 6 discuss the nature of such social groups as the neighborhood and the family in the urban environment; Chapters 7 and 8 deal with the psychology of urban individuals and their typical styles of belief and behavior; Chapter 9 examines the *sub*urban experience; and Chapter 10 summarizes and draws conclusions, indulges in speculations about the urban future, and sets out the moral of the story.

The presentation is organized around a confrontation between three different theories of urban life: first, the most popular theory—that urbanism weakens social cohesion, subjects city dwellers to stress, and culminates in alienation and disorder; then, the opposing theory—that urbanism has little impact on social groups and individuals, certainly far less than the effects of social class, age, and ethnicity; and, finally, a theory that synthesizes these two views, arguing that urbanism does not debilitate social groups, but, instead, that it helps to create them. The predictions of these three theories are evaluated against our best estimate of the facts, across many realms of social life.

This book is intended primarily for students of urban life —most specifically of urban sociology, but also for students of psychology, economics, political science, and urban anthropology. And the topics discussed are certainly of interest to students of urban design, urban architecture, and urban planning. The book presupposes no sociological training; thus the discussion has been kept simple, with little or no intricate analysis, and a conscientious attempt has been made to explain the significance of what might seem to be academic obsessions—for example, the importance of analyzing definitions. But my hope is that the book will also interest professionals in the social sciences and urban studies who are seeking a comprehensive review and analysis of the field. Primarily for them, the notes at the end of the text provide extensive references and some extended discussions of complex or technical issues. For both students and professionals, the result, I hope, is an easily read but also fully documented text.

The Urban Experience began in the form of lectures to a few hundred undergraduates at the University of California, Berkeley. Their responses, positive and negative, have improved it for those who follow them. Discussions with graduate students who have worked with me—especially Mark Baldassare, Kathleen Gerson, Robert Jackson, Lynne Jones, and Ann Stueve—contributed to several of the analyses. Melvin M. Webber lent encouragement and the support of the Institute of Urban and Regional Development at Berkeley. Ann Swidler provided key sociological ideas and strong moral support. Gerald Suttles' comments on the initial draft gave helpful direction in the writing. Charles Tilly's many specific suggestions on various drafts were invariably insightful and markedly improved the book. And Robert K. Merton more than lived up to his fame as a dedicated and peerless editor; working with him has been an altogether edifying experience.

At Harcourt Brace Jovanovich, Judith Greissman managed this production with great expertise, energy, and good cheer. Natalie Bowen saved me from myself with her patient editing. Jeremiah Lighter provided the crisp design. Sally B. Bregman saw the manuscript into print. Lynda Gordon found the photographs that open the chapters. The entire HBJ team provided a lesson in professionalism.

C. S. F.

CONTENTS

THE URBAN EXPERIENCE

1

INTRODUCTION
AN OVERVIEW

For centuries millions of people have left their hamlets and villages to seek a new life in cities. Each of them—a midwestern farm boy toting a shabby valise through the streets of Chicago, a displaced peasant building his shanty on a steep hillside overlooking Rio de Janeiro, or a free-spirited girl in West Africa catching a ride on a mammy-wagon to Accra—must have wondered: What will life be like in the city? What will the city do to me? What sort of person will I become?

This book is about such questions. It deals with the social psychology of urban life—the experiences of people living in cities; how their social relationships are influenced by the urban scene; and the consequences to their selves and personalities of being city dwellers.

The topic of the effects of urban living has generated a large and ancient body of popular opinion and scholarly speculation. The dominant school of thought holds that residing in cities, in and of itself, tends to alter people's mental and social lives, largely for the worse. An opposed theory, favored more by social scientists than by the general public, holds that city life does not have such effects. To the extent that they exist, the contrasts between ways of life in city and country result from the types of groups who choose to live in either place, not from the urban or rural environments themselves. One objective of this book is to pit these two arguments against each other, and to draw out a third theory —one that results from the clash of ideas and facts in the first two. This third theory turns out to be a synthesis of seemingly opposed ideas. It emphasizes the differences between the kinds of social groups found in the city and the countryside, but goes on to argue that the urbanism of the community— essentially, its population size—does have significant consequences for the character of those groups.

A larger purpose of this book is to present and integrate current scientific knowledge about the consequences of urban life to the individual. What does the intensive research of the last decade or two teach us about what cities do to people? Just as important, what do we *not* know? This book provides both a review of our knowledge and a specification of our ignorance about the experience of living in cities.

The subject of urban social psychology is familiar and inevitably important to everyone concerned with urban problems, whether the problems are those currently plaguing the central cities of modern nations or the crises accompanying rapid urbanization in the less developed countries. How many of these difficulties, observers have often wondered, result from urbanism itself? Does population concentration per se disrupt "natural" ways of life? Although these questions have often been raised, they have rarely been answered with more than guesses and anecdotes. Within the limitations of contemporary social science, this book is intended to provide more substantial answers.

Cities and the Human Experience

The crises of the contemporary city are distractingly dramatic, but they should not deter us from viewing the urban experience within a historical context. For millennia, people have had to make personal adjustments to city life. It has been about 5,500 years, according to most estimates, since the first cities arose in Mesopotamia, followed later by similar developments in the Nile, Indus, and Yellow River valleys; around the Mediterranean Sea; in West Africa, Central America, and the Andes. From those earliest urban centers—cities which rarely housed more than 30,000 souls—to metropolises of the modern day, urban civilizations have risen and fallen, but cities and ideas about city life have endured as part of the human experience.

In human terms, some six millennia is a very long time. But from the perspective of natural history, our experience with cities is still short and slight. Our species has lived in permanent settlements of any kind for only the last two percent of its history (about 10,000 years), and the urban era covers only about half of that. Relatively few people have shared in the urban experience until the recent past. Most societies have been totally rural; those that were urbanized at all only occasionally had cities exceeding 30,000 in size, and rarely had any that reached 100,000 (the population of Duluth, Minnesota, in 1970). Even in great ancient civilizations less than ten percent of the populace actually lived within the capital city.

The great urbanization of *homo sapiens* occurred almost yesterday. Demographer Kingsley Davis has estimated that as late as 1850 only two percent of the world's population lived in cities of more than 100,000 persons. But, today, 24 percent do. And the pace of urban growth is accelerating, so that by the end of the century perhaps 40 percent of all people will live in such large cities (Davis, 1955; 1966; 1972). Our urban experience in the last three to five generations, then, is much more intense than in any preceding time.[1]

It is this "urban revolution" which makes the study of the social consequences of city living imperative. From wandering hunters and gatherers, human beings have "suddenly" become city-dwellers. Some writers and theorists worry that the human organism cannot adjust from its original nomadic makeup to that of an urban office-worker. Popular books have argued that cities are unnatural (one author calls them "human zoos") and that their crowding breeds pathological symptoms and behaviors.[2] Of more serious concern is the possibility that human cultures may be slow to adapt because their fundamental values and beliefs were formed during pastoral eras. To what extent, for example, might our picture of the ideal childhood—lived in a small town or on a farm, complete with dog and friendly neighbors—interfere with successfully raising children in a large city? For these reasons, it is both timely and important to take stock of the social psychology of urban life.

It is important for other reasons. For sociologists, it is important because to understand the consequences of urbanism is to gain insights into the general development of modern society. Urbanization has been highly significant in modernization, and the two processes, different as they are, contain parallel features, most especially in the matter of size, or scale (see Fischer, 1975a). Cities compared with villages, and modern societies compared with primitive tribes are immensely large. What happens to social order and to individual psyches with such increases in scale is a question of widespread concern. For all students of communities, the subject is important because the urban dimension is a major one on which communities vary. No single settlement can be understood unless it is put within the context of the entire range of settlements (see Reiss, 1959a; Arensberg, 1965). Other interests also lead directly to an interest in the urban experience. Examples are the currently popular studies of the interaction of people and environment, the professional task of planning new communities, and the concern many citizens have about urban problems.

But better than any of these "good" reasons for studying the social psychology of living in cities is our own curiosity about ourselves. Does urban life alter the way we think and act? If so, how? For better or for worse? And what is the explanation of those alterations?

The Plan of This Book

This section briefly explains the strategic decisions I have made in studying the urban experience, since these form the basis of my approach in this book.

The very use of the word "experience" in the title reflects·
an important decision. In truth, there are many urban experiences, as many as there are urban individuals, for no two
lives are identical. A millionaire being driven down Park Avenue in his limousine and a junkie huddling in a burnt-out
tenement in the South Bronx are both New Yorkers, yet their
experiences are scarcely the same. Nevertheless, as we shall
see, there are similarities even between such seeming oppo-
sites, because of the significant similarities in the individual
experiences urban people have and the ways they react to
them. The social-science procedure for uncovering such similarities is to collect "objective" indicators of people's experiences, using techniques that are sufficiently reliable and valid
for different investigators to arrive independently at the same
conclusions.

In following this approach, I have adopted a behavioral
orientation. This assumes that the nature of people's experiences manifests itself in their behavior, including style of
daily life, interactions with associates, and, for that matter,
responses to social-science instruments (for example, answers to survey questions about moods and feelings). I have
placed much less reliance on personal accounts or unsystem-
atic observation (such as journalistic reports and anecdotes). Such material often provides fascinating illustrations
and worthy leads to further research, but it does not in itself
constitute firm evidence.

The word "urban" in the title of this book also requires
some comment. The obviously related terms "urban" and
"urbanism" both refer to the population size of a community
(that is, a place of settlement); the greater the number of
people residing in a place, the more urban it is and the more
urban are the experiences of its residents. Thus, urbanism is
a *continuum,* a matter of degree (Wirth, 1956). I will often use
the contrasting terms "urban" and "rural," or "city" and
"countryside," but I do not imply any sharp dichotomy by
their use. Such labels are generally used to refer in simple
terms to the relationship between a phenomenon and the
degree of urbanism. For example, the statement "there is
more crime in the city than the countryside" translates into:
"rates of crime increase with increases in community size."[3]

These definitions turn a study of the urban experience

into an inquiry as to whether and how the size of the community in which people live affects their ways of life and
personalities, as those effects are manifested behaviorally
and measured scientifically. The method of inquiry involves
the collection of research reports comparing residents of communities with varying degrees of urbanism on many social-
psychological dimensions: their attitudes, styles of interaction, relationships with friends and relatives, types of deviant
behavior, and so on. My aim is to survey all the important
kinds of social-psychological phenomena, and to establish
their correlation with each kind of urbanism. More ambitious
still, I hope to explain the correlations uncovered by the survey of research evidence.

The strategy of *comparing* communities and persons of
varying degrees of urbanism requires emphasis. Both the
popular and sociological literature often describe some condition within a single urban setting and label it "urban,"
thereby hinting that its urban character caused the condition.
This, of course, is not logically sound. An event or situation
cannot be explained by its so-called urban nature unless it
has been systematically compared with similar events in
places that are more urban and places that are less urban
(see also Wirth, 1956).

As unremarkably simple as this principle is, it is more
often breached than observed. When we read passages such
as the following (which will reappear in the Chapter 6 discussion of friendship), "the awful fact is that modern urban
society, as a whole, has found no way of sustaining intimate
contacts" (Alexander, 1967:243), we must ask the following
questions: Does the author mean to say that this sad condition is not true of modern *rural* society? If so, is he suggesting
that urbanism itself—that is, population size—is the *cause* of
the "awful fact"? If so, has he actually *compared* urban and
rural places with respect to the relative intimacy of the social
ties of their inhabitants? And has his comparison resulted in
evidence that is more objective than his personal impressions? These are the burdens that the comparative method
places on assertions about urban matters. (In this example
the answers to the questions would seem to be yes, yes, no,
and no.)

In comparing urban and rural places and persons, we

should not expect to uncover many large or dramatic social psychological differences. Substantial variations in personality and social relationships are related to the more intimate attributes of individuals: physical constitution, sex, age, education, and so on. It is unlikely, for example, that urban-rural differences in feelings of despair would be greater than differences in such feelings between rich and poor, black and white, or young and old. Compared to factors like these, community size forms only a general, crude, and distant context for people. That is why the contrasts between urban and rural persons are generally modest ones—far too modest to be the total explanation of social psychological variations, but still meaningful enough to help us understand urbanism as a social-psychological variable.

Having established what urban-rural differences exist— or do not exist, as the particular case may be—we must then explain them. If, to pursue the earlier examples, the farm boy newly arrived in Chicago is (on the average) more traditional and less intellectual than the city boys he meets there, or if the young woman from the African bush is friendlier but less clever than the market women she encounters in Accra, how are these differences to be accounted for? Again, one important school of thought holds that there is something intrinsic to cities which alters people—living amidst many other people has serious consequences. Another view is that differences between urban and rural individuals can be largely explained by the personal backgrounds of the people being compared—their age, ethnic heritage, job, and so on—and not by the fact that they live in the city or the countryside. In the next chapter, I will set out in detail the major theoretical approaches to this issue, and I will then refer to them throughout the book.

In pursuing the theoretical controversy, I return repeatedly to the question whether behavior and attitudes associated with urbanism result from the urbanism itself. Does the population size per se of a community, all else equal, create unique experiences and ways of life? Put another way, would moving people from small communities to large ones, and that alone, change their personalities and life styles?[4] Where it is possible to answer this question, it will be through two general techniques. One technique is to examine characteristics of cities in different societies and historical eras. This enables the investigator to study instances in which cities exist but in which factors inevitably associated with them in modern society (mass media and industrialization, for example) do not. If certain experiences are found to be common to the people in these various cities, it is at least possible to assert that they result from population size itself. A second technique involves statistical analyses of data on communities and their residents, in which the statistical tools permit us to control complicating factors, and thereby to simulate a situation in which everything except the population size of the communities is held constant.[5] The following chapters draw upon a large number of studies employing such procedures.

Maintaining a Perspective

The aim of this book, to understand the social psychology of urban life across the entire range of human experience, is unabashedly vast, but its actual scope is more modest because of the limitations of contemporary social science and of the author. I will therefore deal mainly with urbanism in the twentieth century, and that largely in the United States.[6] This constraint upon the available empirical data need not, however, stunt our imagination or foreshorten our perspective. Throughout the book we must bear in mind that many specific features of contemporary cities casually assumed to be inherent to urban life are actually quite different in the cities of other nations and eras. This relativistic perspective not only permits greater accuracy in our understanding, but also places in bold relief those aspects of the urban experience that consistently occur across space and time.

An immense variety of cities exist and have existed, including pre-colonial settlements in West Africa built of grass houses; a city like Aztec Teotihuacan, with its boulevards carefully laid out in geometric patterns; ancient cities in Mesopotamia, with their clay houses built upon the remains of earlier civilizations; and so on up to modern Los Angeles, virtually a country of its own, living on freeways and in backyards. This diversity can hardly be encompassed in a short space, so I shall focus only on the contrast between contemporary American cities and the sort of city—for example, Damascus or Cairo—that existed in the Mediterranean area during the Middle Ages (see Lapidus, 1966; Abu-Lughod, 1971).

The first and most dramatic contrast between these cities is size—size of area and of population. A feudal city such as Damascus could be easily strolled from one side to another in a morning, while the larger metropolises of our period can barely be driven across in the same time. The populations of all but a few of the greatest medieval cities could be dropped into our modern urban centers and make scarcely a ripple. The Los Angeles metropolis was in 1970 over 150 times greater in area and about 14 times greater in population than Cairo at its most glorious around 1500. Yet each was the most urban place of its own time and region, and thus equally a subject for our study.

The streets of modern cities are virtually uniform: two or four lanes of asphalt belong to automobiles, with a border on each side of a yard or two of pavement conceded to pedestrians. The ambiance of the average noncommercial street in a modern metropolis tends to be rather peaceful. There may be a low city hum in the background, punctuated by an occasional baby's cry or motorcycle roar. In some neighborhoods, particularly suburban ones, a pedestrian may be only an occasional sight.

Vastly different were the streets of feudal cities such as Damascus or Cairo. Those streets were (and many still are) very narrow, unpaved or at best laid with stones, often scarcely wide enough for a cart, hemmed in and loomed over by overarching and unstable buildings, cluttered with stalls and benches, and usually following some rambling path understandable only by a long-deceased goat. Most of the city's social life—and much more—was packed into the streets. It was as if the urban institutions of today had emptied their contents into dark and narrow alleys—the hospitals their ill and lame; the schools their teachers and pupils; the prisons their inmates and guards; the stores their merchants, customers, and goods. As if the nursing homes had deposited their charges to beg in the streets, the laundries did their work at public wells, the animals had escaped from the zoos, and sewers ran through the middle of it all. It was a kaleidoscope to the eye, a stench to the nose, and a din to the ear.

Even as late as 1896, a doctor in New York City could complain of

> the useless postman's whistle, the shouting pedlars and hucksters, the yelling "rags and bottles" man, the horn-blowing scissor-grinder and four-in-hand driver, with scores of other noise-makers too numerous to mention, who keep up a continuous din of distracting, nerve-wracking sounds in our residential streets . . . (Girdner, 1896).

In medieval cities, at least, these noises would die down at night, as would everything else. There was little to do and little light by which to do it. Adequate street lighting did not reach London until 1736 (George, 1964: 101), whereas most cities had to suffer much longer with a darkness broken only by an occasional smoky taper. In fact, in the dark of the night, many of these cities were completely shut down, and the gates to their various quarters locked. "Bright lights" indeed!

Anxiety over violent crime pervades modern American city life, yet the contemporary crime problem is far less serious than that of many earlier periods in urban history. For instance, fourteenth-century Damascus was "a world where no man was truly safe except among his kin," and in eighteenth-century Victorian London, certain quarters were openly ruled by criminal gangs (Lapidus, 1966: 85; Tobias, 1972).

The economic activities that support urban populations also vary greatly from era to era and city to city. There are commonalities, of course: administration, specialized crafts, the arts, and supportive services. But the emphases differ. Ancient Peking, for example, was organized around a national bureaucracy. European feudal cities were largely commercial centers facilitating long-distance trade, while some large communities in West Africa were based on agriculture. The cities with which we are most familiar subsisted first on industry and trade, and now subsist increasingly on communications and organizational services.

The social use of urban land is vastly different in modern American cities from what it was through the greater part of urban history. We casually assume that most employed persons work in a district devoted to business and reside in a different and perhaps quite distant neighborhood, commuting regularly between the two places; that they choose their residences largely on the criteria of space, convenience, and cost; that who their neighbors are is determined by who can afford and wishes to live there (with certain exceptions because of practices like racial discrimination). In most of the cities people have built and for most of the time people have resided in them, all this was not so. People lived in or right next to the places where they worked (and virtually everyone except toddlers worked). People lived in neighborhoods partly on the basis of their general class—the rich at the center, the poor pressed against the walls—and, more specifically, on the basis of their occupations, with streets set aside for silversmiths, potters, and so forth; foreigners and ethnic and religious minorities were strictly segregated in special quarters. These "ghettos" were often more than just a result of taste or custom; in many cases they were a matter of law, enforced by walls and gates padlocked at sunset.

These comments barely suggest the great diversity among cities of the past and present world. The American metropolis is distinct in many ways from most of these other cases of urbanism. We have considered size, physical layout, street activity, safety, economic enterprise, and residential segregation, but the full list is much greater. To repeat, the social psychology of urban life presented in this book is, by necessity, largely based on modern American urban life. When evidence at hand makes it possible, the analysis will be extended to cover other urban places, whether ancient Athens, medieval Damascus, or modern Accra. But, again to repeat: Throughout the book, it is important to maintain a cross-cultural and historical perspective that places contemporary facts within the context of the greater urban experience.[7]

2
IMAGES OF CITY LIFE
POPULAR VIEWS AND
SOCIOLOGICAL THEORIES

"Cities are viewed as the seed of corruption and duplicity,
and New York is the biggest City."
Senator Joseph Biden, explaining the resistance of the
U.S. Congress to a request for financial assistance
from New York City.

—*The New York Times*, May 25, 1975

Public opinion about the nature of urban life has practical
consequences. It motivates people to choose or avoid cities,
suggests how visitors and migrants should act in cities, and
fuels political battles between urban and rural interests. It
also has consequences for the study of urbanism. On the one
side, social scientists, just like other members of their society,
are not immune to misleading stereotypes about the city or
countryside; on the other, stereotypes may have the prover-
bial germ of truth to them. Both possibilities must be considered in the sociological study of city life.

Urbanism in Western Culture

Citizens of the Western world are heirs to millennia of legend,
literature, and art focused on cities and city life-styles. The
messages conveyed by those cultural expressions have not
always been consistent or uniform, but the themes that repeat themselves are largely negative ones.

The Bible is representative. The image of the sacred city
appears, of course—Jerusalem, City of Peace, is the residence of God—but it is the image of the sinful city that
predominates. Sodom and Gomorrah, heretical and vice-rid-
den, rather than Jerusalem, are the dominant symbols of the
city. Virtue and justice are distinctly pastoral. The ancient
classical cultures adopted similar themes. In spite of having

15

founded the fabled "polis" in the relatively small city-state of Athens, the Greeks saw country life as altogether more wholesome and virtuous than urban life, and, in any event, they feared large cities (Baroja, 1963). Roman philosophers and poets expressed similar motifs. The poet Juvenal, for example, complained that there was "no place in the city . . . for an honest man," that Rome was run by the moneyed and ill bred, that it produced ulcers and insomnia, and that it subjected the unfortunate resident to larcenous landlords and brash burglars (Juvenal, 1958).[1]

More recent times have seen little change in these descriptions of urban life. Great writers in Europe since the Renaissance have shown some ambivalence; they often depict the city as the site of civilization, literacy, and the arts, in contrast to the "savagery" and "idiocy" of peasant life. Nevertheless, the prevalent image is of the city as the mise en scène of vice and human degradation. The novels of Balzac and Dickens are characteristic examples. Romantic philosophers, such as Rousseau, were also in accord, emphasizing the greater nobility and virtue of rural man (Schorske, 1963; Howe, 1971).

The new American culture of the eighteenth and nineteenth centuries also adopted the negative themes of urban life while underplaying the positive motif of "civilization" found in European thought. Combined with the heroic figure of the frontiersman, these themes gave American thought and letters a powerful antiurban bite. "I view great American cities," wrote Thomas Jefferson, "as pestilential to the morals, health, and the liberties of man," and he saw a then raging yellow-fever epidemic as a potential blessing if it would only reduce the size of the cities. Political figures from Andrew Jackson, Abraham Lincoln, and William Jennings Bryan to recent presidential candidates have often founded claims of virtue on their rural origins. At the other end of the scale, cities have been specifically associated with the "shame" of political machines, the danger of immigrant hordes, and, in its time, the triple threat of "Rum, Romanism, and Rebellion" (see White and White, 1962; Rourke, 1964).

American literature also presents a dominantly negative opinion of city life. "Cities," wrote Emerson, "make men talkative and entertaining, but they make them artificial." And his friend Thoreau went off to Walden Pond to rediscover his soul. Of course, there have been exceptions and qualifications to such attacks on city life. Carl Sandburg, for example, even as he admits to Chicago, "Hog Butcher for the World," that "They tell me you are wicked and I believe them, for I have seen your painted women under the gas lamps luring the farm boys," extols its power and vitality:

> Laughing the stormy, husky, brawling laughter of Youth, half-naked, sweating, proud to be Hog Butcher, Tool Maker, Stacker of Wheat, Player with Railroads and Freight Handler to the Nation (Sandburg, 1960).

Even so, the major motif in American letters was and remains antiurban (see Walker, 1962).

Today's America carries on this tradition, as reflected, for example, in its popular songs, in which for every urban thrill there are many more urban laments and rural yearnings. Science fiction, the distinctive form of prophecy and parable of our time, is replete with plots about a future in which heroes struggle to escape from mammoth, sterile, and dehumanizing cities to the salvation of the countryside (see, for example, Elwood, 1974). Modern American society, like an earlier America, sees urban life as mainly evil.

Of all the urban exemplars, perhaps the most mighty is New York City. The prolific traveler John Gunther described it as ". . . the incomparable, the brilliant star city of cities, . . . a law unto itself, the Cyclopean paradox, the inferno with no out-of-bounds, the supreme expression of both the miseries and splendors of contemporary civilization . . ." (Strauss, 1961: 28). This, of course, is hyperbole; but if the reality of New York does not conform to such hyperbole, the *idea* of New York does. As suggested by the remark of Senator Biden quoted earlier, New York is, in the public mind, the quintessence of "the City." The varied aspects of that idea form a montage of mixed and clashing elements, yet each is electric in itself: New York as the place of senseless, brutal crime; of personal freedom and boundless hopes; of variety, choice, excitement; of callous and uncaring people; of social groups diverse enough to satisfy each individual's unique needs; of crass and crushing materialism; of experiment, innovation, and creativity; of anxious days and frightful nights. New York, concluded British author Anthony Burgess after sojourning there, is "the big growling human condition, complete with baroque music and 50 varieties of sour cream" (A. Burgess, 1972: 39).[2]

From this welter of imagery of the city it is possible to extract a set of organizing motifs, of basic themes.[3] Four, expressed as polarities, suggest themselves: 1) nature versus art; 2) familiarity versus strangeness; 3) community versus individualism; 4) tradition versus change. Each pair presents a characteristic that is associated in Western culture with rural life and the opposite of that characteristic, associated with urban life. The tension in these pairs derives from the fact that neither half is universally regarded as "better" or "worse" than the other. Instead, they pose dilemmas of personal choice. Depending on which horn of the dilemma they have grasped, philosophers and poets have become either pro-urbanists or (as is usually the case) anti-urbanists.

Nature versus Art

The city is art, artifact, a construction of man. To inhabit it is to live in an "artificial" environment, albeit an artistic and intellectual one. Rural life is "natural," closer to nature, "organic." Among the subthemes derived from this theme are instinct versus rationality; body versus mind; outdoors versus indoors; frankness versus guile; crudity versus sophistication. A major element in this motif is the idea of "civilization." It is associated with the city, but in potentially contrary ways. Civilization can mean great sculpture, painting, literature— and the building of a school over a former swamp. It can also mean the imposition of social regulation over natural will, the binding stiff collar of propriety—and the construction of a fast-food outlet where an orange grove once grew. A correlative subtheme is that of chaos versus order, as symbolized by the winding country path contrasted to the grids of city streets (Thrupp, 1963). These all form part of the general polarity between rural nature and urban art, one of the thematic tensions in Western thought on urbanism.

Familiarity versus Strangeness

The countryside is associated with familiar things and familiar persons, with "home"; the city is new, different, full of unexpected things and often incomprehensible people. This theme also has its correlatives. One is the notion of "the stranger." The city is composed of strange people in a specific sense: from the perspective of any particular individual, many persons in the city will look, talk, and act in odd, outlandish ways. Concern over such strangeness expresses itself in xenophobic anxieties about "outlanders," in particular, foreign immigrants clustering in large cities. It can also be celebrated as a source of cultural diversity. E. B. White once wrote: "The city is like poetry: it compresses all life, all races and breeds, into a small island and adds music and the accompaniment of internal engines" (White, 1949: 229; see Lofland, 1973). Another aspect of the theme concerns the variety of opportunities provided by the city—activities, sights, and people to meet. Seen by many as a blessing, it is seen by others as temptation: "The city has many attractions/But think of the vices and sins/When once in the vortex of fashion/ How soon the course downward begins" (Alden, 1887: 34). In modern days, the moral term "temptation" has been replaced by psychologically tinged ones like "complexity" and "rat-race." The essential meaning is the same: the opportunities provided by the city can entrap. Third, there is the subtheme of "excitement." The city provides thrilling sights, sounds, and adventures; the country is routine and deadly dull. But from another perspective, rural life is humanely paced while urban life is garish, overwhelming, and frenetic.

Community versus Individualism

A major concern in much of Western social thought is the tension between "community," in the sense of intimate and enveloping social groups, and "individualism" in the sense of freedom from social shackles. In its pro-rural form, the motif presents country dwellers as happily ensconced in warm, humanly rich and supportive social relationships: the family, neighborhood, town. But in this imagery, city dwellers are strangers to all, including themselves. They are lonely, not emotionally touching or being touched by others, and consequently set psychically adrift. This theme has deeply concerned American writers. A student of urban literature notes: "City fiction has portrayed man searching for a complete self

in an urban world where personal integration or completeness seems to have become impossible. . . . The characters in
urban fiction typically feel that they are strangers moving in
an alien world" (Gelfant, 1954: 23). In its pro-urban form, the
motif presents the country dweller as stifled by conventionality, repressed by the intrusion and social control of narrow-
minded kin, neighbors, and townsmen, while the city resident
is free—free to develop individual abilities, express personal
styles, and satisfy private needs. From both perspectives,
community is identified with rural life, and individualism with
urban life.

Tradition versus Change

The countryside is the treasury of fundamental values and
traditional ways of life, of morality, religion, neighborliness,
and patriotism. The city is where the challenging, the un-
tested, the tradition-shattering, and the deviant flourish. From
the pro-rural perspective, the city is a "den of iniquity," the
breeding ground for sin—dishonesty, blasphemy, venality,
and every sort of crime. From the pro-urban perspective, this
theme involves innovation and creativity: the city produces
original ideas, startling inventions, and modern styles of
dress, behavior, and thought.

These four themes appear throughout Western cultural
expressions about urban in contrast to rural life. In capsule
form, they summarize prevailing ambivalence toward the
city. Each pair can be interpreted in favor of the city, and the
choice made accordingly: for art, excitement, freedom, and
progress. But each can also be interpreted the opposite way:
with the city to be avoided as contrived, grotesque, lonely,
and disturbed. Both interpretations are of the same image;
the difference is in the attitude of the interpreter. By and
large, Western culture—particularly American culture—has
made its assessments *against* the city. Accurate or not, that is
the intellectual heritage bequeathed to us all.

Public Opinion

The images and judgments discussed in the preceding section were those of men of letters; in this section, they will be

those of the general public, as expressed in attitude surveys. These polls, while generally good indicators of the opinions of the adult population, are regrettably limited to only fairly recent years and largely to American samples. They nevertheless provide a means of comparing the images and attitudes of urban life as expressed by artists with those of "people in the street."

A sizable number of surveys have asked people to indicate the type of community in which they would ideally prefer to live. The response, at least among Americans, is loud and clear: the smaller the better. Although people tend to prefer the sort of community in which they currently live, when they wish they were elsewhere, that elsewhere is predominantly a smaller place. For example, a Gallup survey conducted in 1972 asked a representative American sample: "If you could live anywhere you wanted to, would you prefer a city, suburban area, small town, or farm?" The answers were:

City	13%
Suburbs	31%
Small towns	32%
Farm	23%

Even among those currently living there, only twenty percent preferred cities (Gallup Opinion Index [G.O.I.], 1973, #94: 31).[4] A 1969 Harris survey found that two-thirds of big-city residents hoped to live elsewhere by 1979 (Harris, 1970). Moreover, the proportion preferring cities has dropped off precipitously since the mid-1960s. In 1966, 22 percent preferred cities; six years later, only 13 percent. Apparently, the real "urban crises" have had their effects in this realm as in many others.

Americans prefer small communities. What of attitudes in other nations? Data are available for only a few, but they suggest that northern Europeans similarly lean toward the rural—at least the British and Dutch do (Mann, 1964; *Polls,* 1967). However, people in other nations appear to be more divided on this topic, perhaps—as with the French, for example—even slightly pro-urban. Figure 1 presents the results of two similar surveys conducted in the United States and France in 1972 and 1970, respectively. The results indicate that, though Americans are relatively urbanized, they yearn

FIGURE 1

ACTUAL VS. PREFERRED COMMUNITY SIZE
IN THE UNITED STATES AND FRANCE

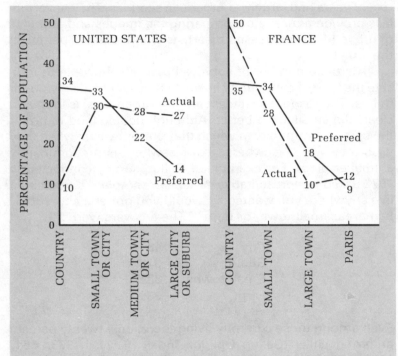

Source (U.S.): Commission on Population Growth (1972), p. 36. The questions asked
were: "Where do you live now?" and "Where would you prefer to live?"

Source (France): Girard et al. (1970), p. 238. The question was: "If you had absolutely
free choice, and were promised the same income in any case, would you prefer to live
in the country, in a town of medium size, in a large town, or in Paris?"

for smaller places, while the French, who are much more
rural, would shift to large and medium-sized cities.[5]

There is little systematic information from the less developed nations of the world on this matter, but rough indications from observations by anthropologists and from popular
sayings and stories are that in those regions the benefits of
city life are viewed as outweighing its drawbacks—"He who
hasn't been to Koumassi [a city of 382,000 in Ghana] won't
go to Paradise" (Hanna and Hanna, 1971: 32–47; Little, 1973).

Ambivalence toward urban life seems to be universal, but the balance of feeling for or against the city differs somewhat from culture to culture. In the United States, the balance swings toward the negative. The attitude shows up not only in residential preferences, but also in evaluations of actual communities. When asked a question such as "Would you say that you are satisfied or dissatisfied with the quality of life in your community?" most Americans respond "satisfied." Consistently, however, the proportion that does so drops off with increments in the size of community. In a 1974 poll, for example, 83 percent of residents in places of under 2,500 responded "satisfied"; but 71 percent of residents in metropolises of over a million did the same (G.O.I., 1974, #110: 12; see also Marans and Rodgers, 1975; Fischer, 1973b).

But this conclusion is only a broad generalization of majority feelings and overlooks minority attitudes. Certain groups of Americans are more pro-urban (or, usually, just less anti-urban) than others. "City-lovers" tend to be more highly educated than most other people, in professional and white-collar occupations or unemployed, quite young or elderly, single or married without children, black, interested in "high culture"—and already living in cities.[6]

Another way of assessing people's preferences is to watch what they do, not listen to what they say. When the investigator examines what people actually do—how they "vote with their feet"—the preceding conclusions differ substantially. Men and women have moved and continue to move overwhelmingly toward urban and especially large urban areas. Throughout recorded history and in all societies, migration has almost always been from countryside to city (Davis, 1966). There are signs that this flow may be currently leveling off in the United States,[7] but it is a pattern throughout our history, even during the urban crises of the 1960s. Why, then, this contrast between ideal and real, between announced desire and actual outcome?

The most important reason is evidently economic. It has been historically true and continues to be dramatically true in most nations that cities provide more and better-paying jobs, and more opportunities for economic advancement than rural areas. In the United States the differences are not as sharp as those in less modern nations, but it is still the case in this country as well that urban residents have slightly higher standards of living, on the average, than people outside the city—the higher cost of living notwithstanding (Alonso and Fajans, 1970; Edel et al., 1975; Hoch, 1972). Furthermore, while some ex-ruralites currently living and working in cities wax nostalgic about the "green, green grass of home," few want to return to the country other than to retire or be buried there (see, for example, Perlman, 1975; Hanna and Hanna, 1971).

These facts about actual behavior in regard to cities need not belie the verbalized attitudes. Instead, the explanation for the one helps to explain the other. Most people (or, at least, most Americans) see residence in cities as a necessary evil—necessary to achieve a desired standard of living, but not desirable in its own right. As long as that is so, they are reluctant urbanites.[8]

There appears to be one escape from the dilemma, and that is the suburb. The suburb has long been seen as a means for achieving the virtues of both country and city, of having the economic and recreational opportunities of urban life together with the land, quiet, and wholesomeness of rural life. The hope has long motivated suburban expansion and for just as long has been part of the sales pitch used by suburban developers (Donaldson, 1969; Warner, 1962; Tarr, 1973). It is explicit, for example, in the bucolic names chosen for suburban developments: Park Forest, Sleepy Hollow, Mountain View. The wish to have the best of both worlds also finds expression in responses to surveys. In one poll, when people expressing a preference for living in rural areas were then asked whether they wanted their rustic home to be far from a medium or large city or near it (within thirty miles), the great majority (74 percent) answered "near" (Fuguitt and Zuiches, 1973). Now, a village or small town within thirty miles of a large city is essentially a suburb. That seems to be what most Americans want, and, indeed, that is where many Americans are continuing to move. Metropolitan areas in the United States grew 16.6 percent in population between 1960 and 1970; virtually all of that growth was in the suburbs (Zimmer, 1975) and the trend continues (Bureau of the Census, 1975).

In summary, soundings of general public opinion echo the voices of the spokesmen for Western (and especially for American) culture: the theme is ambivalently anti-urban. In part, this popular viewpoint reflects concern about the choices examined in the previous section—strangeness, change, and the like. In part, it expresses discontent with other features of urban life, which will be discussed in the next two chapters: noise, pollution, crowds, crime, and so on. Nevertheless, migration to the city continues to be the world-wide norm, mainly because of the economic opportunities it provides. This discrepancy between the yearning for small-town life and the desire for urban advantages creates among many an unfulfilled desire to leave the city; and it creates among many a fulfilled desire for the best of rural and urban, which they see represented by suburbia.

Much like the heritage of our culture, these public attitudes are based partly on certain assumptions about the nature of urban life. One purpose of this book is to test those assumptions. But, well-founded or not, the popular opinions form an inescapable part of the intellectual baggage both reader and author bring to this investigation. They also have a much more important consequence: as we saw in the growth of the suburb, they help determine the very shape of the future metropolis.

Sociological Approaches

Now that we have described cultural values and popular attitudes toward urban life, we begin our inquiry into the nature of the urban experience by considering the theorizing of social scientists about the consequences of urbanism. The purpose of developing such theories before looking at the "real world" is to provide the investigator with a set of concepts needed to organize his or her perceptions of what would otherwise be a bewildering complexity. Properly developed, these concepts focus attention on the most critical features of the "real world." To begin a major study without a good theory or theories is like being dropped into a dark jungle with neither map nor compass.

But before reviewing those theories, we must consider, once again and more exactly, the problem of defining "urban." For it turns out that some of the disagreement and confusion about the nature of the urban experience stems from differences in interpretation of the terms "urban" and "city." Surely, little progress can be made in understanding city life if we do not understand what the word "city" means.[9] The four broad types of definitions are: demographic, institutional, cultural, and behavioral.

Demographic definitions involve essentially the size and density of population (for example, Tisdale, 1942). In the present book, a community is more or less "urban" depending on the size of its population; a "city," therefore, is a place with a relatively large population.[10] (This general definition will be used until Chapter 9 when, in discussing suburbs, the meaning of "city" will be further delimited.) *Institutional* definitions reserve the term "city" for communities with certain specific institutions. For example, to be a city, a community must have its own autonomous political elite; or, it must have specific economic institutions, such as a commercial market. *Cultural* definitions require that a community possess particular cultural features, such as a group of literate people. And *behavioral* definitions require certain distinctive and typical behavioral styles among the people of a community—for example, an impersonal style of social interaction—before the community is labeled a "city."

The demographic definition has at least three advantages: One, the numerical criterion is common to virtually all definitions of "urban" or "city"; even those focusing on other variables employ size. Two, the purely demographic definition does not beg the question as to whether any other factor is necessarily associated with size; that remains an open issue. And three, the demographic definition implies that "urban" and "city" refer to matters of degree; they are not all-or-nothing variables.[11]

What theories are there about the social-psychological consequences of urbanism in the sense of the demographic definition—population concentration? Here and throughout the rest of the book, we shall center on three major theories of urbanism, two of which confront each other directly, and a third which attempts their synthesis:

1. DETERMINIST THEORY (also called *Wirthian* theory or the *theory of urban anomie*) argues that urbanism increases social and personality disorders over those found in rural places.
2. COMPOSITIONAL (or *nonecological*) THEORY denies such effects of urbanism; it attributes differences between urban and rural behavior to the composition of the different populations.
3. SUBCULTURAL THEORY adopts the basic orientation of the compositional school but holds that urbanism does have certain effects on the people of the city, with consequences much like the ones determinists see as evidence of social disorganization.

Before discussing each theory in detail, we should consider the history of social thought from which they all emerged.

The most influential and historically significant theory of urbanism received its fullest exposition in a 1938 paper by Louis Wirth (thus the term, "Wirthian") entitled "Urbanism as a Way of Life" (Wirth, 1938). This essay, one of the most often quoted, reprinted, and cited in the whole sociological literature, needs to be examined carefully. It is heir to a long tradition of sociological theory.

The events that formed the focal concern of social philosophers during the nineteenth and early twentieth centuries have been termed the "Great Transformation" (Polanyi, 1944). Western society was undergoing vast and dramatic changes as a result of the Industrial Revolution and its accompanying processes of urbanization, nationalization, and bureaucratization. These early social scientists (Marx, Durkheim, Weber, Simmel, Tönnies, and others) sought to understand the forms of social life and the psychological character of the emerging civilization—our civilization.

The analysis they developed greatly emphasized the matter of *scale.* Innovations in transportation and communication, together with rapid increases in population, meant that many more individuals than ever before were able to interact and trade with each other. Instead of a person's daily life being touched at most by only the few hundred people of one village, in modern society an individual is in virtually direct contact with thousands, and in indirect contact with millions.

This "dynamic density," to use Durkheim's term, in turn produces *social differentiation,* or diversification, the most significant aspect of which is an increased division of labor. In the preindustrial society, most workers engaged in similar activities; in modern society, they have very different and specialized occupations. In a small, undifferentiated population, where people know each other, perform the same sort of work, and have the same interests—where they look, act, and think alike—it is relatively easy to maintain a consensus on proper values and appropriate behavior. But in a large, differentiated society, where people differ in their work and do not know each other personally, they have divergent interests, views, and styles. A pipefitter and a ballet dancer have little in common. And so, there can be little consensus or cohesion in such a society, and the social order is precarious. Further ramifications of social differentiation, it was thought, included the development of formal institutions, such as contracts and bureaucracy; the rise of rational, scientific modes of understanding the world; an increase in individual freedom, at the cost of interpersonal estrangement; and a rise in the rate of deviant behavior and social disorganization.[12]

The essence of this classic sociological analysis is the connection of the structural characteristics of a society, particularly its scale, to the quality of its "moral order." That turns out, not coincidentally, to parallel the focal interest of urban sociology: the association between structural features of communities—particularly scale—and their moral orders (Fischer, 1975a). In fact, the city has long played a significant role in classic sociological theories. It was seen as modern society in microcosm, so that the ways of life in urban places were viewed as harbingers of life in the emerging civilization.[13] At the same time, the classic theories have had a significant role in influencing the study of cities, having been borrowed from liberally in the formation of the determinist approach.

The development of urban theory moved from Europe to the University of Chicago during the first third of this century. There, the Department of Sociology, under the leadership of Robert Ezra Park, a former journalist and student of the classical German sociologist Georg Simmel, produced a vast and seminal array of theoretical and empirical studies of urban life, based on research conducted chiefly in the city of Chicago. In an influential essay published in 1916, Park followed the lead of the classic theorists by arguing that urbanism produced new ways of life and new types of people, and that sociologists should venture out to explore these new forms in their own cities, much in the style of anthropologists studying primitive tribes (Park, 1916). Another strong motivation for such research was the social turmoil then accompanying the rapid growth and industrialization of Western cities, a realm of civic activity in which Chicago about 1916 was no doubt a leader. The serious social problems accompanying these developments demanded study and explanation.

The varied studies of Chicago resulted in a remarkable series of descriptions of urban ways of life. The "natural histories" depicted many different groups and areas: taxi-hall dancers, hobos, Polish-Americans, juvenile gangs, the Jewish ghetto, pickpockets, police, and so on (see Short, 1971; E. Burgess and Bogue, 1964). A theme running through the findings of these various studies was that the groups, whether "normal" or "deviant," formed their own "social worlds." That is, they tended to be specialized social units in which the members associated mainly with each other, held their own rather distinctive set of beliefs and values, spoke in a distinctive argot, and displayed characteristic styles of behavior. Together these studies described a city which was, to quote Park's famous phrase, "a mosaic of social worlds which touch but do not interpenetrate." As we shall see, the explanation for the urban phenomena observed by Chicago's sociologists was drawn largely from the classic theories of the Great Transformation.

Determinist Theory

Some leads to a determinist theory of urbanism can be found in Park's 1916 paper, but the full exposition of this theory was achieved in Wirth's essay 22 years later.[14] Wirth begins with a definition of the city as "a relatively large, dense, and permanent settlement of socially heterogeneous individuals"—an essentially demographic definition. He then seeks to demonstrate how these inherent, essential features of urbanism produce social disorganization and personality disorders— the dramatic aspects of the city scene which had captured the attention of the Chicago School. Wirth's analysis operates on essentially two levels, one a psychological argument, the other an argument of social structure.[15]

The psychological analysis draws heavily upon a 1905 paper by Georg Simmel, a teacher of both Park and Wirth. In his essay "The Metropolis and Mental Life," Simmel centered on the ways that living in the city altered individuals' minds and personalities. The key, he thought, lay in the sensations which life in the city produces: "The psychological basis of the metropolitan type of individuality consists in the *intensification of nervous stimulation* which results from the swift and uninterrupted change of inner and outer stimuli" (Simmel, 1905: 48, italics in the original). The city's most profound effects, Simmel maintained, are its profusion of sensory stimuli—sights, sounds, smells, actions of others, their demands and interferences. The onslaught is stressful; individuals must protect themselves, they must adapt. Their basic mode of adaptation is to react with their heads instead of their hearts. This means that urban dwellers tend to become intellectual, rationally calculating, and emotionally distant from one another. At the same time, these changes promote freedom for self-development and creativity (see Levine et al., 1976.) The social psychologist Stanley Milgram has recently translated Simmel's analysis into modern language drawn from information theory. The threat of city life is posed in terms of "psychic overload," which must be met by developing means of diverting "inputs." However, the argument is essentially the same (Milgram, 1970; see also Meier, 1962; Deutsch, 1961).[16]

Wirth's treatment of this process follows Simmel's and begins with the assumption that the large, dense, and heterogeneous environment of the city assaults the hapless city dweller with profuse and varied stimuli. Horns blare, signs flash, solicitors tug at coattails, poll-takers telephone, newspaper headlines try to catch the eye, strange-looking and strange-behaving persons distract attention—all these features of the urban milieu claim a different response from the individual. Adaptations to maintain mental equilibrium are

necessary and they appear. These adaptations liberate urbanites from the claims being pressed upon them. They also
insulate them from the other people. City dwellers become
aloof, brusque, impersonal in their dealings with others, emotionally buffered in their human relationships. Even these
protective devices are not enough, so that "psychic overload"
exacts at least a partial toll in irritation, anxiety, and nervous
strain.

The interpersonal estrangement which follows from urbanites' adaptations produces further consequences. The
bonds that connect people to one another are loosened—
even sundered—and without them people are left both unsupported and unrestrained. At the worst, they must suffer
through material and emotional crises without assistance,
must deal with them alone; being alone, they are more likely
to fail, to suffer physical deterioration or mental illness, or
both. The typical picture is one of an elderly pensioner living
in a seedy hotel without friends or kin, suffering loneliness,
illness, and pain. But this same estrangement permits people
in the city to spin the wildest fantasies—and to act upon those
fantasies, whether they result in feats of genius or deeds of
crime and depravity. The typical picture here is one of a
small-town boy suddenly unshackled by conventional constraints, and possessing unlimited options—including a life of
creative art or a life of crime. Ultimately, interpersonal estrangement produces a decline of community cohesion and
a corresponding loss of "sense of community." These are the
psychological changes and further consequences, Wirth
argued, that follow from increases in urbanism.

In his analysis of social structure, Wirth reaches essentially the same conclusion as he does in his psychological
analysis, but he posits different processes. Through economic processes of competition, comparative advantage, and
specialization, the size, density, and heterogeneity of a population produce the multi-faceted community differentiation
mentioned earlier. This is manifested most significantly in the
division of labor, but it exists in other forms as well: in the
diversity of locales—business districts, residential neighborhoods, "bright-lights" areas, and so on; in people's places of
activity, with work conducted in one place, family life in another, recreation in yet a third; in people's social circles, with

one set of persons co-workers, another set neighbors, another friends, and still another kin; in institutions, with the alphabetized diversity of government agencies, specialized school systems, and media catering to every taste. An important aspect of this community differentiation is that it is reflected in people's activities. Their time and attention come to be divided among different and disconnected places, and people. For example, a business executive might move from breakfast with her family, to discussions with office co-workers, to lunch with business contacts, to a conference with clients, to golf with friends from the club, and finally to dinner with neighbors.

The differentiation of the social structure and of the lives of individuals living within that structure weakens social bonds in two ways. At the community level, people differ so much from each other in such things as their jobs, their neighborhoods, and their life-styles that moral consensus becomes difficult. With divergent interests, styles, and views of life, groups in the city cannot agree on values or beliefs, on ends or on means. As community-wide cohesion is weakened, so is the cohesion of the small, intimate, "primary" groups of society, such as family, friends, and neighbors—the ones on which social order and individual balance depend. These groups are weakened because, as a result of the differentiation of urban life, each encompasses less of an individual's time or needs. For instance, people work outside the family and increasingly play outside the family, so that the family becomes less significant in their lives. Similarly, they can leave the neighborhood for shopping or recreation, so that the neighbors become less important. Claiming less of people's attention, controlling less of their lives, the primary groups become debilitated. Thus, by dividing the community and by weakening its primary groups, differentiation produces a general loosening of social ties.

This situation in turn results in *anomie,* a social condition in which the norms—the rules and conventions of proper and permissible behavior—are feeble. People do not agree about the norms, do not endorse them, and tend to challenge or ignore them. Yet some degree of social order must be, indeed is maintained even in the largest cities. Since personal means of providing order have been weakened, other means must be used. These other means—rational and impersonal procedures that arise to prevent or to moderate anomie—are called *formal integration.*[17] For example, instead of controlling the behavior of unruly teenagers by talking to them or their parents personally, neighbors call in the police. Instead of settling a community problem through friendly and informal discussions, people organize lobbying groups and campaign in formal elections.[18]

This sort of formal integration avoids chaos and can even maintain a well-functioning social order. However, according to the classic theories that Wirth applied in his analysis of cities, such an order can never fully replace a communal order based on consensus and the moral strength of small, primary groups. Consequently, more anomie must develop in urban than in nonurban places.

The behavioral consequences of anomie and of the shedding of social ties are similar to those eventually resulting from overstimulation. People are left unsupported to suffer their difficulties alone; and they are unrestrained by social bonds or rules from committing all sorts of acts, from the simply "odd" to the dangerously criminal.

These, then, are the arguments with which Wirth explained what seemed to the Chicago School to be peculiarly urban phenomena—stress, estrangement, individualism, and especially social disorganization. On the psychological level, urbanism produces threats to the nervous system that then lead people to separate themselves from each other. On the level of social structure, urbanism induces differentiation, which also has the consequences of isolating people. A society in which social relationships are weak provides freedom for individuals, but it also suffers from a debilitated moral order, a weakness which permits social disruption and promotes personality disorders.

Compositional Theory

The determinist approach has been challenged on a number of fronts. The most significant challenge has been posed by compositional theory, perhaps best represented by the work of Herbert Gans (1962a, b; 1967; see also Lewis, 1952; Reiss, 1955). The position of this school has been summarized by another exponent, anthropologist Oscar Lewis:

> Social life is not a mass phenomenon. It occurs for the most part in small groups, within the family, within neighborhoods, within the church, formal and informal groups, and so on. . . . [Consequently,] the variables of number, density and heterogeneity . . . are not crucial determinants of social life or personality (Lewis, 1965: 497).

Compositionalists emerged from the same Chicago School tradition as the determinists, but they derived their inspiration largely from that part of the Chicago orientation which describes the city as a "mosaic of social worlds." These "worlds" are intimate social circles based on kinship, ethnicity, neighborhood, occupation, life-style, or similar personal attributes. They are exemplified by enclaves such as immigrant neighborhoods ("Little Italy") and upper-class colonies ("Nob Hill"). Wirth himself described such an enclave in his book on the Jewish ghetto in Chicago (Wirth, 1928). The crux of the compositional argument is that these private milieus endure even in the most urban of environments.

In contrast to determinists, social scientists such as Gans and Lewis do not believe that urbanism weakens small, primary groups. They maintain that these groups persist undiminished in the city. Not that people are torn apart because they must live simultaneously in different social worlds, but instead that people are enveloped and protected by their social worlds. This point of view denies that ecological factors —particularly the size, density, and heterogeneity of the wider community—have any serious, direct consequences for personal social worlds.[19] In this view, it matters little to the average kith-and-kin group whether there are 100 people in the town or 100,000; in either case the basic dynamics of that group's social relationships and its members' personalities are unaffected.

In compositionalist terms, the dynamics of social life depend largely on the nonecological factors of social class, ethnicity, and stage in the life-cycle. Individuals' behavior is determined by their economic position, cultural characteristics, and by their marital and family status. The same attributes also determine who their associates are and what social worlds they live in. It is these attributes—not the size of the community or its density—that shape social and psychological experience.

Compositionalists do not suggest that urbanism has *no* social-psychological consequences, but they do argue that both the *direct* psychological effects on the individual and the *direct* anomic effects on social worlds are insignificant. If community size does have any consequences, these theorists stipulate, they result from ways in which size affects positions of individuals in the economic structure, the ethnic mosaic, and the life-cycle. For example, large communities may provide better-paying jobs, and the people who obtain those jobs will be deeply affected. But they will be affected by their new economic circumstances, not directly by the urban experience itself. Or, a city may attract a disproportionate number of males, so that many of them cannot find wives. This will certainly affect their behavior, but not because the city has sundered their social ties. Thus, the compositional approach can acknowledge urban-rural social-psychological differences, and can account for them insofar as these differences reflect variations in class, ethnicity, or life-cycle. But the compositional approach does not expect such differences to result from the psychological experience of city life or from an alteration in the cohesion of social groups.

The contrast between the determinist and compositional approaches can be expressed this way: Both emphasize the importance of social worlds in forming the experiences and behaviors of individuals, but they disagree sharply on the relationship of urbanism to the viability of those personal milieus. Determinist theory maintains that urbanism has a direct impact on the coherence of such groups, with serious consequences for individuals. Compositional theory maintains that these social worlds are largely impervious to ecological factors, and that urbanism thus has no serious, *direct* effects on groups or individuals.

Subcultural Theory

The third approach, *subcultural theory* (Fischer, 1975b), contends that urbanism independently affects social life—not,

however, by destroying social groups as determinism suggests, but instead by helping to create and strengthen them.
The most significant social consequence of community size
is the promotion of diverse *subcultures* (culturally distinctive
groups, such as college students or Chinese-Americans). Like
compositional theory, subcultural theory maintains that intimate social circles persist in the urban environment. But, like
determinism, it maintains that ecological factors do produce
significant effects in the social orders of communities, precisely by supporting the emergence and vitality of distinctive
subcultures.

Like the Chicago School in certain of its works and like
compositionalists, the subcultural position holds that people
in cities live in meaningful social worlds. These worlds are
inhabited by persons who share relatively distinctive traits
(like ethnicity or occupation), who tend to interact especially
with one another, and who manifest a relatively distinct set
of beliefs and behaviors. Social worlds and subcultures are
roughly synonymous.[20] Obvious examples of subcultures include ones like those described by the Chicago School: the
country club set in Grosse Pointe, Michigan; the Chicano
community in East Los Angeles; and hippies in urban com-
munes. There are more complex subcultures as well. For
example, on the south side of Chicago is an area heavily
populated by workers in the nearby steel mills. These workers
together form a community and occupational subculture,
with particular habits, interests, and attitudes. But they are
further divided into even more specific subcultures by ethnicity and neighborhood; thus there are, for example, the recently immigrated Serbo-Croatian steelworkers in one area
and the earlier-generation ones elsewhere, each group somewhat different from the other (Kornblum, 1974). In both subcultural and compositional theory, these subcultures persist
as meaningful environments for urban residents.

However, in contrast to the compositional analysis,
which discounts any effects of urbanism, subcultural theory
argues that these groups *are* affected directly by urbanism,
particularly by the effects of "critical mass." Increasing scale
on the rural-to-urban continuum creates new subcultures,
modifies existing ones, and brings them into contact with
each other. Thus urbanism has unique consequences, includ-

ing the production of "deviance," but not because it destroys social worlds—as determinism argues—but more often because it creates them.

The subcultural theory holds, first, that there are two ways in which urbanism produces Park's "mosaic of little worlds which touch but do not interpenetrate": 1) Large communities attract migrants from wider areas than do small towns, migrants who bring with them a great variety of cultural backgrounds, and thus contribute to the formation of a diverse set of social worlds. And 2), large size produces the structural differentiation stressed by the determinists—occupational specialization, the rise of specialized institutions, and of special interest groups. To each of these structural units are usually attached subcultures. For example, police, doctors, and longshoremen tend to form their own milieus—as do students, or people with political interests or hobbies in common. In these ways, urbanism generates a variety of social worlds.

But urbanism does more: It intensifies subcultures. Again, there are two processes. One is based on *critical mass,* a population size large enough to permit what would otherwise be only a small group of individuals to become a vital, active subculture. Sufficient numbers allow them to support institutions—clubs, newspapers, and specialized stores, for example—that serve the group; allow them to have a visible and affirmed identity, to act together in their own behalf, and to interact extensively with each other. For example, let us suppose that one in every thousand persons is intensely interested in modern dance. In a small town of 5,000 that means there would be, on the average, five such persons, enough to do little else than engage in conversation about dance. But in a city of one million, there would be a thousand —enough to support studios, occasional ballet performances, local meeting places, and a special social milieu. Their activity would probably draw other people beyond the original thousand into the subculture (those quintets of dance-lovers migrating from the small towns). The same general process of critical mass operates for artists, academics, bohemians, corporate executives, criminals, computer programers—as well as for ethnic and racial minorities.

The other process of intensification results from contacts

between these subcultures. People in different social worlds often do "touch," in Park's language. But in doing so, they sometimes rub against one another only to recoil, with sparks flying upward. Whether the encounter is between blacks and Irish, hard-hats and hippies, or town and gown, people from one subculture often find people in another subculture threatening, offensive, or both. A common reaction is to embrace one's own social world all the more firmly, thus contributing to its further intensification. This is not to deny that there are often positive contacts between groups. There are; and there is a good deal of mutual influence—for example, the symbolism of young construction workers growing beards, or middle-class white students using black ghetto slang. It is, however, the contrast and recoil that intensify and help to define urban subcultures.

Among the subcultures spawned or intensified by urbanism are those which are considered to be either downright deviant by the larger society—such as delinquents, professional criminals, and homosexuals; or to be at least "odd"— such as artists, missionaries of new religious sects, and intellectuals; or to be breakers of tradition—such as life-style experimenters, radicals, and scientists.[21] These flourishing subcultures, together with the conflict that arises among them and with mainstream subcultures, are both effects of urbanism, and they both produce what the Chicago School thought of as social "disorganization." According to subcultural theory, these phenomena occur not because social worlds break down, and people break down with them, but quite the reverse—because social worlds are formed and nurtured.

Subcultural theory is thus a synthesis of the determinist and compositional theories: like the compositional approach, it argues that urbanism does *not* produce mental collapse, anomie, or interpersonal estrangement; that urbanites at least as much as ruralites are integrated into viable social worlds. However, like the determinist approach, it also argues that cities *do* have effects on social groups and individuals— that the differences between rural and urban persons have other causes than the economic, ethnic, or life-style circumstances of those persons. Urbanism does have *direct* consequences.

Summary

The intent of this chapter is twofold: to describe the popular views of urban life that variously color any study of the city, and to list the three key sociological theories with their predictions about the urban experience. We have noted a few reasons why contemporary public opinion, particularly in America, is largely anti-urban; other reasons will be considered in the next chapter. But there can be no doubt that one source of these views is the image of the city projected in Western thought since ancient times. We noted four major themes in that cultural heritage—nature versus art, familiarity versus strangeness, community versus individualism, and tradition versus change. Each of these can be interpreted as being for or against city life, and most have been interpreted against the city. The classic determinist theory of urbanism draws on many of the same themes, in a sense arguing that the strangeness of urban life creates a pervasive individualism which in turn leads to deleterious consequences for the individual and the society. Against this determinist position, compositional theory argues that urbanism has no major social-psychological effects. Subcultural theory, the third and synthesizing approach, argues that these effects do occur—not, however, because social groups break down, but rather because they are created.

These conceptions, popular and sociological, state the question of this book with some force: What are the major social-psychological consequences of urban life? In the next chapter we begin to discover the answers.

3

URBAN LIFE

THE PHYSICAL CONTEXT

The visitor's first impressions of a city are of its physical
nature. I confess that I never fail to be awed by Manhattan—
to be left gaping at its buildings grazing the clouds; to be
swept up in its massive street-corner crowds; to be slightly
dazed by its cacophony of horns, truck brakes, and construction machines; to be mildly alarmed by the speed with which
its soot gathers under one's collar; and, not least, to be left

wide-eyed by the exotic and beautiful objects to be found in its galleries and stores. All the great cities—London, Paris, and the few others in their class—leave impressions much like this, though each is spiced with its own special flavor.

How is the urbanism of a community related to these physical features? And, what are the consequent effects of these physical dimensions on individuals? The debate between the determinist and compositional theorists begins here, on the issue of whether the physical context of the urban experience affects psychological states.

The Ecological Variety in Cities [1]

The urban visitor who stays a while soon learns that the city is not uniform in its physical aspects; rather, that its various subareas often differ radically from each other. For example, a tourist in San Francisco driving on Geary Street from its downtown intersection with Market Street all the way across the northern part of the peninsula to Geary's western terminus at the Pacific Ocean sees in rapid succession: a financial district full of modern glass-and-girder office buildings; a slightly older area of expensive shops and large department stores; a small district devoted to theater and night-life; a seedy strip of bars and hotels for transients; an area of new construction with high-rise luxury apartment buildings mixed in with low-rise public housing projects; a hospital district; and a long stretch of commercial street surrounded by residential neighborhoods of well-kept duplexes and triplexes.

This variety within cities is familiar enough, and it is also important because the physical differences in the various locales of a city are accompanied by social differences in the people who live in these locales and the activities that take place in them. Together, the various kinds of differences mean that *the urban experience is plural.* People living in the same city will be affected in very different ways by the place in which they live—sprawling suburb, inner-city ghetto, penthouse—and by the place in which they work—downtown department store, or a factory on the city's outskirts. These internal variations are not random—they occur in systematic patterns common to many cities. Although, as we have seen in Chapter 1, there is great diversity in the types of cities throughout urban history, we can usefully distinguish between preindustrial cities (or, cities established largely before industrialization) on the one hand, and modern cities on the other. Each type tends to have its own characteristic pattern (Sjoberg, 1960).

Preindustrial cities tended to be small, densest near the center and declining in density with distance from that point.

At the center were usually found the main market, the temple, and the residences of the rulers. Other members of the elite lived nearby. Around them resided well-to-do merchants, small shopkeepers, artisans, and craftsmen. The further out from the center, the lower the quality of the dwellings and the rank of the residents, until near the city wall and beyond were found the laborers and the poor. The pattern was not simply circular, however; it was significantly "cellular" in spatial structure. Various streets or sections ("quarters") of the city held the residences of particular ethnic groups (a form of segregation that continues today) and of particular occupations, such as the "street of the leatherworkers." In the preindustrial city, occupation and ethnicity usually overlapped a good deal. Sometimes, the quarters were walled apart, with gates locked at night (for instance, the Jewish ghetto). Often, there were settlements just outside the walls and linked to the city, such as the residences of the long-distance traders. Many of these preindustrial forms can still be seen in nations of the developing world and in the centers of European metropolises.[2]

The layout of modern cities differs from that of preindustrial ones in at least three major ways:

1. Home and work place have been separated. Silversmiths or merchants of earlier days worked and lived at the same location; today they live at one place and work at another, perhaps many miles away.
2. Social classes have become more separated. Although there was residential segregation in preindustrial cities, it was not based primarily on income. Rich and poor artisans lived near one another (though in dwellings of different quality); the rich and poor members of an ethnic community shared a common quarter. In modern cities, the major differences between neighborhoods depend largely on the rents their inhabitants can afford to pay.
3. The relationship between centrality and social rank has been partly reversed. Whereas status used to decline with distance from city-center, it now tends to increase.

These changes occurred in most Western nations during a period—the mid-nineteenth century through the first few decades of the twentieth—in which the economic bases, social composition, and technologies of urban social structures were in rapid flux. Whatever the various forces that have produced the physical layout of modern cities, the changes could not have occurred without the invention and spread of cheap and efficient means for short-distance transportation. Beginning with horse-drawn buses on cobbled streets through individual automobiles on paved highways, it became immensely easier for people who could afford it to get around the city. In Boston, during the 1870s and '80s, trolley lines extending radially west from the compact center city opened up large strips of land for profitable home building, areas that have since become suburbs such as Cambridge, Belmont, Watertown, and Brookline (Warner, 1962). Within thirty years, trolley lines in Cairo had similarly opened up land for settlement, in this case, desert to the east (Abu-Lughod, 1971: Ch. 9).

These changes in transportation made it possible for many people to obtain spacious dwellings in attractive surroundings while not overextending the household budget or the breadwinner's commuting time. It also became possible for the middle class to separate its residences and its children from the "dangerous classes." These options were meaningful, of course, only to those who could afford them (Chudacoff, 1975: 67 ff).[3]

The ecological form of the modern city is most clearly seen and best known in the United States. A concentric-circle pattern serves as a crudely accurate description (in contrast to the cellular pattern of the preindustrial city). In the center circle are usually found concentrations of bureaucratic enterprises (financial institutions, corporate headquarters) and specialized retail stores. The next ring usually includes manufacturing and warehouse districts. Around these business areas are deteriorated neighborhoods housing low-income families and transients. Unlike the preindustrial city, the general tendency in modern cities is for residential areas to be higher in quality the farther they are from the center. Also, the farther out, the less dense the neighborhood, the smaller the proportion of minority residents, and the higher the social rank of residents.

This circular pattern is only a gross simplification. Many factors modify any simple pattern of concentric circles: topographical features such as hills and lakes; cultural values making for the preservation of old neighborhoods; political forces influencing availability and use of land; historical iner- tia (exemplified by former industrial towns that have become engulfed in the suburban expansion of large cities), and the direct effects of transportation lines. This last factor is espe- cially important, for social groups tend to move outward along road and rail lines, creating pie-shaped wedges of class or ethnic enclaves. The confluence of these various forces complicates the circular pattern: Luxury apartment buildings appear near city centers, for example, and office structures in outlying areas.

A noteworthy instance of a specialized subarea, men- tioned in the last chapter, is the steel-working community of South Chicago. The district is unique in the city: a series of steel mills was built along a stretch of the Calumet River, and over the years workers have moved in to be near their jobs. The local neighborhoods are shaped partly by the plants themselves—the mills, servicing railroads, and slag heaps slice up the community. The neighborhoods are also marked by the history of immigration to Chicago and its steel mills. As different waves of newcomers reached South Chicago, they moved to newly built sectors of the community, or often replaced one another in older neighborhoods. For example, "Slag Valley," once largely South Slavic, became increas- ingly Mexican (Kornblum, 1974: Ch. 1).

These general descriptions of urban patterns have been based largely on studies of physical features and economic activities. Other patterns of ecological differentiation have been found by examining the characteristics of residents in various neighborhoods of a city. Such studies of North Ameri- can cities indicate that neighborhoods are generally differen- tiated simultaneously in terms of three characteristics of their residents:

1. ECONOMIC STATUS—the most important characteristic, residential areas being ranked by the cost of living in them.
   As we noted earlier, the social class of residents tends to
   increase with distance from city-center, and even more
   definitely, classes are segregated by sector (for example,
   East Side versus West Side).

2. FAMILY STAGE—another major distinguishing trait; unmarried and childless residents tend to congregate, usually in center-city apartment neighborhoods; and families with children also live in characteristic neighborhoods, usually in areas of detached dwellings in outlying areas.
3. RACE AND ETHNICITY—the third characteristic that distinguishes neighborhoods. The segregation of blacks is most obvious, but in many cities other groups are also concentrated, the Spanish-speaking or the Italian, for example.[4]

We know a good deal more about North American ecological patterns than about those in other regions. Studies of cities abroad have yielded complex results. Social class seems always to be a criterion that differentiates neighborhoods. Occasionally, family stage is also important. Ethnicity or race is less commonly a differentiator (in some cases because there is great ethnic homogeneity, and perhaps in others because of government policies that integrate housing). Unique features of nations or cities often produce distinct neighborhoods. In British cities, for example, because government projects are such a large segment of home construction, many areas are distinguished basically by whether they are public housing developments or private estates (Rees, 1972). In general, metropolises outside North America tend to exhibit many features of the preindustrial city, but they also appear to be changing toward the modern form. For example, residential segregation by social class is increasing (Hoyt, 1969; Schnore, 1965).

The moral to be drawn from all this and to be kept in mind as we proceed is that, just as cities vary a great deal internally, so will individual experiences of the city. Urban life is not the same for the resident of an elegant townhouse in Manhattan as it is for the owner of a small frame house in Brooklyn. Let us remember this plurality of the urban experience even as we search for sweeping generalizations.

Crowds

Putting up with crowds, their jostling, their noise, their heat, and their abrasion, seems to be an integral part of urban life.

Manhattan sidewalks at lunch hour, Los Angeles freeways at rush hour—these are unavoidable images of urbanism. Common experience tells us bluntly that the larger a community, the more its residents and visitors must put up with crowds. The problem for the sociologist is that we do not know the extent to which this is true. Lacking any specific studies on the matter, we do not know how much of an average urbanite's life is spent in a crowd, nor how that experience differs from small-town experiences. But before we dismiss this issue as being trivially obvious, several points should be considered.

If we could find those mythical figures, the average urbanites, we would probably see that they spend only brief periods of their typical day in crowds, most notably as they commute to and from work. Other than that, they live in a relatively uncrowded home and probably work in a relatively uncrowded office. Even the work trip may be only mildly crowded, at least in the sense that an automobile provides a sheltered and private space. In virtually every large city, only a minority of workers commute by mass transit, and their number has been declining (Schnore, 1963; Blumenfeld, 1971). We do know that overall "crowding" of industrial cities has been *declining* since 1900. Even as cities have been growing in population *size,* they have been declining in population *density*—in crowding. For example, urbanized areas in the United States averaged 5,411 persons per square mile in 1950; they averaged 3,539 persons per square mile in 1970, a reduction of 35 percent in twenty years. This growth in numbers combined with a drop in density means of course that people have spread out their homes; and it means that the directions and destinations of those people have also been spread out. Work and shopping places are less concentrated in the center, more dispersed in outlying areas (Zimmer, 1975; Kasarda, 1975). As a result, relatively fewer people are going in the same direction or to the same places at the same time, which implies less crowding.

Our images of daytime crowding may be exaggerated; we do not really know the hard facts. We do know some facts about nighttime crowding—that is, statistics on the number of persons per room and the number of persons per dwelling unit. The statistics indicate that, if anything, urban residences are *less* crowded than nonurban ones. For example, in 1970,

American housing units outside metropolitan areas were overcrowded (having more than one person per room) in 9.3
percent of the cases. Central-city units were overcrowded in
8.5 percent of the cases, and suburban units, in 7.1 percent
(Bureau of the Census, 1971a; Carnahan et al, 1974).[5] Of
course, these statistics, like most others reported in this book,
refer to averages that can conceal enormous variations—
there are city dwellers who are severely cramped and rural
persons who live in spacious houses. Nevertheless, on the
average, household crowding is more a rural than an urban
problem.

     These considerations should moderate any hasty asser-
tions about city life and the crowd. Obviously, urbanites are
more likely to find themselves in large crowds than ruralites,
if for no other reason than the difficulty of gathering many
people together in sparsely populated regions. (In Chapter 7,
we will explore the psychological effects of such large crowds
on city dwellers.)

Physical Environment

Modern cities are the bane of the environmentalist. They suck
the earth of energy sources and then contaminate the air with
the remains; they draw off riverfuls of water and send it back
befouled to the bays. Trees give way to concrete, animals are
run off by cars, and silence succumbs to traffic noise. And in
the end, the citizen of the city is physically sickened by it all.
Ghastly as these aspects of the modern city seem, the city of
today is as pure as an alpine meadow when compared to the
cities and even the villages of earlier times. Preindustrial
cities may not have consumed the amount of natural resources that modern cities do, but they were vastly fouler
environments.

     Cities as glorious as Athens and as grand as Rome were
open running sewers. Their narrow stone alleys were used
not only as pathways for foot and carriage traffic and as
places of business for sidewalk merchants and hawkers, but
also as troughs for animal and human wastes. The most
polluted cities were the early industrial ones that relied on
coal energy. Although cities have not been as soot-covered
since, substantial improvements did not occur until the twen-

tieth century. As late as 1866, the streets of New York City were cleaned by letting hogs run wild. Noise was loud and constant. When the technology permitted, multistory buildings rose along these narrow alleys, casting them and the buildings' inhabitants into constant gloom. The air was full of odors, fumes, and the ashes of fires—some intended, and some not, as when London burned in 1666 and Chicago in 1871. The density of buildings and of the people within them, combined with the absence of sanitation and the presence of chickens, goats, and other animals as boarders, made epidemics a regular event.[6]

Some preindustrial cities and some quarters of others were more pleasant than this general description implies. Yet it is not an unfair portrait, and it helps us understand why cities had higher death rates than birth rates until the twentieth century, and thus depended on migration from rural areas just to maintain their populations. The change wrought by modern sanitation was revolutionary, turning cities from net consumers to net producers of people. It has been estimated that in Cairo the construction of a sewage system alone saved five of every thousand lives each year (Abu-Lughod, 1971: 123–31). Compared to their pasts, most cities today could be advertised as health spas.[7]

Heat

However, modern cities are scarcely pure, natural environments. For one, they bring about artificial changes in the weather. Cities tend to produce "heat islands," a result of a number of urban characteristics. Large numbers of people active in a restricted area produce heat. Buildings pressed close together reflect, trap, and absorb sunlight and warmth, while simultaneously retarding cooling winds. Their construction materials absorb and conduct heat, radiating it back at night. All cities produce these effects, but modern cities add on heat from industry, home furnaces, and especially automobiles. Pollution particles in the air then help contain the heat within the city. In general, cities are notably warmer than their surrounding countrysides, although there can be great variations, sometimes as much as 20°, between various neighborhoods within a city.

The consequences for city residents are mixed. Winters

are milder, but summers are made more uncomfortable. Probably, in some cases of already sickly city dwellers, the extra heat has meant a losing margin between life and death (Lowry, 1967; Bryson and Ross, 1972; Bach, 1972).

Noise

Noise levels can be safely assumed to increase with size of community (Elgin et al., 1974; G.O.I., 1974, #110: 11). However, two qualifications should be noted. First, noise levels differ greatly within urban areas. Indeed, noise is not so much a problem of metropolitan life as it is of life in the center city and near major arteries (Beranek, 1966). Second, it is clear that the technology currently exists to significantly reduce the level of noise in our cities by, for instance, the better muffling of automobiles and construction machinery (Stevenson, 1972). All that is needed is a collective decision to spend some money on the problem. But even then, noise will be to some extent an inevitable concomitant of urban life.

The major source of noise and public irritation with noise is transportation, especially autos and trucks. They contribute the most to the ambient noise level and the most to people's complaints. Two other major sources are construction activity and the pandemonium of playing children (Stevenson, 1972; Goldsmith and Jonsson, 1973).

Studies of the consequences of living in a noisy environment indicate that some loss in hearing sensitivity is common, and that psychosomatic symptoms such as headaches and nervousness can also result. Noise may even be a factor in increasing mental hospital admissions (E.P.A., 1971; Beranek, 1966; Goldsmith and Jonsson, 1973). A study of school children living in a high-rise building near a busy highway indicated that the closer the children were to the noise, the more their hearing was weakened, and the lower their reading ability (S. Cohen et al., 1973). A series of experimental studies in which college students were subjected to various kinds and levels of noise revealed that the type of noise which is especially damaging is unpredictable and uncontrollable noise (such as the persistent crying of a neighbor's baby or the roar of motorcycles without mufflers). Predictable noise, unless quite loud, can often be adapted to (Glass and Singer, 1972).

Since urbanism probably increases ambient noise levels, and since noise tends to reduce hearing sensitivity, it should follow that the larger the community, the higher the incidence of hearing impairment. However, that does not seem to be the case. Tests given to over 7,000 6–11-year-old children revealed only a tiny, insignificant superiority in the hearing sensitivity of small-town children compared with that of city children (National Center for Health Statistics, 1972). A U.S. Census Bureau survey of over 250,000 persons revealed that the proportion whose hearing was so poor as to impair their regular activities tended to be *lower* in metropolitan than in nonmetropolitan areas (N.C.H.S., 1969a). These findings suggest that the connection between urbanism and experiencing severe noise, while real, is not very substantial. Nevertheless, noise remains a serious complaint which people have about the urban environment (Lansing, 1966). And, in cases where residents are directly exposed to high noise levels, such as the apartment-house children, it does cause serious damage.

Filth

A third environmental issue is pollution—less decorously, dirt and filth. Cities produce enormous amounts of pollutants, and the brief description of the preindustrial city offered earlier in this chapter indicates that the problem of solid waste disposal has plagued cities (literally and figuratively) for many centuries. To the usual solid wastes, modern cities have added cellophane wrappers, nonreturnable bottles, and Sunday newspapers. Even so, a brief look at the evidence indicates that, today, cities probably fare better with regard to sanitation than rural areas, which often lack organized garbage collection and sewage treatment plants. And about four times as many nonmetropolitan housing units as metropolitan units lack indoor plumbing (Bureau of the Census, 1971).

The pollution of the air, however, is an obvious urban problem. A recent study commissioned by the National Academy of Sciences reported that air pollution was fifteen times greater in large cities than in rural areas (*Los Angeles Times,* September 11, 1972). This, too, is not a new problem: "Hell," wrote Shelley, "is a city much like London, a populous and smoky city." But instead of the coke and peat smoke of an earlier London, modern cities have chemical smogs, complete with high levels of dangerous lead and microorganisms (Chilsom, 1971; McDermott, 1961).

The effects of air pollution are costly in terms of cleaning bills, corroded materials, and employee illnesses—estimated for Detroit, for example, to be $20,000 per person annually (Hawley, 1971: 247). And the effects are dangerous: the National Academy study claimed that Americans in large cities suffered lung cancer deaths at twice the rate of rural persons. Bronchitis, emphysema, and other respiratory diseases have been attributed to smog. And air pollution during heat inversions has been blamed for mass deaths, including a record-breaking 170 in New York City in 1953 (Revelle, 1970; McDermott, 1961).

Physical Health

What price must the city dweller pay in life and lungs for this heat, noise, and dirt? Historically, urban life has been hazardous to human health. Poor sanitation combined with high densities constantly bred epidemics, so that death was more common in cities than birth. However, with the medical advances of the modern age, this urban-rural difference in health seems to have disappeared, even perhaps reversed in favor of the city dweller (see Cassel, 1972).

It is not easy to assess such differences from official statistics. For one thing, sick people from rural areas or small towns often go to cities for treatment, sometimes to die there. And, in general, diagnoses of the causes of death tend to be more accurate and sophisticated in larger than in smaller communities.[8] Nevertheless, we can combine such information with other data—such as the periodic health survey conducted by the United States Public Health Service. In all, contemporary statistics suggest that the once clear-cut urban-rural differences in health no longer exist; that the advantages of people in the salubrious environment of small communities are offset by the advantages of people in access to medical care in large communities.

The United States health surveys indicate, for example, that persons in metropolitan areas are somewhat *less* likely than residents of nonmetropolitan areas to suffer impairment of their regular activities because of a chronic condition, whatever the condition—whether heart trouble, mental or nervous tension, arthritis, back strain, hypertension, or the like. At the same time, the surveys indicate that living in a large community somewhat *increases* the likelihood that residents will contract temporary, acute illnesses restricting activity or requiring medical care, particularly upper respiratory conditions (colds, flu, pneumonia, and so on), and also increases slightly the probability of being injured in a traffic accident (N.C.H.S., 1967a; 1969a; 1971). British mortality statistics indicate similar patterns (Mann, 1964). The same American surveys show that urban residents are substantially more likely to visit doctors and health centers, and to visit more specialized ones, than are people living outside the cities. While this may reflect in part their greater susceptibility to colds and the like, it also indicates a greater opportunity for the diagnosis and treatment of potentially chronic conditions.

Housing

Of the many nightmare scenes associated with city life in the public mind, one of the most depressing is the tenement: four or five creaky flights high, dark and dense with both people and rats, tilting and tearing at the seams, its denizens turned miserable and malevolent by their surroundings. The history of cities reveals that this description may indeed be not a caricature but a reality, for the housing situation of city dwellers, while perhaps not individually far worse than that of their rural cousins, must have seemed worse because of the density with which the hovels pressed together and the absence of open space sufficient to provide a sense of relief. Perhaps the worst period of urban housing in Western history was the era of industrialization during the nineteenth century. Cities were engulfed by unprecedented and unprepared-for tidal waves of immigration from the countryside. The newcomers, whose cheap labor fueled modernization, were packed and crammed into whatever makeshift housing was available. Even while a newly rising middle class was discovering the pleasures of suburban life, the poor and laboring classes lived in conditions such as those described in the following passage describing the home of some of New York City's "cellar dwellers" in the 1840s:

> Typical of overcrowded cellars was a house in Pike Street which contained a cellar ten feet square and seven feet high, with one small window and an old-fashioned inclined cellar door; here lived two families consisting of ten persons of all ages. The occupants of these basements led miserable lives as troglodytes amid darkness, dampness, and poor ventilation. Rain water leaked through cracks in the walls and floors and frequently flooded the cellars; refuse filtered down from the upper stories and mingled with the seepage from outdoor privies. From such an abode emerged the "whitened and cadaverous countenance" of the cellar dweller (Ernst, 1949: 206).[9]

As the statistics we will examine indicate, much of the squalor of this period of Western urban history has ended, though a suffering minority in center-city ghettos must still contend with conditions that are not much improved. Yet the popular image remains, modernized perhaps into a picture of high-rise concrete "bunkers," cramped, sterile, and lifeless, save for the occasional mugger stalking the halls. In this section we will examine the reality of urban housing, beginning with some basic statistical facts.

Figure 2 compares metropolitan to nonmetropolitan housing, and within metropolitan areas, center-city to suburban housing. Our earlier warning about statistical averages deserves repetition: Averages mask much internal variation. For instance, to say that there are 5.0 rooms in the median metropolitan dwelling unit glosses over the fact that some metropolitan areas average higher, some lower, and that within metropolises, center cities average 4.7 rooms and suburbs 5.3. Similarly, within center cities, there are neighborhoods which average far above 4.7 rooms and some far below. We continue to use averages because they are the best way to summarize great masses of data, but we should also continue to be conscious that they summarize a great deal of diversity.

Figure 2 demonstrates that

FIGURE 2

HOUSING STATISTICS FOR THE
UNITED STATES BY PLACE OF RESIDENCE (1970)

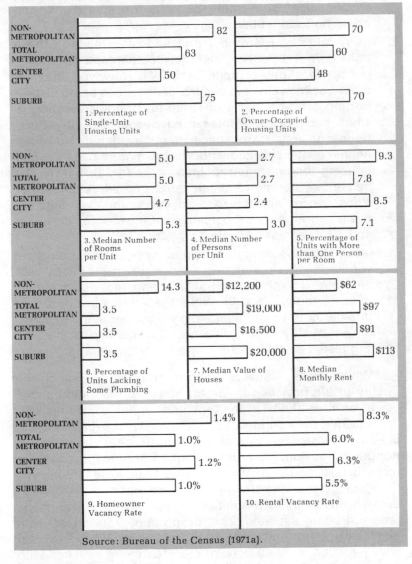

Source: Bureau of the Census (1971a).

1. Metropolitan housing more often consists of apartment and rental housing than nonmetropolitan housing (graphs 1 and 2). The difference is due particularly to center cities, where half the units are apartments and about half are rentals.

2. The number of rooms per unit and of persons in these units do not differ between metropolitan and nonmetropolitan locations (graphs 3 and 4). However, they do differ between city and suburb, center cities being disproportionately the locale of small households residing in small housing units (measured by number of rooms; figures on actual floor space are not available). However, neither center cities nor suburbs have more overcrowded housing than nonmetropolitan areas (graph 5). The 9.3 percent of nonmetropolitan units exceeds even center cities, except for a few extreme cases, and even they are not much higher: 9.9 percent for Chicago, for example, and 10.3 percent for New York City.

3. Metropolitan housing units appear to be in better physical condition than nonmetropolitan units, more often with plumbing (graph 6), and selling and renting at higher prices (graphs 7 and 8). While these rents are no doubt due partly to the generally higher cost of living in cities, they probably reflect differences in quality as well (as suggested by the vacancy rates in graphs 9 and 10).

While these statistics cannot completely reveal the quality of life provided by urban housing, they should cast doubt on the validity of the tenement image presented earlier. Further, they suggest that the quality of urban housing is—*on the average*—as high as, if not higher than, that of nonurban housing. Nevertheless, urban Americans tend to be more dissatisfied with their housing than rural Americans. For instance, in a 1969 Gallup poll, 84 percent of the interviewees who lived in communities of less than 2,500 persons reported being satisfied. This proportion dropped off with increasing community size until, in metropolitan areas of over a million, only 60 percent reported being satisfied with their housing (Fischer, 1973b). Although no studies have yet explained this difference in satisfaction, it is unlikely to be a result of differences in housing quality, given the statistics just presented. Instead, it probably represents a spillover of the general dislike for city living (Marans and Rodgers, 1974; Fischer, 1973b), and, more specifically, of the dislike North American people have for apartment living. The spacious, single-family house is their overwhelming preference, as demonstrated by their responses to surveys and their buying patterns.[10] At best, apartments are viewed as acceptable temporary quarters for young singles, or as convenient arrangements for elderly widows and widowers.

Given the fact that the single-family house is probably as close to a universally accepted ideal as there exists in our pluralistic American society, what are the consequences, besides some discontent, of apartment living? Estimating these consequences is complicated by two general difficulties: First, people who live in apartments bring to their homes attitudes and characteristics different from those of house dwellers. The former are more likely to be either young adults or quite elderly, unmarried, childless, of low income, and minority group members. Moreover, the buildings they inhabit are usually located in the less affluent neighborhoods. So, it *is* true that apartment areas are more often problem areas (suffering high rates of crime and poor health, for example) than neighborhoods of detached dwellings. And it *is* the case that apartment residents more often suffer personal problems than house-dwellers. But these facts are not enough to demonstrate that apartment living *caused* the problems. Residents may bring those problems with them. Demonstrating a causal relationship requires a far more complex analysis in which the traits of residents and other factors are held constant. The second difficulty results from the fact that residence in a house is the ideal in American society, so that apartment dwellers may be chronically upset simply because they lack one of life's "good things."[11]

Yet a number of studies have been conducted which permit us to draw some conclusions. One is that housing conditions in general have little direct impact on social or psychological states. While moving from an extremely poor dwelling unit to a more adequate one is likely to have beneficial effects on health, other changes, such as extra rooms, are unlikely to have significant consequences (Schorr, n.d.; Michelson, 1970).

A similar conclusion emerges from studies of apartment living in particular: few, if any, significant consequences. There is evidence that residence on the higher floors may create a problem of managing children. Either the children are downstairs and out of sight—something parents object to, although we do not know whether the children object—or they get under foot, producing some degree of parent-child conflict and anxiety (R. Mitchell, 1971; Cooper, 1972; Michelson, 1970: 161). In general, however, there is little evidence to support the contention that apartment living per se, ruling out serious overcrowding and the personal characteristics of the residents, has any noteworthy effects on personality, family, or social life (R. Mitchell, 1974; 1971; 1975; Booth, 1975; Michelson, 1973a).[12]

Two consequences in particular are often thought to result from apartment living: higher crime rates and personal isolation. It does seem that the design of many high-rise buildings is conducive to criminal acts. The buildings include hidden areas not easily kept under constant surveillance, such as elevators, stairwells, and blind corridors, which can harbor muggers, rapists, and addicts. The point is, however, that the high-rises do not cause their residents to commit crime; rather, their designs often allow nonresidents to enter the buildings and assault inhabitants (Newman, 1973; compare Gillis, 1974). And, of course, residents of high-rise buildings that are designed for tight security, or that are located in affluent neighborhoods do not often suffer these attacks.

The belief that apartment dwellers are isolated and lonely souls is deeply embedded in American folk wisdom. Research on the question suggests that the notion is both true and false. Generally, though not always, persons living in apartments are less likely to know, interact with, or be close to their neighbors than persons living in detached homes (see, for example, Gates et al., 1973; see also Chapter 5). Yet this does *not* mean that they are isolated and friendless, only that their friends tend not to live nearby. A careful study conducted in Toronto by William Michelson (1973b) of persons moving into apartments and of those moving into detached dwellings indicated that the apartment residents had less contact with their neighbors than the house residents. This was not, however, a result of building type, but, rather, a result of the characteristics that the individuals brought to their homes. In particular, families with working wives tended to gravitate toward apartments, and such families are precisely the ones that have relatively little contact with their neighbors, since the wife is not at home during the day and the couples share a less sedentary way of life. More important still, the apartment dwellers had as many social ties as the house dwellers, but their friends and relatives were more geographically dispersed. Apartment buildings may or may not discourage neighborliness—that is probably a function of other considerations, such as how homogeneous the apartment residents are—but there is no reason to believe that they estrange and isolate their inhabitants.[13]

Even if there is little evidence that apartment living is physically or socially harmful, there is still much evidence that it is more annoying and generally less satisfying (at least for North Americans) than living in a house. Persons living in multiple-family units more often report being bothered by noise from their neighbors, feeling inhibited in their behavior, noticing a lack of privacy, and generally feeling that their housing desires are unfulfilled (Lansing and Hendricks, 1967; Marans and Rodgers, 1974; Michelson, 1973a).

Facilities and Services

In one of its frequent introspective examinations of the quality of life in the "Big Apple," *The New York Times* published an article by a refugee New Yorker living in Vermont. The author states that on a visit back to New York,

> I kept hearing this tempting ad for a Czechoslovakian restaurant. . . . When the ad went on to say that this particular place had been chosen by the critic of the *Times* out of all the Czech restaurants in New York as the very best, I could have broken down and cried. We hardly get a choice of doughnut stands in Vermont; New Yorkers idly pick and choose among Czech restaurants (January 30, 1972).

This is the same city that provides a unique official service, reported by *The Wall Street Journal* as follows: "How do you get rid of a dead elephant? Move it to New York: City's offal truck will take expired rhinoceroses, yaks or mules offal your hands" (October 3, 1972). The point is obvious: the immense variety of facilities and services that a great city can provide.

The fact that cities offer arrays of services unavailable in smaller communities is important. It forms part of the theme of "strangeness" discussed in Chapter 2. And it is one of the images of urban life that turns out to be resoundingly true. Figure 3 presents the results of a survey conducted in the 1930s (still the most comprehensive one available) of the services and facilities present in cities of different sizes, showing the approximate size of a city required before it becomes almost certain that a given service is available there. For example, 95 percent or more of cities above 100,000 had bookstores; the smaller the city below that figure, the less likely it was that a bookstore could be found. These data demonstrate the positive association between community size and services.

More recent but less complete studies indicate the same. Whatever the service—retail stores, specialty goods, religious denominations, doctors—the more urban a place, the greater the number and variety of services, particularly specialized ones (Berry, 1967). Economists have estimated that a population of about 200,000 to 250,000 is necessary for a community to provide a "comprehensive range" of services (H. Richardson, 1973: 131).[14]

Though informative, these statistics do not demonstrate that rural people actually have less *access* to services than urban people. Although a hardware store or a veterinarian may be available in a neighboring village only a short drive away, there are indications that residents of small communities do suffer from limited access to services. The National Health Survey cited earlier queried respondents on their frequency of visits to and from doctors. In 1963–1964, families in metropolitan areas averaged seventeen contacts a year with doctors; nonmetropolitan, nonfarm families averaged fifteen; farm families averaged thirteen. More dramatic were the differences in contact with specialists. Metropolitan families reported about twice as many such contacts as did nonmetropolitan, nonfarm families with pediatricians, dermatologists, gynecologists, and the like. The ratio was about three and four to one in comparison with farm families

FIGURE 3

CITY SIZE NECESSARY FOR THE CERTAIN PRESENCE
OF SPECIFIED SERVICES (c. 1930)

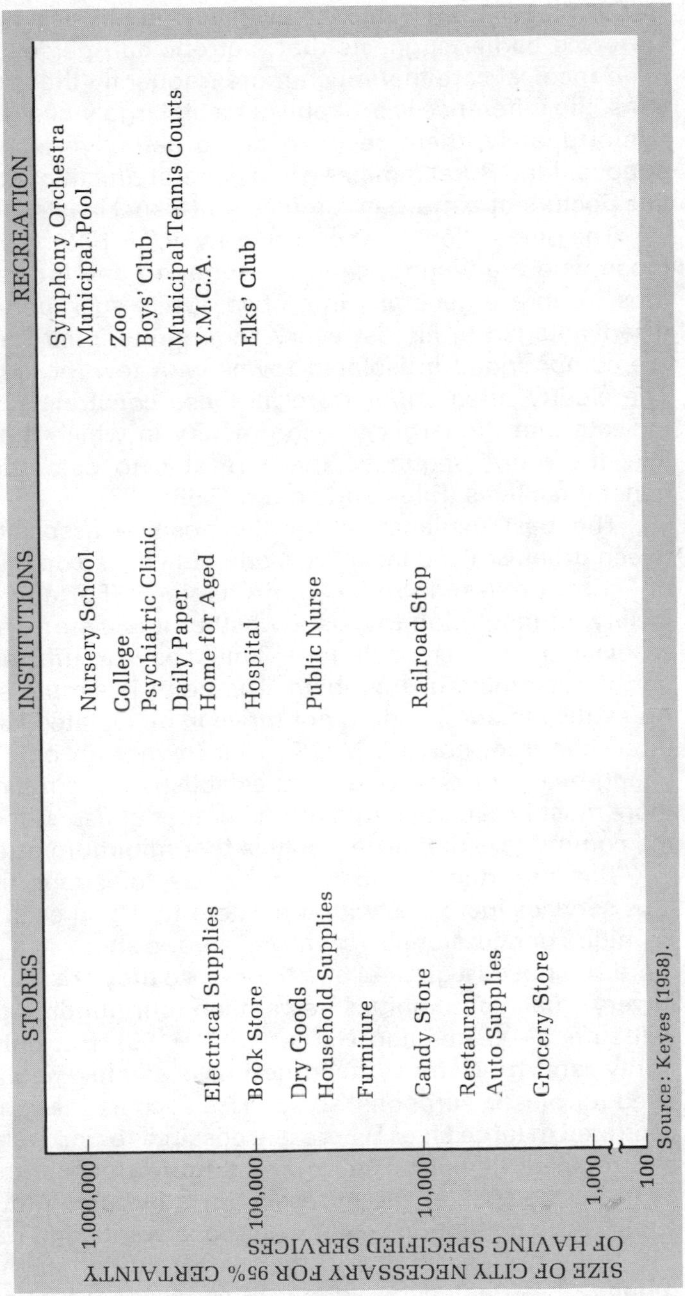

SIZE OF CITY NECESSARY FOR 95% CERTAINTY OF HAVING SPECIFIED SERVICES	STORES	INSTITUTIONS	RECREATION
1,000,000			Symphony Orchestra Municipal Pool Zoo Boys' Club Municipal Tennis Courts Y.M.C.A. Elks' Club
		Nursery School College Psychiatric Clinic Daily Paper Home for Aged	
100,000	Electrical Supplies Book Store	Hospital	
	Dry Goods Household Supplies	Public Nurse	
	Furniture		
10,000	Candy Store	Railroad Stop	
	Restaurant Auto Supplies		
1,000	Grocery Store		
100			

Source: Keyes (1958).

(N.C.H.S., 1969b).[15] Since the evidence on physical health we reviewed earlier suggests that metropolitan persons do not *need* medical care that much more frequently than rural persons, the difference is probably a result largely of availability. (Unfortunately, there seem to be no definitive tests of this supposition.) Rural families go to general practitioners if they see doctors at all; urban families go to specialists.

The phrase "only a short drive away," is bitterly ironic for those who are without cars, or money to pay for transit, or those who are generally immobile. While such persons are disadvantaged in almost every community, their handicaps are compounded in isolated towns with few local services. The elderly often suffer from all these constraints. Studies indicate that the larger the community in which the elderly live, the more frequently they are able to use stores and general facilities (Riley and Foner, 1968: 127).

The best explanation for the positive association between urbanism and facilities is probably based on the notion of "critical mass" introduced in Chapter 2. For any service, facility, or institution to exist—whether it is a store, fraternal association, theater, or church—it must have a sufficient number of customers or members. The point is simple enough: An exotic restaurant could not thrive in an isolated hamlet of three hundred, nor a Y.M.C.A. in a town with only twenty young men. For a service to be established and maintained, there must be a certain minimum number of users; the larger the community, the more easily is that minimum attained.

The importance of community size for supporting various services increases with the extent to which each service is unique or occasional. Virtually everyone shops in a grocery store and needs a general practitioner, so they are found even in very small communities (fewer than four hundred persons will suffice—Yeates and Garner, 1971: 165). But only a minority cares much for symphonic music, and few people have need for plastic surgeons, so services such as these are concentrated in large cities where it is possible to find a sufficient and regular clientele. The rarer and more unusual the want or need, the greater the necessity for a large community to support the institutions satisfying those wants and needs.

There are exceptions to the rule of the larger the community, the greater the variety of services, exceptions that prove (test) the rule, by demonstrating the effects of critical mass. Prostitution, for example, is a commercial service disproportionately concentrated in cities. Yet the small town of Hurley, Wisconsin—"the city that brought sin to Wisconsin" —once had an estimated four hundred prostitutes when its population was only 3,400, a ratio of one prostitute for every eight residents. The reason for this curious statistic was the iron mines outside the town, which employed many young, single males. Such a mass of customers for the services of so many prostitutes can usually be found only in cities, but in this unique case they were concentrated in a rural area (Reiss, 1955: 51). Another more common exception is services for students, such as book stores and inexpensive coffee houses. They can often be found in a small college town or a state university town in a rural area, because campuses contain an unusually large number of young adults. In general, however, these services are to be found only in more urban communities.

Exceptions like these, due to concentrations of particular populations, appear in many small communities. But it is principally in the larger communities that such distinctive clienteles—single male laborers, college students, Italian-Americans, symphony fans, dog-breeders, adherents of mystical sects, and so forth—are usually found and all found together. Consequently, it is in the larger communities that facilities and services, from the very general to the very specialized, are also found.

This conception is crucial to the theoretical argument which states that the facilities and services found in cities are not incidental correlates of city life, but result from the sheer aggregation of people, the very factor that defines urbanism. In that sense, access to services can be said to be an intrinsic part of urban life. This does not imply that all cities always have more of all services than smaller places do. We have noted exceptions; moreover, many other factors besides population size determine access to facilities, for example, the affluence of the population. Nevertheless, as a strong and general rule, the larger a community, the greater the availability of services, particularly specialized ones.[16]

What consequences does this plenty of services and facilities have for the individual? Hard conclusions are not available, but speculations are. One hypothesis, drawn from Simmel's analysis examined in the last chapter, suggests that all these services provide a multitude of options and choices, which in turn require decisions by city dwellers. This profusion of decisions is taxing for human beings and leads to stress, strain, tension, and irritation. Having to choose among many stores, restaurants, movies, and so on becomes a psychic burden, while having little or no choice is actually relaxing (Milgram, 1970; Meier, 1962). This may be so. But perhaps people do not suffer from making decisions, especially when it involves deciding among attractive alternatives; perhaps boredom is the greater threat. Having to choose one of Baskin-Robbins' 31 flavors of ice cream may perhaps create strain, but having to settle for vanilla every day might be experienced as worse still. Or it may be that urbanites, no less than ruralites, are creatures of habit. Instead of agonizing over choices, they return to the same places (and same flavors) as a matter of routine. In that case as well, freedom of choice would not be psychologically enslaving.

Another hypothesis is that the presence of these facilities and services creates among certain parts of the urban population feelings of relative deprivation. In store windows, fancy restaurants, and on fashionable streets, people see objects and life-styles they do not have but, having seen them, wish they did (Durkheim, 1897; Merton, 1938a, 1964; Pettigrew, 1967). In smaller communities, with fewer and less visible signs of affluence, people are less often confronted by unattainable objects of yearning. In that sense, ignorance is bliss. For example, one city planner has suggested that the reason large cities seem so expensive is not because their costs of living overreach their pay scales, but because they offer such an unusual number of desirable ways to spend money, far more than anyone could hope to satisfy (Alonso, 1971). Though the thesis that urban services evoke a sense of relative deprivation is intriguing and plausible, there are no more than the barest indications to support it (Fischer, 1973b).

A third hypothesis is that specialized services and facilities nourish and sustain a variety of special social worlds. For example, the availability of art museums, art stores, and art schools makes a flourishing art community more likely. Or the existence of synagogues, Hebrew schools, delicatessens, and Jewish newspapers makes a vigorous Jewish community more likely. Obviously, the relationship is reciprocal: a critical mass of the artistically inclined is necessary for the art institutions to develop; and a critical mass of Jews is needed for the Jewish institutions to develop. However, these services—newspapers, clubs, stores, and the like—help turn what is only a mass, just numbers, into a meaningful and robust social group. Artists become an art *community;* Jews, a Jewish *community.*

Definitive evidence that urban facilities produce such consequences does not exist, but research on immigrant groups in cities indicates that the development of ethnic services is an important ingredient in maintaining group identity and cohesion. A study of immigrants to Montreal found that groups with the greatest number of ethnic churches, newspapers, and organizations maintained the most cohesive social ties (Breton, 1964; see also the discussion of ethnicity in Chapter 6).

Fourth and finally, it might be hypothesized that the greater the number of facilities and services in a community, the happier its people. Perhaps, but there is not much evidence to support this. While persons bereft of services may complain, there is little evidence that this deficit haunts the lives of most ruralites in any major way.[17]

One or more (or none) of these speculations about the results of the availability of services in urban places may be true—they are as yet unproved. What does seem clear now is that residents of large communities have easier and more frequent access to a greater and more specialized variety of services and facilities than those in smaller places. This fact forms part of the physical context of urban life, and must inevitably affect the individual urban experience.

Summary

The purpose of this chapter has been to describe the ways in which living environments differ by size of community, and to examine their consequences. The physical setting of urban life produces somewhat more encounters with crowds, but probably an extreme amount for only a relatively few. It provides a moderately noisier and dirtier environment, features that make urban areas undesirable places to live for most persons. However, as far as we know, these aspects of the urban environment do not produce a state of physical health in modern urbanites that is any worse than that of ruralites. On the whole, today's metropolitans appear as healthy, if not more so, than nonmetropolitans. There is one psychological effect of city pollutants—annoyance—that for some people is a prime reason for not living in the city.

Urban areas, particularly their center cities, are characterized by high-density housing, notably apartment buildings. These dwellings are probably of better quality than much nonurban housing. And there is little scientific reason to endorse the popular suspicion that apartment living has negative social or psychological consequences. Nevertheless, people—particularly North Americans—generally dislike apartment life. Whatever this distaste is based on—whether myths about apartment living, or a desire for outdoor space, home ownership, a secure playing area for young children, freedom from noisy or intrusive neighbors, or any other reason—it explains this dissatisfaction with urban housing. But urban areas do have a clear advantage in one regard: the larger the community, the greater the availability and diversity of services and facilities.

Conclusion

If we apply these facts to the determinist/compositional debate, the following conclusions seem justified: the physical features of city life—layout, crowds, environmental changes, housing, and facilities—certainly do affect people. They can irritate them, entertain them, and sometimes make them ill. However—and this is a big "however"—by and large these effects are not the kind with which the determinist theory is concerned. There is little evidence here that the city alters people's basic psychological conditions, that it "disorders" or isolates them, producing urban anomie. In this sense, then, the compositional analysis is more correct: mental stability and social order persist in spite of many annoyances.

In one realm at least there do appear to be some meaningful social consequences of the city's physical nature. That is the support which urban facilities provide to the life of small social worlds. Partly as a consequence of these services, small, specialized, and unique subcultures emerge and thrive. In this manner, subcultural theory incorporates and extends the compositional approach to a more accurate interpretation of the effects of the urban physical context.

With respect to all these dimensions of the physical scene, it should be remembered that the urban experience is a plural one. Metropolises are internally very heterogeneous, so that any generalization must always be specified. Some sectors of an urban area are more crowded, or noisy, or dirty than others. Some have high housing density; some, even in center cities, have spacious houses. Some neighborhoods have a wealth of services and facilities easily at hand; others suffer a dearth of services. This internal physical variety should not be overlooked, as it both reflects and generates internal social variety. It is to that social context we turn next.

4

URBAN LIFE
THE SOCIAL CONTEXT

"Every day the people sleep and the city dies; every day
the people shake loose, awake and build the city again."
—Carl Sandburg

Once having assimilated impressions of its physical features,
the visitor to the city soon begins to notice the special characteristics of its people. Particularly at a busy intersection, the
visitor will probably be struck by the variety of people he or

she observes. Compared to almost any small town, the city will appear to be a Noah's Ark of colors, languages, physiognomies, costumes, styles, and activities. A statistically-inclined observer would soon notice a relatively high proportion of certain types of people, such as young adults, members of racial minorities, men in suits carrying briefcases. All these people are the human bricks and mortar from which the city is built.

The urban dwellers and what they do collectively form a major part of the urban experience for each individual among them. To describe the nature of that experience, we must therefore describe the social context of urban life.

The social context must also be considered in order to explain the urban experience. The compositional theory of urbanism argues that the social-psychological differences between city and country result from the different personal traits of the residents of each place. So if urbanites are, say, more "offbeat" than ruralites, it is because urbanites tend to be younger, and young people are generally more unconventional than their elders. As we have seen, compositional theory denies that urban people per se are more offbeat than ruralites.[1] Determinist theory focuses on other features of the social context than personal traits—for example, novel experiences and the consequent psychological strain. And subcultural theory directs attention to the social context by focusing on contacts between people from different social worlds and the effects of these contacts. To evaluate any of these arguments, we must be clear about the differences in social composition of urban and rural places: We need to know who the urbanites are and what they do.

Social Composition: Who Are the Urbanites?

The differences between urban and rural populations in gender, age, economic status, and ethnic makeup have several implications. They *cause* a distinct urban social psychology. That is, certain beliefs or behaviors may result from residence in the city, not because of the city as such, but because of the people who live there. For example, city dwellers might become more "sophisticated," because they would encounter a greater number of highly educated people whose attitudes influence them than elsewhere. Compositional differences can also be *consequences* of urban life. For example, aspects of the urban experience may delay marriages for city dwellers, or it may make them wealthier than ruralites. Either consideration, cause or effect, makes these socio-demographic differences important. This section examines the various compositional differences in some detail.

Gender

No generalization can be made about urban-rural differences in sex composition that is valid internationally. Instead, a distinction must be drawn between the developing nations of Africa and Asia and Western nations, particularly the economically advanced ones. In Africa and Asia, cities typically have a heavy preponderance of men who have moved there to fill strenuous jobs. Calcutta, for example, has three males for every two females (Bose, 1965), with similar male-female proportions existing in West African cities (Little, 1973). This ratio leaves at least a third of the males without mates. In Western societies, however, there are less extreme imbalances of the other kind, with more females than males living in the cities (Jones, 1966).

Several factors contribute to these patterns: land-inheritance rules that push younger sons off the land, for instance, and labor laws, such as those in white-ruled African nations, that compel young black males to move to mining towns but restrict the movement of females (Hanna and Hanna, 1971; Little, 1973). In general, the international differences in urban sex ratios appear to result from differing demands for labor. Like Western nations a century ago, cities in industrializing societies have great need for strong manual laborers, and young men migrate to fill those jobs, leaving the elderly and the women behind in the villages. In economically developed countries, the greater urban demand is for light, clerical labor. Young women, especially at low wages, are regarded as ideal for those jobs (McGee, 1975).

Serious and dramatic consequences can result from the concentration of unmarried people that is produced by this heavy imbalance in the sex ratio. One is the expenditure of effort and wealth by deprived urbanites to find a mate. In many parts of Africa, an urban worker will labor to accumulate enough resources to permit a return to his village, where he can obtain a wife to bring back to the city. Similar efforts were undertaken frequently by immigrants to American cities, even when their home villages were thousands of miles away.

Second, being unmarried promotes footlooseness, among other things, and weakens social commitments. These young unmarried persons, familiarly known as "singles," form a somewhat unintegrated mass within the city. Perhaps it was their notable presence that led the Chicago School to think that urbanism itself produced isolation.

A third consequence is that young singles, especially males, are prone to unconventional behavior and are likely to patronize and enrich unconventional institutions such as prostitution and "swinging-singles" bars. These individuals are also the ones most likely to commit crime. Sex-ratio imbalance thus variously influences a city's ongoing activities.

Age and Stage in the Life Cycle

In all countries, urban persons are, on the average, younger than nonurban persons. But even at the same age, they are also less likely to be married; or, if they are married, to have children; or, if they have children, to have many of them. This disproportionate number of youthful and unencumbered residents forms an urban "surplus" of people between 15 and 45. During that wide range of years many individuals move from farms and villages to the cities, leaving the children and the elderly behind. The contrasts are most dramatic in the developing nations of the world, where the great waves of rural-to-urban migration continue to roll. But even in the United States around 1970, the difference persists: metropolitan areas have nine percent of their population over the age of 65, while small towns of 1,000 to 2,000 population have fourteen percent (Bureau of the Census, 1971a). And in many nations, the urban-rural difference in age is much sharper.[2] The social order of a society is much affected by the age structure of its population, so that a difference even as slight as that in the United States can have serious implications for economics, politics, and life-styles.

As mentioned, urban populations include larger proportions of people who have never been married or who are divorced than rural populations; and among married people in Western societies, the general pattern has been for urbanites to want and have fewer children than rural dwellers. The United States still shows this pattern, though differences have moderated (Slesinger, 1973; G.O.I., 1974, #107:28; Robinson, 1963).

Urban-rural differences in the proportions of the population at various stages of the life cycle largely result from the character of migration to and from the cities. Young, unmarried, or childless persons have greater freedom from the obligations that restrain others from moving. They are more likely to have the physical or technical skills needed to fill the urban jobs. Often, city life is for them only a brief sojourn to accumulate capital before returning to the village for permanent and affluent residence. Finally, young persons are the ones most attracted to the "bright lights" and the lively congregation of their kind (see Jacoby, 1974: 13ff.).

The consequences of differences in age and life-cycle stage are substantial. First, because of their larger families and older citizens, rural places are burdened with economically unproductive residents. In rural areas of the United States in 1970, each 100 persons between the ages of 15 and 64 had to support 69 persons below 15 or over 64. In metropolitan center cities, however, the burden was 59 (Taeuber, 1972: 103–5), and this difference is not an extreme example. Second, the disproportionate presence of young individuals without families to support means that the activities and behavior to which they are especially prone—including support for public entertainments such as movies, liberal opinions on social questions, avant-garde life-styles, and criminal activity—will be particularly evident in urban areas. All these activities then become part of the urban context, helping to shape the experience of every resident in the city.

Ethnicity, Religion, and Race

The more populous a community in almost any country, the higher the proportion of minorities (those racial, religious, and national groups that include less than a plurality of a nation's populace—for example, Catholics in the United States). Put another way, the minority groups of any society will tend to be concentrated in its cities. In the United States in 1970, eight percent of the rural population, eleven percent of the small-town population, but twenty percent of the metropolitan population was foreign-born or of foreign-born parentage. For example, 93 percent of all Greek-born or Greek-parentage Americans lived in metropolitan areas, while only

70 percent of the general population did (Bureau of the Census, 1972: Table 108). Similar though less sharp patterns exist in this country with regard to religion and race (Bradburn et al., 1970: Ch. 6). Kenya provides another example. In 1964, only 3 percent of its total population was non-African, in contrast to 42 percent of the population of the city of Nairobi (Hanna and Hanna, 1971: 109). Nations and historical periods vary in the degree to which minority urbanization occurs, but it remains the common pattern.[3]

Two basic processes probably explain the correlation between community size and ethnic variety. First, the larger an urban settlement, the more central it is to transportation. A direct consequence is the recruiting of minorities engaged in trade. For example, in West Africa, members of the Hausa tribe are minorities in many cities located along old caravan routes, from which they conduct long-distance trade (Cohen, 1969). The position of cities on these transit lines also means that they are ports of entry for immigrants. Many of the newcomers choose—or as with some Irish immigrants in Boston, were compelled—to remain at those disembarkation points (Handlin, 1969). New York City is a classic example of such a port of entry; Buenos Aires is another, with over two-thirds of its population between 1869 and 1930 foreign-born (Germani, 1966: 2).

Second, even for cities that do not bestride long-distance transportation routes, size provides a wide and diverse hinterland from which to draw migrants. On the average, the larger a community, the larger and more culturally diverse the region it influences, and, therefore, the more heterogeneous its incoming population.

Such ethno-religious variety is a major explanatory factor for the competing theories of urbanism. According to the compositional theory, urban minority populations explain to a large extent the behavioral differences between rural and urban communities that are otherwise thought to result from city life itself. According to Wirth's determinist analysis, the cultural heterogeneity of cities is one source of psychological and social strains. The threatening problem of dealing with people who differ in customs and beliefs leads individuals to withdraw and communities to develop formal institutions to preserve social order. But it could be argued that, especially in large cities, individuals are able to live almost entirely within the bounds of their own ethnic group, have only rare encounters with people of other groups, and thus develop an urban parochialism. Put another way, the sizes of ethnic groups distinct from the majority, particularly in very large cities, may guarantee that their members live solely within their own groups, and thus individuals may have *less* contact with people differing from themselves than do residents of smaller communities.[4] An Italian-American in a large city, for instance, could grow up within the confines of the parish and the parochial school, almost never encountering non-Italians. Such a consequence of ethnic heterogeneity would lend weight to the subcultural argument that cities generate and intensify social worlds.

The consequences of ethnic heterogeneity for the community as a whole would seem to be competition and conflict arising from the presence of groups with disparate values and interests. Consensus over community ends and means becomes harder to achieve; deep cleavages are more likely to develop. This is an expectation derived from both Wirthian and subcultural theories, and one that appears to be borne out. For example, the likelihood and severity of racial conflict in the United States has been found to increase with the size of community (Morgan and Clark, 1973). This problem of intergroup relations will be taken up again later; it is an important feature of urban variety.

Social Class

Two kinds of urban-rural comparisons are relevant to social class: one, the contrast between urban and rural communities in the average social-class *rank* of their residents—in educational achievement, occupational prestige, and income level; two, the relative extent of class *differentiation* in large and small communities—the number of substantially distinct ranks along the dimension of social class.

In general, the larger the community, the higher the average educational, occupational, and income levels of its residents. Cities contain proportionately fewer people at the low

FIGURE 4

DISTRIBUTION OF INCOME

FOR METROPOLITAN, SMALL URBAN, AND RURAL FAMILIES (1970)

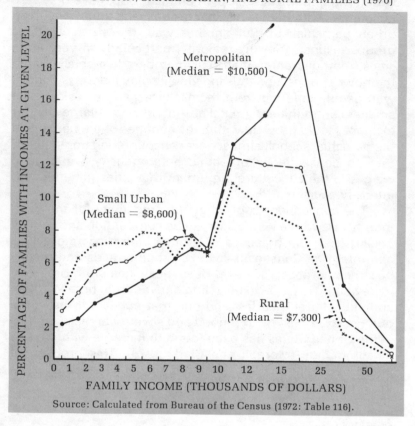

Source: Calculated from Bureau of the Census (1972: Table 116).

end of these scales and proportionately more at the high end. For example, Figure 4 presents the 1970 distribution of family incomes in the United States for metropolitan, small urban (between 2,500 and 50,000 population), and rural places. The graph shows that the larger the community, the greater the proportion of families whose incomes exceeded $10,000; the smaller the community, the greater the proportion who fell below $7,000 (see also H. L. Richardson, 1973; Alonso and Fajans, 1970). A similar pattern exists with regard to education (Bureau of the Census, 1972: Table 110), and occupational prestige (Blau and Duncan, 1967). These gaps between urban and rural class levels are even larger in developing nations (Cantril, 1965).

Note two qualifications about these figures: One, they represent summary statistics that veil a great deal of internal variation. Some small towns are quite affluent, others are miserably poor; urban neighborhoods vary in a similar manner. We are reporting *averages.* Two, these comparisons refer to percentages; in absolute numbers, a large community will of course contain many more rich and many more poor families than a small one.

This urban advantage in social rank is open to various explanations. It may be spurious, a result of the fact that city dwellers tend to be young, and young people tend to be better educated and to earn more money. This is part of the explanation, but not the whole. It has been suggested that, historically, the city dweller has waxed fat on exploitation of the rural peasantry (Mumford, 1961). This may be true, but does not adequately explain contemporary differences. More than one economist has argued that the higher income of city dwellers is a "bribe" the market system pays workers for putting up with pollution, crime, and urban life in general (for example, Hoch, 1972; but see Alonso, 1975). The most likely explanation seems to be that concentration of population provides higher efficiency, economies of scale, occupational and industrial specialization—all of which interact to upgrade the urban economy and ultimately increase the affluence of the urban population (Alonso, 1971; H. L. Richardson, 1973). While urbanites do not always hold higher class positions than comparable ruralites, they do so in the majority of cases.

These urban-rural differences in educational, occupational, and income levels have important consequences, both practically and theoretically. From the practical point of view, if sociology has demonstrated any fact of social life, it is that the social class of an individual is the most crucial determinant of the opportunities, experiences, beliefs, and behavior of that individual. One consequence, therefore, is that city dwellers generally have slightly greater access to the good things in life, because of their rank. Another is that most urbanites enjoy a social setting composed of a more affluent set of neighbors than otherwise comparable rural people. In many ways, the metropolis seems largely constructed for the affluent, as in the case of sprawling suburban developments, the locations and designs of which presume ownership of a car. In a sense, the urban environment is the affluent environment.

From the theoretical point of view, the class difference points up the importance of distinguishing the effects of urbanism from the effects of social class. If urban dwellers are found to differ from ruralites in experience or behavior, our first question, compositionalists remind us, must be whether the differences can be explained by class rather than by residence in the city. Only when the former is ruled out can the latter be accepted.

The concentration of people stimulates diversity in economic activities, with a proliferation of specialized lines of work (such as neurosurgeons, Persian rug salesmen, concert pianists). This is especially true at the higher managerial levels. With the greater array of occupational types, especially white-collar and professional ones, finer gradations within social ranks become possible and actual. Thus, people in larger communities can distinguish a greater variety of class levels than can those in smaller towns.[5]

There are, however, large settlements with little economic and class differentiation—for example, precolonial African towns largely populated by farmers (Krapf-Askari, 1969; Bascom, 1963). But descriptions of cases such as these suggest that smaller villages in the hinterlands are even less differentiated, so that the generalization still holds. A description of ancient India illustrates what is probably an almost universal pattern: "The distinguishing mark of a town or city in the ancient texts was that *only* there did one find all the castes resident. It was in the city alone that the more specialized castes, the learned Brahmins and astrologers, as well as the artisans producing luxury goods, could be maintained" (Rowe, 1973:213). Class differentiation seems to be a consequence inherent in urbanism.

The potential effects of class heterogeneity parallel those

of ethnic heterogeneity: either urban confusion over values, or urban insularity. In either case, as we will discuss in Chapter 5, there are greater chances for class conflict in larger communities.

Migrants to the City

As we know, the flows of human migration have been cityward throughout recorded history. There has been much movement to and fro, but over extended periods the pattern has been consistently from rural to urban places. Until recent times, cities would have declined and died without the constant transfusions of rural migrants. Lewis Mumford, the noted urban critic, has put it forcefully:

> The chronic miscarriages of life in the city might well have led to a wholesale renunciation of city life and all its ambivalent gifts, but for one fact: the constant recruitment of new life, fresh and unsophisticated, from rural regions, full of crude muscular strength, sexual vitality, procreative zeal, animal faith. These rural folk replenished the city with their blood, and still more with their hopes (Mumford, 1961: 54).

In his own manner, Mumford points to a critical urban fact: The population of cities is composed heavily of people from rural regions.[6]

Why do migrants come to the city? As suggested earlier, the motive is overwhelmingly and consistently economic: they want a better job, higher wages, better schooling, a materially better life (or they want to join a relative who has moved for those reasons). Supplementary motivations exist as well: the "bright lights" of the city, a wish to reunite with kin, and the desire to escape constricting families. But the essential lure is economic improvement.[7]

Who are the migrants? What distinguishes them from the people they left behind, and the ones they have come to join? Before a composite picture of the migrants can be drawn, two crucial distinctions must be made. First, some migrants to the city arrive alone, but others arrive in families. During eras of industrialization, the former are usually male; sometimes they are attached to a work cadre. Many Italian and Greek immigrants to American cities followed this pattern, while the Irish and Jews tended to come in families. The consequences are that single migrants are usually transitory (though often they are the pioneers of a later family migration). Sojourners in the city, single migrants intend to return to the village and usually do. The single migrants are also the ones most likely to experience loneliness, instability, and deviance. The second important distinction is that some migrants have associates in the city to which they are moving, but others do not. The great majority do, but those who do not will more often be isolated, move on, and become drifters (see Thernstrom, 1968; 1973).

With these distinctions in mind, we can make general statements about the characteristics of migrants. They are principally young adults, largely accounting for the age distribution discussed earlier. More important, migrants are generally not average. That is, they differ from the people left behind—they are sometimes less capable, sometimes more capable, but different. In some cases, migrants are unemployed, unemployable, social outcasts, misfits, even psychologically disturbed. Their failure is a reason to move. However, in more cases, migrants are better educated, smarter, more highly motivated than the people who stay behind. Reaching for an opportunity is also a reason to move (Tilly, 1970b; Hanna and Hanna, 1971:Ch. 3; Bagley, 1968).

One of the studies which found that migrants were especially skilled was conducted in Peru. It compared fifty pairs of brothers; in each pair, one brother had stayed in (or returned to) the home village, while the other had moved to the city. In most pairs, the brothers agreed that the one who had migrated was harder working in school and was more daring, independent, and intelligent (Bradfield, 1973). Many anthropologists have studied the rural migrants who build shanty-towns on hillsides overlooking Latin American cities. The researchers' impression is that these migrants are relatively resourceful, innovative, and enterprising, compared both to those who stayed behind and to the native urbanites (for example, Mangin, 1967; Perlman, 1975).

Misfits move to cities for obvious reasons (they are pushed out), and for less obvious ones (they can find a com-

patible group among the urban multitudes). The talented,
who may occasionally also be outcasts, move to cities partly
because they have the skills called for in urban jobs, partly
because they have that extra measure of drive which permits
them to sunder old ties and take new risks, and partly because they are the most frustrated in environments of limited opportunity. Whether this selective migration occurs for
any or all these reasons, it has clear consequences: Cities receive some portion of the rural misfits, but they also receive
probably a much greater portion of rural talent, leaving the
villages to suffer brain-drains and youth-drains.

What happens to the migrants when they arrive has been
intensively investigated over the last few decades. The dominant viewpoint, related to urban anomie theory, used to be
that rural migrants to cities suffered great social and psychological shocks and strains, adjustment traumas, alienation,
and social disorganization, which led to deviant behavior. The
migrants therefore became an unstable and volatile mass, a
potential mob. This thinking was reflected, for example, in the
McCone Commission Report on the 1965 racial disturbances
in Watts, Los Angeles. The Commission attributed the violence to unassimilated black migrants from the rural South
(Governor's Commission, California, 1965).

However, little empirical evidence was found to support
this theory. Instead, research done on several continents supports the view that, especially after the first year or two,
migrants to cities are at least as adjusted, satisfied, and integrated as the city-born. They are also generally uninterested
in returning to the village, except to retire or to be buried. (In
the case of American racial disturbances of the 1960s, later
research demonstrated that, in fact, it was *city-reared* blacks
who were more often participants in riots than the rural newcomers.)[8]

A critical reason for the inadequacy of the disorganization theory is that the popular image of the migrant to the city
—a lonely soul, just off the train, friendless and overwhelmed
in the great metropolis—is highly inaccurate. Only a relative
handful of newcomers arrive without their families, and
without associates in the city. All the others have decided to
move and where to move largely because someone already
there has drawn them in. Those associates—whether kin,

friends, or friends of friends—provide shelter, orientation to the city, and connections to obtain a job. Even more, these urban acquaintances provide a network of ties in a social world composed of people much like the migrant. In this compatible milieu, the migrant finds social support to aid satisfactory adjustment to the urban experience. Moreover, most migrants continue to maintain ties to the home village, through visits and third parties.[9]

A study conducted in the *favelas* (shantytowns) of Rio de Janeiro demonstrates the general point. Of those who had migrated to Rio, all but three percent either knew someone already there or had traveled there with someone. And six of every seven migrants had obtained a job within three months of arrival, usually through a friend (Perlman, 1975).

Of course, the move to the city is frequently an unhappy one. Many migrants do not "make it." They quickly return to their villages. The ones who remain, however, do not form an unintegrated and anomic mass. Instead, more often than not, they tend to be skilled, determined, and involved in meaningful social worlds.

This body of research on migrants has led some theorists to suggest a hypothesis directly opposed to the previously prevailing ideas: Cities do not change migrants; migrants change cities. They "ruralize" the city by converting sections of it into versions of rural villages. The city becomes infused with the values and life-styles of the countryside. This compositional thesis, for which some evidence can be found in urban ethnographies, turns the determinist theory on its head (Halpern, 1965; Cornelius, 1971).

It would not do to end this section without mentioning a recent trend—reverse migration. In the mid-1970s, there are some migrants in the United States who are moving from the city to the countryside. Little is known about them, but it appears that most are not really leaving the city at all, but are merely moving into the exurbs. These are regions just beyond the formal boundaries of the metropolitan area from which it is still possible to commute to an urban job (Reed, 1975a). Some others are unemployed factory workers who are seeking jobs in the small towns they had left behind, perhaps encouraged to do so by the opening up of light industry in rural areas. A good proportion have retired from the labor market and find regions such as the Ozarks enjoyable and cheap places to live (Reed, 1975b). And some, a smaller number, are young persons tired of urban "hassles" and searching for "clear skies, dense woods, quiet streets, few cars, fruitful soil and good fishing, direct communication . . . [and] community life" (Efros, 1975).

Strangers

The stranger is one of the most dramatic figures in the urban literature. While the resident of a small town is depicted as living in a world of friends and family, the urbanite is often portrayed as cast adrift in a world of strangers:

> . . . The city, whatever else it may be, is a world peopled in large measure by strangers. It is a place where people are continually brought together who do not, and, in most cases will never, know one another *at all.* It is a place where, on its sidewalks and in its parks, on its buses and subways, in its restaurants and bars and libraries and elevators, in its depots and terminals, people are surrounded by persons whom they do not know and with whom their only basis for relationship is that they happen to occupy the same territory at the same time (Lofland, 1972:93-94).

The precise meaning of the term "stranger" is somewhat elusive. In a sociological tradition founded by Simmel (1950), a stranger is an outsider visiting or residing temporarily in a community. The classic case is the Jew in medieval European towns (see discussion by Levine, 1975). We will discuss this kind of stranger in Chapter 6. The meaning of "stranger" in the passage just quoted is quite different: it refers to the individual whom the observer does not know personally, who is *unfamiliar.* Later in this section, we will consider yet another meaning: the stranger is the person who appears *unusual* or "odd" to the observer.

As a general rule, the larger a community, the more often individuals are in the presence of persons they do not personally know. Speculations about the consequences of living among strangers are at the heart of the urban theories of Simmel, Wirth, Milgram, and others that we examined in Chapter 2. These presumed consequences can be divided into two categories: direct consequences and adaptations in reaction to these direct consequences. The first category includes the cosmopolitanism and sophistication that come from encountering exotic strangers; a breakdown in normative expectations—the result of misunderstandings and disagreements between individuals of different cultures; psychic overload from continuous encounters with unfamiliar and odd individuals; and what one author calls "the urban unease," a general anxiety about the threatening styles of strangers (Wilson, 1968; but see Eisinger, 1973; Foster, 1974).

In the second category, adaptations to the above, are some of the anomic consequences predicted by determinist theory: self-isolation; formal, impersonal relations with strangers; an emphasis on status symbols; and distrust. Furthermore, these adaptive styles come to permeate people's entire lives, including their relationships with people they know. The questions of whether adaptations such as these do occur with regard to *strangers* is partly trivial—by definition we can hardly have a personal relationship with a stranger. It is also partly serious, though yet to be researched: Are urban people colder and more hostile to strangers than rural people? This question will be posed again in Chapter 8. The matter of what effects strangers have on city dwellers' conduct of their *personal* lives will be dealt with in Chapters 6 and 7.

Much of the literature on "the stranger" seems to confuse the two meanings of the term we have distinguished—the individual who is not personally known to another, and the one who appears unusual to another. Of course, a stranger can be both simultaneously, but the analytical distinction is important. The native Americans who met the first Europeans to land in the Western Hemisphere encountered "strangers" in both senses. The critical factor in the natives' reactions, however, was not that the Spaniards were personally unfamiliar to them, but that the explorers were strange, odd, unusual, bizarre.

Urban life no doubt involves more frequent experiences with people who are simply *unknown* than does rural life (though we do not know the degree to which this is so). But the importance of this difference remains unclear. Perhaps being among people who are unknown but not unusual has little effect. Unknown people fade into the background, or urbanites learn a polite etiquette to deal exclusively with them. Lyn Lofland, in a study of encounters among strangers in public places, concludes that city dwellers maintain their usual personal styles of behavior with their friends, but that they also learn special styles of behavior for public encounters with unknown people (Lofland, 1973).

More critical is the probability that urban life involves more frequent encounters than rural life with people who are *unusual* (because of the heterogeneity just discussed in this chapter). "Strangers," in this sense, are often individuals who are clearly identifiable as members of particular ethnic, class, age, and life-style groups. In this regard, Edward Bruner's observations about the adjustment of rural Indonesians to life in the big city are relevant. The essence of becoming urban, he suggests, is learning to distinguish among unusual strangers, to learn which ones are members of which distinct groups and what that implies for dealing with them (Bruner, 1973b); Lofland calls this distinction "categoric knowing." An American example underlines the importance of the unusual compared with the simply unfamiliar: When a stranger in an affluent white suburb is himself white and well-dressed, little will happen around him; but if the stranger is black and shabbily dressed, a great deal will happen—perhaps including the arrival of the police. The suggestion is that the presence of distinctively different "others" is a more significant aspect of the urban experience than is the presence of unknown others.

What consequences can follow from life in the presence of very different others? They are the consequences of different social worlds, or subcultures, touching each other. For one, urbanites systematically avoid and ignore their odd fellow citizens. Residential segregation encourages that outcome, and even in mixed neighborhoods, people usually go their own separate ways (Molotch, 1969; Suttles, 1968). Beyond that, contrasts, competition, and conflicts between "us" and "them" can be expected. It is the case that group conflict increases with urbanism (see Chapters 5 and 6). At the same time, mutual influence and exchange of a positive nature occurs in a great range of areas, including dress styles, foods, and political attitudes. Put grossly, part of the urban

experience involves being both offended by and positively
influenced by "odd" people. This interpretation leads directly
to a subcultural interpretation of urbanism.

The role that the stranger plays in urban life partly involves being personally unknown, but it more significantly
involves being "categorically known"—known to be a member of a group that is different, "foreign," and perhaps threatening. An apt illustration is San Francisco's No. 30 bus, where

> . . . nobody looks out the window to sightsee.
>
> Instead, the regulars sightsee each other—colorful South of
> Market types, reciprocally sightseeing exotic Orientals, Ital-
> ians, bohemians and immaculate Marina dowagers an endless
> wonder, each to each.
>
> And especially wondrous to all the regulars are the irregu-
> lars—the train riders up from the mysterious Peninsula for
> lunch at the Palace: and the pickpockets who ride the short
> Sutter Street segment, from W. and J. Sloane's to the Stockton
> Tunnel turnoff, where they drop their incriminating emptied
> billfolds in the sidewalk planter, and hike briskly back for an-
> other ride (Wallace, 1975).

Activities

Urbanites are surrounded by people in a social environment
that includes the activities in which those people engage—
their leisure and work activities.

Little is known about urban-rural differences in leisure
activities. On the basis of scanty evidence, rural people, especially farmers, seem to have slightly less leisure time than do
others. This may be a result of their lower income, their
greater number of children, or both (Reiss, 1959b; Leevey,
1950). In recent years, the use of leisure time, by Americans
at least, does not appear to differ much between residents of
large and small communities (Brail and Chapin, 1973). One
reason for this is that television-watching is a favorite pastime of about half the population, rural to urban. The small
variations in leisure activity are the sorts one might have
anticipated: residents of more rural places incline toward at-
home or outdoor pursuits such as gardening, while members
of more urban communities lean toward public entertain-

ments, such as dining out or seeing movies (De Grazia, 1962:461; G.O.I., 1974, #105:12-13; Swedner, 1960). In any event, there seems little in the data on leisure pursuits to warrant flights of speculation about social-psychological differences.

Small communities vary greatly in their predominant work activities. There are manufacturing towns, mining towns, college towns, and military towns. There are villages in which residents reap wheat, and villages in which they reap tourists (see Berry, 1972). Large communities tend to be economically diversified and thus more similar to one another. Within a large community, however, there is plenty of variety in its various districts: business, wholesale, theater, or red-light (see, for example, Herbert, 1972). In spite of both these types of variety, some broad statements can be made. In very general terms, small communities engage in "primary" industry, medium-sized communities in "secondary" industry, and large communities in "tertiary" industry.

Residents of small villages tend to specialize in the primary activity of working natural resources: farming, fishing, mining, and lumbering. Of course, not all employed village residents work at such jobs. Some—storekeepers, bankers, barbers, etc.—provide basic services to the primary workers. In small cities, manufacturing (secondary) industries become more prominent, as well as somewhat more specialized (tertiary) services—hospitals, colleges, government agencies, etc.—for people in the hinterland. Large cities are notable for such tertiary work, their residents performing both blue- and white-collar services for entire regions. In addition to manufacturing plants, large cities contain the major financial and governmental institutions, corporation headquarters, centers of mass communication media, and transportation centers. Finally, in the few "supercities," such as New York, Paris, and Tokyo, are located specialized services for the whole world: the centers and suppliers of art, science, and knowledge. As we saw in the last chapter, the more specialized a service, the more centralized it is in large cities (Schnore, 1967; W. R. Thompson, 1965; Berry, 1967).

In simplified terms, the shift from primary through secondary to tertiary industry means a shift from land- to machine- to paperwork. These three kinds of industry shape the

immediate social environment by determining the jobs that
are available and the kinds of people who form the population. Thus, urbanites face a complex and specialized work
setting, which may include greater opportunity for advancement, more interesting jobs, or perhaps more subdivided,
alienating jobs than the simpler rural work setting provides.

Crime

One threat above all dominates the news and nightmares of
American cities: crime, particularly crime against the person.
In *Little Murders,* his horrific play about New York, Jules
Feiffer has his protagonist say:

> You know how I get through the day? . . . in planned seg-
> ments. I get up in the morning and I think, O.K., a sniper didn't
> get me for breakfast, let's see if I can go for a walk without
> being mugged.
> O.K., I finished my walk, let's see if I can make it back home
> without having a brick dropped on my head from the top of a
> building. O.K., I'm safe in the lobby, let's see if I can go up in
> the elevator without getting a knife in my ribs.
> O.K., I made it to the front door, let's see if I can open it
> without finding burglars in the hall. O.K., I made it to the hall,
> let's see if I can walk into the living room and not find the rest
> of my family dead.
> This goddamned city! (Feiffer, 1968: 88)

Once again, New York City serves as the quintessential symbol of the American city. Exaggerated as it is,[10] Feiffer's
image symbolizes a stark reality: the seriousness of urban
crime generally in the United States, the notable risk of being
a victim in its urban centers, and the reasonable fears of its
city-dwellers.

The kinds of criminal activities in today's newspaper
headlines are not new. An 1889 Horatio Alger novel describes
Seventh Avenue in New York in terms of its "unenviable
notoriety as the promenade of gangs" that attacked passers-
by (*The New York Times,* January 28, 1973: 31). Towns and
cities of seventeenth- and eighteenth-century England, notably London, routinely included a separate criminal quarter.
Citizens were beset by roving gangs of criminals in almost

purposeless attacks, and Dickensian schools for the training of child criminals flourished (Tobias, 1972). The people of medieval Damascus suffered from the "Zu'ar"—organized youth gangs who dressed distinctively, and who controlled their own neighborhoods as criminals, assassins, looters, and, occasionally, mercenaries (Lapidus, 1966). In general, they resembled a melange of Hell's Angels, Mafiosos, soldiers of fortune, and Robin Hoods, all rolled into one.

These accounts of pre-modern urban crime could be multiplied many times over. In fact, cities now are *less* crime-ridden than earlier ones; for example: there has been a general *decline* in American urban crime in the last hundred years or so (Lane, 1969; Ferdinand, 1967). Why, then, do Americans perceive an increase? Two probable explanations are that, despite the general decline, there has been a rise in crime since the Second World War, and that the public's standards for public morality keep rising so that more and more misbehavior becomes defined as "criminal" (Graham, 1969; Lane, 1969).

Historical perspective is all very well. But crime today is experienced as a menacing reality, particularly in American cities. It is also a reality that virtually all rates of crime in the United States increase with the size of the community. Figure 5 presents the rates of various crimes in cities in 1970, expressed as ratios of rural rates. The figure indicates, for example that the number of all violent crimes per person was 9.6 times greater in the largest cities than in rural places, and that the murder rate, though half the rural rate in small cities, was three times greater in large cities. The risk of suffering serious crime was, and still is, substantially higher in large communities than in small ones. (The same is true for Canada; Statistics Canada, 1973.)

We must keep in mind that these official statistics have numerous deficiencies. For instance, because people do not report most crimes, the actual rates are usually two or more times greater than indicated in the figures. But independent studies support the central conclusion that urban crime rates are substantially higher than rural ones. For example, a Gallup poll conducted in 1972 asked a sample of Americans whether they had been victims of crime in the previous

FIGURE 5

CRIME RATES BY CITY SIZE,
EXPRESSED AS RATIO OF RURAL RATES (1970)

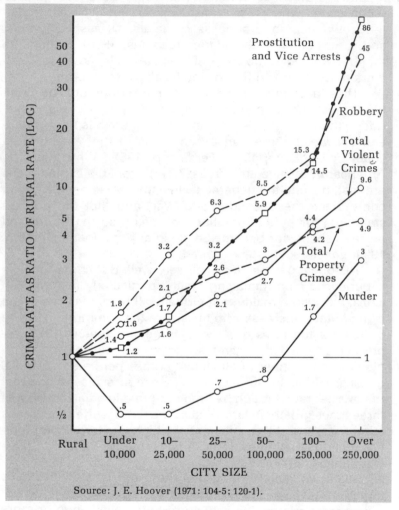

Source: J. E. Hoover (1971: 104-5; 120-1).

twelve months. Thirteen percent of central-city residents had
had their homes broken into, six percent of suburbanites, and
only three percent of residents in small communities. The
proportions of households experiencing one or more serious
crimes were 33 percent, 19 percent, and 13 percent, respec-

tively (G.O.I., 1973, #91; 1975, #124; see also Ennis, 1967).[11]

How does this pattern of urban criminality in modern America compare with those of other historical eras and other nations? We must immediately note the tremendous variation in urban crime from country to country and from time to time. Some of the world's largest cities, such as Tokyo, Hong Kong, and Rome, have crime rates, especially for crimes of violence, that fall *below* those of small towns in America.[12] In European history, there have been periods when cities were homes for mayhem and misdeed, and others in which cities were ruthlessly cleansed of the "criminal element," leaving them far safer than the surrounding countryside (Mulvihill and Tumin, 1969:707).

In spite of this great variety, there is a general pattern: Rates of *property crime* increase worldwide with size of community. I know of no society for which the opposite has been reported. Rates of *victimless crime*, or "vice," also increase everywhere with population size. Figure 5 shows, as a case in point, that arrest rates for prostitution and vice were 86 times greater in the largest cities than in rural areas (rates of occurrence are not available). However, with regard to *crimes against persons*, or violent crimes, there is no general rule. In some cases, such as the United States, they are particularly urban, though even here the pattern has emerged only since the Second World War (McCarthy, et al., 1975: Table 1), and murder is still relatively less probable in small cities than it is in rural places. In other nations and times rates of criminal violence are predominantly rural or equal in communities of different sizes.[13]

In order to understand this pattern, some basic facts about crime should be laid out. Crimes are, in general, committed by all social classes—perhaps at equal rates if tax evasion, price-fixing, influence-peddling, and other crimes of the affluent are fully included. However, the crimes that worry people most (burglary, robbery, and violent crimes) are disproportionately committed by individuals in the lower social classes, males, and members of deprived minorities. In contemporary America, blacks are particularly prone to commit serious crimes. In other times, it has been other subordinate groups. For example, in 1859, 55 percent of the people arrested for crimes in New York City were Irish-born (Glaab and

Brown, 1967:96). In most serious crimes, both criminal and victim are members of the same social groups: 90 percent of American urban murders, 89 percent of rapes, even 52 percent of armed robberies, occur between members of the same race. Furthermore, the large bulk of violent crimes occur between people who know each other. Ninety percent of homicides occur between relatives or friends; in about half the rapes, the victim knew her attacker by sight (Mulvihille and Tumin, 1969; Wolfgang, 1970). A major reason many crimes are not reported is that the victim felt it was a "private matter." If statistics on these unreported incidents were available, the proportion of robberies and violent crime committed by friends and relatives would be even higher (Ennis, 1967; Reynolds and Blythe, 1974).

Various explanations have been offered for the higher crime rate in cities. One is that there is simply more to steal in cities; this would account for the consistent urban-rural differences in property crime, and is the simplest explanation of the difference. Another is that cities provide greater opportunities for escaping detection and apprehension; perhaps so, though quite often criminals are recognized as such in their communities.[14]

These explanations of urban criminality are specific to crime, and are therefore less complete and interesting than hypotheses derived from more general theories about the effects of urbanism on human behavior. There seem to be three major hypotheses of this sort, each of which is based on different assumptions about the causes of crime, and each of which is related to a theory of urbanism.

1. *Criminal behavior results from social and individual "disorganization."* When the social restraints against crime weaken, or when people are psychologically disoriented, individuals are likely to burgle, mug, embezzle, and the like. Thus, the reason cities have more crime is that they weaken mental stability and social order (Wolfgang, 1970). This is, of course, a *determinist* analysis.

2. *Criminal behavior is a rational response by individuals to their circumstances.* This assumption differs radically from the first. When people need or want something, and when they find themselves constrained from getting it legitimately (they are unemployed or unskilled, for example), and when illegitimate action is seen as potentially successful, then the

chances are relatively high that they will commit crimes (Merton, 1938a). The explanation for the higher urban rate of crime, then, is that a higher proportion of urbanites than ruralites face constraining circumstances (or opportunities for success at crime, or both). This is essentially a *compositional* analysis. But, although its assumption about the cause of crime is probably correct, this interpretation does not suffice as an explanation for rural-urban differences. One problem with it is that there are proportionately fewer poor people in large than in small communities.[15] Another is that the differences between rural and urban rates are so great that one must incorporate direct effects of urbanism into any explanation of them.

3. *Criminal behavior is a result of social learning and social support.* Criminal behavior is rational, but it also depends on association and organization. Most criminals, especially full-time professionals, depend on organized markets for selling "hot property," organizations to protect them, and associates to train, aid, and befriend them (Cloward and Ohlin, 1961). This assumption, of course, contradicts the disorganizational assumption—crime is seen as a product of social cohesion, not a product of social breakdown. This third, organizational assumption is consistent with evidence that most crimes are committed or supported by groups, and that people learn to be criminals.[16]

It is, of course, also quite consistent with subcultural theory, which explains the correlation between urbanism and crime in the following way: Large population size provides a "critical mass" of criminals and customers for crime in the same way it provides a critical mass of customers for other services. The aggregation of population promotes "markets" of clients—people interested in purchasing drugs or the services of prostitutes, for example; and it provides a sufficient concentration of potential victims—for example, affluent persons and their property. Size also provides a critical mass of criminals sufficient to generate organization, supportive services (such as fences, "bought" policemen, and a criminal underground), and full-time specialization. An English police officer in the 1830s wrote: "The thieves in a village are not the same as the thieves in town. They [the village thieves] all work occasionally" (Tobias, 1972: 68).

This explanation is another instance in which a subcultural analysis reverses a determinist analysis: The higher rates of urban than of rural crime are largely the result not of the breakdown of community, but—quite the opposite—of the *creation* of communities that support criminality.

The organizational argument might explain why cities generally have disproportionately high incidences of property and vice crimes. But can it explain their rates of violent crimes—crimes against persons? Remember that violent crimes are *not* usually more common in urban than in rural places. This means that there is no general relationship between urbanism and violent crime, only the relationship in modern America. The American circumstances might be explained by national character, for (compared with other Western countries) the United States is generally a violent society. Probably more significant in explaining urban violence in the United States are the critical masses of specific violence-prone populations in its cities. These are ethnic or regional groups usually less than three generations removed from particular regions that have traditions of great bloodshed (such as the American South), and in which violence is a particularly common method of settling disputes. These groups have been termed "subcultures of violence." Although the idea that there are cultures which promote violence has been severely challenged, it nevertheless helps explain both the fact that violence is very much a family affair and the fact that there are great variations between societies in rates of violence. American cities thus suffer subcultures of violence on top of subcultures of crime.[17]

Choosing among these theories, while perhaps interesting, will provide little immediate comfort to the city resident who continues to suffer from crime and its effects. One of these effects, which afflicts people who never actually become victims, is anxiety about crime. This anxiety is, for instance, by far the greatest worry New Yorkers have about living in their city (Burnham, 1974). Surveys, as well as some elections, show that the entire American urban public is more anxious about crime than are people in small-town America. In some center-city neighborhoods, anecdote has it, not only has fear of crime led people to lock themselves indoors at night, it has even led some, especially the elderly, to avoid leaving home at any time (see Ginsberg, 1975).

In a 1971 poll, fourteen percent of rural Americans felt that it was unsafe for them to walk outside at night. The proportion feeling this way increased with community size, and in the center cities of America's largest metropolises, 57 percent felt that it was unsafe. A similar pattern emerged when respondents were asked whether they thought it was important to lock their doors when they left home: 37 percent of the rural sample said it was, and the proportion rose to 81 percent for center-city residents (Marans and Rodgers, 1975: Table 18; see, also, G.O.I., 1975, #124). Put simply, part of the urban experience is to feel anxiety about crime.

Crime is disproportionately an urban activity, then, and is thus a relatively characteristic feature of the urban context. Understanding the association between urbanism and criminality is a key to understanding urban life in general. Compositional theory seems to be inadequate in this case; determinist theory explains the association by assuming that crime results from social disintegration. Subcultural theory assumes the opposite, that crime is largely a result of emergent subcultures, and this, we have argued, is a more adequate explanation of urban crime than the others.

Summary

There is one dimension of the urban context we have not discussed: ambience—the pace, the rhythm, the taste, and feel of a place; the quality that differentiates New York from Paris, as well as a large city from a small town. This is a dimension hard to capture by scientific techniques. Balzac warns us, for instance:

> . . . Paris is indeed an ocean. Sound it: you will never touch bottom. Survey it, report on it! However scrupulous your surveys and reports, however numerous and persistent the explorers of this sea may be, there will always remain virgin places, undiscovered caverns, flowers, pearls, monsters—there will always be something extraordinary, missed by the literary diver (Balzac, 1962: 17).

In our survey of social composition, we found that urban populations, compared with those of smaller communities, generally tend to be younger; less often married; composed of smaller families; more heterogeneous with regard to ethnicity, religion, and social class; and of higher social status. We found that urban populations in the Western hemisphere comprise slightly more females; in the Eastern, somewhat more males. We also found that urbanites are more likely to engage in bureaucratic or professional work. A composite portrait of an American urban type drawn from these facts might look something like this: An unmarried 22-year-old Jewish Peruvian female with a Ph.D., earning a high salary as a neurosurgeon for a large and bureaucratic medical center. Of course, she is hardly a typical urbanite, since there are millions of them who are old, Anglo-Saxon, male, Protestant, uneducated, married, with children, and holding menial jobs or no jobs at all. But the portrait does stress the ways in which urbanites tend to differ from ruralites.

These differences imply three major points: 1) the composition of the metropolitan population forms part of the environment for individuals living in the city. 2) In many cases, this composition is the consequence of urbanism, of the concentration of population (though perhaps not in the ways determininst theory would suggest). For example, urban affluence probably results from the economic efficiencies of concentration. 3) These traits may mislead investigations into the social-psychological effects of urbanism. We must always consider that differences between urban and rural individuals may result from their demographic traits rather than from characteristics of their communities.

We also found that great numbers of urban residents, particularly in nations undergoing industrialization, were once rural residents. Their processes of adjustment, more or less successful for most of those who stay any period of time, are a major part of the urban experience. The migrants tend to be a superior selection of the rural population. The fact that newcomers from the countryside who settle in are able to adapt and integrate themselves successfully into city life challenges the popular theory that the disorientation of rural migrants explains urban disorder. Actually, migrants are less likely than natives to contribute to conflict in the city. At the same time, for migrants and city-born alike, an important feature of most urban settings is the presence of multitudes of rural migrants who variously affect the experience of all.

Finally, the character of the stranger is a pervasive aspect of the city's social context, in that each individual is often surrounded by people whom he or she does not personally know. More critical still is that these strangers represent particular subcultures, subcultures that may have a positive influence on the individual or that may conflict with the individual's own subculture. This diversity of subcultures is a key to understanding the urban scene.

5

SOCIAL GROUPS IN THE CITY
SECONDARY GROUPS

The reflective visitor to the city, once having assimilated its
stark physical features and appreciated its complex social
makeup, will no doubt begin to speculate about consequences. What does all this mean—the hustle and bustle, the
businesses and stores, the variety of races and religions, and
all the rest—but most of all, the sheer size? What does it mean
for the lives of city dwellers and the kinds of persons they
are? To pursue this curiosity, the visitor might do well to

begin a regular schedule of city-watching from a favorite and well-placed vantage point. For the lucky ones, that observation post could be a seat in a sidewalk café in Paris or Barcelona in the spring, where scrutinizing passers-by could alternate with sips of expresso and perusal of the back pages of the local newspapers. (Our visitor would not be conspicuous since city-watching is a favorite pastime of the natives, too.) In short order, the observer would begin to notice not only distinctive individuals, but distinctive groups among the passers-by: families on outings; a group of businessmen on their way to a working lunch; some adolescents engaged in horse-play. These observations might lead to the specific query that introduces the topic of this chapter and the next: What is the fate of social groups in the city?

For the sociologist, this is a critical question. Individuals do not interact in any significant way with the masses of people who form the city; instead, they live their lives in a much smaller frame, with the relatively few people who populate their social worlds. These worlds—ethnic enclaves and professional circles, for example—are composed of *social networks,* sets of people who tend to see one another, care for one another, and depend on one another. It is a cardinal principle of sociology that people neither truly experience nor act on the environment as separate individuals; instead, their experiences and actions are mediated by social networks.

To know how the urban setting affects people, we must therefore know how that setting affects the social networks in which they are involved. That is why the theoretical controversy about urban life focuses on the quality of social relationships as the key issue. Determinist theory holds that cities weaken the cohesion and reduce the importance of personal social networks in favor of impersonal institutions, which brings about anomie and deviant behavior. (Wirth [1938: 153] wrote: "The superficiality, the anonymity, and the transitory character of urban social relations . . . [leads to the loss of] the spontaneous self-expression, the morale, and the sense of participation that comes with living in an integrated society. This constitutes essentially the state of *anomie,* or the social void. . . .") Compositional approaches argue that personal networks are largely unaffected by factors such as community size, and that, therefore, individuals are unaffected too. (Reiss [1955: 47]: "No matter what the size of a community may be, when a person acts in small situational contexts his behavior is apparently subject in large degree to direct primary controls.") Subcultural theory suggests that urbanism does affect social networks by facilitating the growth of some social worlds within which these networks are imbedded and by altering others, with complex effects on individuals (see Chapter 2). All these theories, however, assume the critical importance of social networks.

Social networks can be usefully divided into common-
sense groups based on content—kinship, friendship, neighboring, and the like. This chapter will consider *secondary
groups*—social networks that are not most intimate to individuals, in which not all facets of their personality are involved.
Individuals join these groups (sometimes called *Gesellschaf-
ten,* "associations") to pursue specific ends. In this list are
included the community as a whole, formal associations,
class and occupational groups, special-interest groups, and
neighborhoods. Chapter 6 will consider *primary groups*
(sometimes called *Gemeinschaften,* "communities")—social
networks that do involve individuals intimately, with which
they are fully identified, and which are ends in themselves—
ethnic groups, friends, and kin. For both these sets, the key
question is: How does the urban setting affect the structure
and cohesion of the social networks to which people are
attached?[1]

The Community

The largest and least intimate social group in a community is
of course the entire community itself. The term "community"
has several meanings. Here it refers to a group of people who
reside in the same settlement. Often the term is used to mean
the quality of the relationships within such a group (the "real
community" of intimacy and commitment for example). It is
also often used to refer to some particular set of people who
interact with one another (the "academic community"). But
our concern in this section is the association between the size
of a community—the population of a settlement—and the
quality of relationships within that community as a whole. In
particular, we will ask two connected questions about urbanism and the community. First, how does urbanism—the size
of the group—affect the cohesion of the community? Are
large communities, for example, less harmonious and less
likely to act in a unified way than small ones? Second, how
does urbanism affect the attachment of the individual to the
community? For instance, are people in large towns less loyal
to and less involved with their communities than people in
smaller towns?
Simple arithmetic provides one answer to these ques-

tions. Residents of a village (say, 1000 persons) can reasonably expect to know personally all or almost all the families in the community. But residents of even a modestly sized city (say, 25,000) cannot hope to know more than a small fraction of their fellow citizens.[2] As size increases, the chances of a community being bound together by personal relationships among all its members drops rapidly. To the extent that cohesion requires such relationships, it would seem to be doomed in great urban communities.

Other arguments do not depend on arithmetic when they speak of "the eclipse of community" in the urban setting (Stein, 1960). Determinist theory suggests that both the structural differentiation of urbanism and individual adaptations to the stress of the city threaten the solidarity of the community.[3] Interestingly, subcultural theory makes a similar prediction, though without assuming that anomie is integral to the process. As its size increases, the community becomes less united, not because people drift apart, but because distinctive, smaller groups emerge. These groups—occupational-interest groups, life-style groups, and political groups, for example—clash with one another, creating conflict in the community, and they draw the allegiance of their members away from the community as a whole. Compositional theory seems to make no prediction at all, except perhaps that size has no independent effect on community solidarity.

What kind of criteria can be used to test the proposition that community cohesion and community involvement are reduced by urbanism? A survey conducted in England asked each respondent "if there was an area around his home which he felt he belonged to," and if so, what its size was. In communities of under 30,000, people tended to identify the entire town as "home," while in populous cities "home" was a set of nearby streets (Royal Commission, 1969: 151-62). More generally, the rate of emigration can be taken as an indicator of residents' feelings of attachment to their communities. Evidence suggests that there is not much difference in this respect between large and small communities.[4] Probably the best expression of the group dynamics of a community is its politics. While there are some problems in using politics as an index of the social relationships of the community,[5] it does have certain advantages. Politics is at least nominally relevant to all adult members of the community; it tends to reveal the extent of community harmony or division; and it is one way individuals demonstrate their involvement in the community or their disengagement from it.

The two general questions about urbanism and community life are therefore translated into two specific questions about urbanism and community politics: How does urbanism affect the political system of a community? And, how does urbanism affect the involvement of individuals in community politics?

Political systems are affected by differences in community size (see Dahl and Tufte, 1973). In essence, they follow the principle of structural differentiation—the larger the community, the more distinct are political roles and functions from other parts of the community. Villages have part-time mayors and council members who hold monthly meetings in school auditoriums, while cities have full-time professional administrators who are housed in large office buildings. The city government is more formal, complex, and bureaucratic. It is also more significant in people's lives and, in general, more effective than small-town governments (see Prewitt and Eulau, 1969; Aiken and Alford, 1974; Dahl and Tufte, 1973: 87).

More significantly, as community size increases, so do political disagreements and divisiveness. To be sure, small towns are often rent, sometimes violently, by arguments and feuds (Konig, 1968). But the general rule is that the larger the community, the more disagreement there will be about values and goals. There will also be more conflict, more contested elections, more lobbying by interest groups, and a higher turnover in administrations. The likelihood of intergroup violence also increases with the size of the community. Thus, urbanism is related to a decline in community cohesion.[6]

Individual involvement in community affairs is influenced by two particular factors (besides anomie or the emergence of subcultures). One is the relative importance to residents of a town's public affairs and the interest those affairs generate. Larger communities have an advantage in this respect, since their political controversies involve greater expenditures of resources and more significant aspects of residents' lives. The second factor works to the disadvantage of large communities. Once again, it is a matter of simple arithmetic: The population of a town or city may increase fairly rapidly, but the number of decision-making positions (mayor, council member, friend of council member, or "community elder") increases more slowly. Thus, the larger the town, the smaller the proportion of its residents who can fill one of these roles.[7] Generally, the average individual can have less impact on public affairs in urban than in rural communities, so the likelihood is that individual involvement in urban politics will not be as deep. (On these two countervailing forces, see Greer, 1962: 149-51.)

Studies of political interest confirm, in general, that the larger a community, the less interested and active its citizens in local politics. These urban-rural differences in political in- and miniscule in others (England), but they form the prevailing pattern. However, the relatively smaller interest of urbanites in local affairs does not mean that they are politically apathetic. They tend to be interested instead in national and international affairs. (This preference is partly, but not entirely, due to the urbanites' higher level of education.) Thus, urbanism tends to turn people away from local to translocal affairs.[8]

Studies of voting habits find roughly the same pattern. In economically developed nations, as size of community increases, voter turnouts for local elections drop off, but turnouts for national elections increase slightly. In the less developed nations, the larger the community, the smaller the turnouts for both types of elections.[9] The explanation for these national differences seems to lie in the nature of voting as a political act. In the American experience, fierce political battles increase voter interest and result in large election turnouts. This does not seem to be the case in many villages of other nations, where voting is more of a social ritual, often enforced by village elders. A study conducted in Japan showed that in the villages even politically apathetic citizens went to the polls, but that this was not the case in the cities, where there were no village elders to pressure citizens to vote (B.M. Richardson, 1973; see also Kesselman, 1966).

The larger a community, then, the less interested its citizens tend to be in its politics. And when they are interested, they are much more divided. Is this evidence of the urban anomie predicted by determinist theory? It appears not. First, we have seen that city dwellers are no more apathetic on the average than rural residents; instead, their attention is cen-tered elsewhere. Second, controversy and contention, al-though evidence of a divided community, are not evidence of anomie; instead, political disputes indicate that people are aggressively pursuing their group interests. (For a case study illustrating this process, see Glazer and Moynihan, 1970.) Subcultural theory accounts for this urban divisiveness—it results from the presence of a variety of social groups large enough to challenge the rule of the majority. Subcultural theory also explains the decline of interest in the local com-munity. The large subcultures of cities challenge allegiance to the community, a group that is based primarily on geogra-phic proximity. People's commitments are located in cultural and economic subcultures with concerns that transcend the community—for example, racial groups or national unions. What connection urbanites do maintain with their communi-ties can hardly be based on personal relationships with all their fellow urbanites. It is most likely an indirect connection, mediated through the very subcultures that have divided the community.

Formal Associations

According to determinist theory, rural people maintain their connections to their communities through a multiplicity of informal and intimate relationships. The personal relation-ships of urbanites being fewer and weaker, they must rely more on formal associations, such as sports clubs and mutual loan societies, to maintain ties to their community and to achieve their ends. Unmarried persons in small towns are "fixed up" with each other by mutual, matchmaking friends, while in the big city they must more often rely on leisure-time organizations for meeting potential spouses. The deter-minist expectation is that urbanites belong to and rely on formal associations to achieve their ends more than do ruralites.[10]

In contrast, compositional theory maintains that there should be no marked urban-rural differences in formal rela-tionships, or, if there are any such differences, that they can be accounted for by differences in social class. Subcultural theory predicts that people will join formal associations more frequently in large communities, not because these associations are an alternative to personal relationships, but because they are a *certification* of them. When the number of acquaintances who share a hobby becomes large enough, they may form a club. The club does not replace the original relationships; it makes them official.

One often observed process seems at first to support the determinist expectation. Rural migrants to cities commonly establish formal associations soon after their arrival. In some ways, these associations seem to substitute for rural kinship groups. Leaders of such urban organizations occasionally exercise the authority that in rural areas is reserved for family elders. But studies of these associations suggest that their formal quality is usually only a veneer, applied (often for political purposes) to a set of essentially informal relationships based on ethnicity or village background. For instance, a group of migrants to the city who have come from the same village may wish to participate in the annual carnival parade. In order to do so, they need official recognition from the municipal authorities; so they constitute themselves as a formal club, complete with officers. This kind of group is usually not very "formal" in the sociological sense.[11]

A series of studies done in Western nations casts further doubt on the determinist hypothesis. Some researchers have estimated the number of memberships in formal associations held by individual residents of large cities, and found that most of them belonged to no associations or only one besides their church. Comparative studies done in America, Canada, Mexico, Great Britain, Italy, and Germany show that rates of membership in formal associations did *not* differ by size of community. Research also indicates that association members have generally low rates of participation (such as attending meetings), and such participation is equally low in both large and small communities.[12]

Perhaps, a determinist might say, the critical issue is the functional significance of formal associations, rather than questions of membership or even degree of participation in them. In large communities, while such organizations may be proportionately rarer, they may be psychologically more important to individuals than they are in small communities. There is little evidence to test this proposition; there are indications that people by and large use their formal affiliations to cultivate informal personal ties, not as substitutes for these ties. Membership in an organization is often valued because the association provides a place to pursue and develop friendships. The scanty data available suggest that the formal organizations of cities come not to replace or overshadow, but perhaps only to supplement persisting informal subcultures (Gutkind, 1969).[13]

Social Classes and Occupational Groups

In the previous chapter, we saw that the larger a community, the more numerous and distinct its social classes (that is, the more differentiated its class structure). The question here concerns the extent to which those social classes—strata of people at roughly the same level of income and job prestige —form bases for meaningful social groups. Does urbanism affect the likelihood that members of the same social class will maintain personal relationships with one another, identify themselves as members of a class, and act in unison?

According to determinists like Simmel and Wirth, the answer is yes, because, much like formal associations, social classes based on economic status are part of a functionally integrated society. Grouping around class and occupational interests is consistent with the impersonal relationships urbanites are assumed to have.[14] Compositionalists like Gans would presumably argue that class affiliation was equally important in communities of different sizes (at least, once the personal characteristics of residents have been controlled). Subcultural theory implies, again in common with determinist theory, that the probable existence of class- or occupation-based groups does increase with urbanism—not, however, as part of an increasing formalism, but as a result of the critical masses that foster the emergence of many types of subcultures.

Studies of communities generally find that class is a basis for personal ties and community divisions in all places, from villages to metropolises. The many studies of small towns show class cleavages to be deep and divisive. Research in an American farming community in the 1940s found that the rural tradition of mutual assistance was expressed frequently, but that all the exchanges of neighborly aid (with harvesting, for example) were among farmers of comparable income. That is, help was class segregated (Kimball, 1965). A small mining town was constantly in conflict in the 1950s because of bitter and often violent class divisions (Lantz, 1971). Newburyport, Massachusetts, a town of 17,000 in the 1930s, was the subject of a famous sociological study the major point of which was that personal relationships in the community were kept largely within class lines (Warner et al., 1963). A similar conclusion was drawn by a study of men in the large city of Cambridge, Massachusetts in the 1960s: they drew their friends for the most part from their own social classes (Laumann, 1966; see also Dollard, 1957, and G. M. Foster, 1960).

Class serves as a basis for social divisions virtually everywhere, but the question for us is: Does the *degree* to which this is true vary by community size? There are some indications that class distinctiveness and cohesion do increase with community size in the bits of evidence that come from studies of conflict between social classes. An analysis of voting patterns in four states found that political differences between social classes increased with urbanism. In small communities, blue- and white-collar workers were similar in their party preferences, but in the larger towns, white-collar workers voted predominantly Republican and blue-collar workers voted predominantly Democratic. It would appear that, as size increased the numbers in each class, the likelihood that voters' contacts would be exclusively with members of their own class also increased, thereby making them more "class-conscious" (Ennis, 1962).

Other forms of class conflict, some of them violent, also increase in frequency with community size. For example, worker-days lost in labor strikes increase disproportionately with the population size of metropolitan areas.[15] Studies conducted by Charles Tilly and his associates on collective violence in Europe indicate that cities were disproportionately the sites of such violence, which in turn was largely the direct or indirect expression of class divisions (Tilly, 1974; Tilly et al., 1975; on Africa, see Jenkins, 1968). Such conflict and disorder has been interpreted by many determinists as indicative of societal breakdown and anomie. Park (1916: 109), for example, wrote: "Strikes and minor revolutionary movements are endemic in the urban environment," and: "The community is in a chronic condition of crisis," because "human relations are likely to be impersonal and rational." However, the evidence suggests that the urban tendency to class violence results from organization and cohesion within economic groups in the city, not from disorganization and collapse (Tilly et al., 1975). That is, cities generate class conflict by "intensifying" competing economic groups.

Urbanism increases the solidarity of social classes, then, making it more likely that they will be the sources of personal relationships and the bases of collective action. What appears to underlie this pattern is the fact that urbanism enlarges the importance of *occupation* as a basis of social affiliation. Indeed, social class as such may be most important in modest sized towns, where, for example, the lawyers, bankers, and doctors might jointly form a single clique. In cities, however, each occupation is probably more apt to form its own group; and, in the larger cities, the process probably evolves to the point where tax lawyers, trial lawyers, and divorce lawyers each have their own separate set. The hypothesis is that the larger cities have larger numbers of people in the community in each occupation and this, combined with the effect of job similarity on the formation of personal relationships, produces small social worlds based on occupation. Each occupationally distinct set of people forms internal allegiances, develops a characteristic outlook and style—in short, becomes a potentially viable subculture. As Park noted long ago: "In the city every vocation, even that of beggar, tends to assume the character of a profession and the discipline which success in any vocation imposes, together with the associations it enforces." (Park, 1916: 102).[16]

What evidence is there for this hypothesis? It is evident that small towns with few people in most occupations are not likely to develop occupational subcultures. But it does not necessarily follow that occupationally-based social groups emerge in large cities. Several sociological studies indicate that they do.

The longshoremen of Portland, Oregon, present a clear example. A longshoreman-turned-anthropologist has described how members of this occupational group not only work together but also see each other socially, largely belong to the same nationality groups, marry each other's sisters, and recruit relatives into the union. (They are not, however, likely to be neighbors—a point that will be important later in this chapter.) Accompanying these dense relationships is a distinctive identity, style of behavior, and set of habits and beliefs. In short, they form an occupational subculture (Pilcher, 1972).

Union Democracy, one of the classics of sociology, offers another example in the social world of printers in New York City. Like the Portland longshoremen, they are socially intertwined and quite distinctive, and they form a viable subculture that, in turn, is divisible into successively more distinctive groups according to religion (Lipset et al., 1956). Even prostitutes, criminals, and skid-row alcoholics have social circles and subcultures of their own in cities (Oelsner, 1971; Bahr, 1973).

All the preceding occupations are to some degree special; for instance, they have irregular or unique working hours. Unfortunately, we have few studies on "average" nine-to-five workers. Nevertheless, the argument is both simple and plausible: People get to know other people whom they meet at work, or deal with as professional colleagues; they also share common backgrounds and interests with others in their line of work. This is true everywhere. But what occurs with an increase in population is that the size of an occupation becomes sufficient to permit, even to encourage, the formation of subcultures by which each occupation becomes a somewhat separate and self-sufficient social world. People establish the major portion of their personal relationships within the group of their work colleagues, they become involved in the institutions of the subculture (its organizations, meeting-places, newspapers, etc.), and they tend to exhibit its particular style of behavior in such things as their dress, language, and attitudes.

The development of occupational subcultures in cities also contributes to the paradox of diversity mentioned in the last chapter: The urban setting is heterogeneous, but if each of the various occupational groups is sufficiently large and self-contained, its members may often not have any serious relationships with persons from other occupational groups (or, as we sometimes say in academe, from the "real world").

Special-Interest Groups

People constantly join together in order to pursue a common interest—chess, politics, charitable works, scuba-diving, or opera-going. Sometimes such groups are formalized—as in political parties, or chess clubs. More often they are informal —the group that plays basketball together on Sunday mornings, the amateur musicians who jam on Saturday night, the regular customers at a local bar. These are groups in which the commonality is produced by some special activity. Are such groups more likely to form in larger communities than in smaller ones? If so, what implications follow?

Earlier, we examined some fragments of data about formal associations. Even less information is available on informal associations. In the absence of hard evidence, we must therefore fall back on reasonably informed speculation. In Chapter 3, we saw that the advantage of cities in providing services and facilities came about because cities could command sufficient numbers of clients—critical masses of clients —to support specialized institutions and occupations. The present analysis of special-interest groups pursues the same logic. Large populations concentrated in small areas permit people with particular pastimes, political causes, or life-styles to get together in viable groups.

Homosexuals provide one example of people who often wish to meet and enjoy each other's company in their own milieu. It is apparently common for homosexuals to drift from smaller communities to the large metropolises, such as San Francisco, New York, Los Angeles, and Chicago, because it is easier to follow their inclinations in the more urban places (see Mileski and Black, 1972; Hoffman, 1968). The cities provide a large enough pool of fellow homosexuals to provide for liaisons and friends, and services and locales, such as "gay bars." The larger cities also appear to be more tolerant— an attitude that itself is in some part a result of the size of the homosexual community. (In San Francisco, politicans take serious account of the homosexual vote.)

Assuming that special-interest groups are relatively both more common and more important in larger than in smaller communities, what consequences follow? The answer depends on how we interpret special-interest groups.

For the determinist school, special-interest groups in the urban setting involve impersonal, utilitarian relationships. Members are engaged with each other almost exclusively on an instrumental basis as means to an end.[17] Illustrations include the group that plays basketball together regularly, and the coffee-house intellectuals who debate one another each night over cups of espresso. In both examples, the determinist interpretation suggests, the activity is the essence, if not the totality, of the relationships; personal interaction—that is, people treating each other as unique individuals—is relatively rare. Moreover, these instrumental ties come to challenge and replace personal ones. For example, people would prefer to discuss their anxieties in encounter groups rather than with their friends or family; the coffee-house savants do not deign to discuss their ideas with their neighbors. The intimate web of relationships common to rural life fades as a consequence, replaced in the city by shallow, single-purpose ties. "The growth of cities," wrote Park (1916: 110), "has been accompanied by the substitution of indirect, 'secondary,' for direct . . . 'primary' relations in the association of individuals in the community."

An alternative assumption about special-interest groups, one held by both compositional and subcultural theory, is that they *supplement* personal ties. They sometimes usurp functions otherwise performed by intimate associates—for example, in the case of the girl who plays chess with fellow chess buffs rather than with her father. But such activities are not the central functions of the family or of other intimate groups. And, sometimes, special-interest groups can provide a source of primary ties, a way of making friends. In either case, the groups do not undermine intimacy.

These two analyses are speculative. In the next chapter, when we discuss friends and family, we will be better able to assess the effects of urbanism on intimacy. Before that, we must consider the unique type of group known as the neighborhood.

The Neighborhood

Neighbors, a set of people who live in close physical proximity, are often seen by the general public and scholars alike as a "natural" social group. Like the family, the neighborhood commands early the intense loyalties of its residents and their intimate involvement with one another.[18] In this view, isolation from the neighborhood portends an individual's alienation; disintegration of the neighborhood threatens social disorganization (see Nisbet, 1967; Durkheim, 1893: 300). We will examine here the effects of a community's size on the vitality of its neighborhoods. This examination will lead us to reconsider the assumption that the neighborhood is a core social group.

The popular concept of the neighborhood often also includes the notion that the quality of neighborhood life—that is, the degree to which neighbors form an intimate and active social group—is seriously reduced by urbanism. In this view the city is exemplified by apartment-house neighbors who never greet each other, much less know each other's names, while the small town is seen as the heartland of neighborliness. More than one recent presidential candidate has used his small-town upbringing to certify his ability to apply a spirit of "neighborliness" to America's urban problems. Residents of large cities have seemingly accepted their unneighborly image—so much so that contrary incidents are viewed as exhilarating exceptions. *The New York Times,* for example, prints stories of apartment-house or block parties as heartening beacons in the generally gloomy neighborhood life of the city.

This view of the urban neighborhood is central to the determinist theory. Like other primary groups, the neighborhood is weakened by urbanism. The Chicago School thought that, with the exception of ethnic enclaves, "in the city environment the neighborhood tends to lose much of the significance which it possessed in simpler and more primitive forms of society," and that "where thousands of people live side by side for years without so much as a bowing acquaintance, these intimate relationships of the primary group are weakened and the moral order which rested upon them is gradually dissolved." (Park, 1916: 98, 111). Ties to the locality are loose or sundered; people are independent of and anonymous to their neighbors—it is all part of the general anomie and isolation of urban life.

How do the facts match up with both the popular and scholarly impressions? Compared with residents of smaller communities, do city dwellers less often know, interact socially with, and care about their neighbors? In general, the answer is yes. Most relevant studies indicate that, on the average, the larger the community, the less the involvement with neighbors. For example, an American survey conducted in 1968 asked respondents, "About how many people in this neighborhood do you know by name?" In nonmetropolitan places, only three percent of the interviewees said fewer than three; seventy percent said either that they knew over twenty of their neighbors or "all" of them. In the center cities of large metropolitan areas, the results were quite different. Twenty-two percent responded with fewer than three, and only 27 percent said twenty or "all." Similar reports come from other studies in the United States and abroad.[19]

These findings do not indicate an absence of neighboring and neighborhood vitality in cities. Indeed, some prime examples of vibrant local groups studied by sociologists come from large cities: Boston's North and West Ends (W. F. Whyte, 1955; Gans, 1962b), London's East End (Young and Willmott, 1957), New York's Greenwich Village (Jacobs, 1961), and Chicago's Addams Area (Suttles, 1968). Descriptions of these places show that neighborhoods can thrive in the center of the metropolis. Yet as Suzanne Keller (1968), a noted student of the neighborhood, has pointed out, these locales are in some ways out of the mainstream (a point to which we will return). The pattern of the mainstream, where most people and places are found, has less neighborhood "groupness" in larger than in smaller communities.

The Neighborly Individual

How might we explain this general pattern? One explanation is the determinist thesis of general urban anomie. However, a simpler explanation is provided by the compositional school—that is, differences in the characteristics of urban and rural residents explain this difference in neighborhood involvement. Neighborly types of people tend to live in small communities, and people who are not prone to neighbor end up in cities. (It is not the city per se that reduces neighboring.) To explore this proposition, let us consider the distinguishing traits of the neighborly individual.

First, neighborly people are likely to be long-time residents of the neighborhood. Although people newly arrived in the area often exhibit a flowering of sociability, that bloom tends to fade. Time permits the meetings and remeetings that root people to a place. Second, the neighborly type is likely to be raising a family. Children serve to keep their parents in a neighborhood in a variety of ways: Because of their children, parents search for amiable places to live and take on local responsibilities (such as the PTA); children meet the next-door children, causing the parents to meet; and raising children often means that someone is home during the day. Third, the neighborly type is likely to be older. Aside from length of residence and family stage, youth contributes to roaming, and age contributes to resting. Fourth, the likely-to-neighbor is a person who tends to be at home during the day —a retiree, or, most likely, a homemaker; and, being at home means having more opportunity (and more need) to see the people nearby. Finally, one important trait involves not the individual alone, but the neighborhood itself: commonality. Sharing common values and common needs creates bonds between all people, including neighbors. Such shared interests usually arise from common statuses—age, occupation, ethnicity—and similar life-styles. Thus homogeneity contributes to neighboring.[20]

This list of characteristics explains, at least in part, why urbanites tend to neighbor relatively little. On most counts, city dwellers are less likely to have traits associated with neighboring than people outside the city. Instead, urbanites are more likely to be without children, younger than the average, working, and living in heterogeneous neighborhoods.

But these characteristics do not completely account for the very sizable differences between large and small communities in neighborhood life.[21] It appears that there is something additional, related to urbanism itself, which decreases social interaction in the large locality. Urban anomie is the determinist's suggestion for what that "something additional" is. I propose an alternative explanation, one which requires us to examine further the concepts of "neighbors" and "neighborhood."

Any set of people who happen to live near one another

may be called "neighbors." This loose meaning of the word, as in "just neighbors," must be distinguished from a tighter meaning—an intimate social group composed of people who live nearby (what many might consider to be "real" neighbors). An intimate, or at least personal, group arises from a set of "just neighbors" under certain specific conditions. Those conditions are less commonly found in cities.

The first condition that generates social bonds out of "just neighbors" is functional necessity. That is, people in a locality join together to meet certain local needs. There are, for one, internal functions: in rural areas, harvesting, barn-raising, road maintenance; in cities of an earlier era, street cleaning, maintaining the well; in both places, enforcing the norms of proper behavior. There are also external functions— foreign relations, so to speak. In many political systems, rewards are divided territorially, areas must compete with each other, and people are treated by others partly on the basis of where they live. These, too, are problems calling forth neighborhood cooperation.[22]

Cities of an earlier era had much more distinct neighborhoods than modern cities do, and thus can provide us with an illustration of the way these factors work to promote cohesion. Consider medieval Damascus again. Each section of that city contained about five hundred persons, who usually shared an ethnic or occupational identity. The city administration recognized the various quarters as autonomous entities, with sheikhs appointed from each quarter to represent it to the municipal government, to help administer the collective taxes, and to ensure the enforcement of ordinances. The quarters were so distinct and self-reliant that it was not uncommon for fierce battles to erupt between them. Little wonder, then, that they were "small, integrated communities, . . . analogues of village communities inside the urban agglomeration" (Lapidus, 1966: 95; see also Abu-Lughod, 1971: 71-9).

Other dramatic examples of achieving neighborhood unity through conflict come from urban shantytowns in Latin America. The residents, called *favelados* in Brazil, are treated as outcasts by their national governments and are thus forced to rely on their own communal resources for providing necessary public services (Leeds, 1973; Cornelius, 1973). In North America, neighborhood cohesion is occasionally produced by a threat from outside, such as highway construction, ethnic invasions, or school busing (see Coleman, 1971: 673).

These internal and external functions that can bind neighbors together do not necessarily bind them with ties that are personal. Rather, they can be specifically instrumental ones. Rudolf Herberle (1960: 9) has described the traditional rural German neighborhood in this way: "Neighborhood, as a social relationship, is originally indifferent in regard to emotional-affectual attitudes of neighbors to one another. Neighbors will do certain things for each other, whether they like each other or not." The point is that functional interdependence generally leads to instrumental relationships among neighbors. These, in turn, make it more likely that personal relationships will also emerge—but they do not guarantee that they will.

The second condition that can produce personal bonds among neighbors is the existence among them of other relationships besides living near one another. Relatives, co-workers, members of similar religious or ethnic groups will tend to have close ties. Being neighbors may help strengthen those ties, but the source of the intimacy is not the neighbor relationship itself. A rural village provides an example. The anthropologist Conrad Arensberg (1968a) discovered a great deal of cooperation among the countrymen of a remote Irish farming village during the 1930s. But when he carefully examined who actually helped whom, he found that "in every case an extended-family relationship was involved." These farmers were greatly intermarried, so that by helping their kin, they were simultaneously helping many of their neighbors. It was the kin tie, however, that called forth the mutual assistance.

A third condition that encourages local interaction is simply the absence of an alternative. In cases where other social contacts are too distant in time or cost, people must either form personal connections with their neighbors, or have none at all. People whose mobility is restricted, such as the elderly, or who are isolated, as in the countryside, face this choice. Usually they choose to neighbor.

These three conditions—functional interdependence, prior relationships, and lack of alternatives—increase the likelihood that people will have personal relationships with those who live nearby. And the larger the community (and the more modern the society), the less likely it is that each of these conditions will be found. Consequently, neighborhood inter-action declines with increases in urbanism.

Urbanism and the Neighborhood

In modern cities, the responsibility for many internal func-tions such as safety, street-cleaning, and education rests at a higher level than the neighborhood. (Of course, this can be a problem when the city fails to serve certain neighborhoods. The cry of "community control" is then often raised.) City-wide allegiances also dissipate the unity derived from dealing with external relations. Racial, religious, class, and ideolog-ical divisions that cross-cut the entire city compete with terri-torial divisions for the interest and commitment of the resi-dents. As Heberle (1960: 9) puts it:

> The reciprocal obligation between neighbors is a conse-quence of their proximity and interdependence. Where interde-pendence ceases because of the availability of services as in the city, proximity no longer constitutes the basis for a cate-goric social relationship. Neighbors may now choose to what extent they want to associate with each other.

Instrumental ties among neighbors and the emergence of personal ties out of them become less probable.

The second condition—the proximity of kin, co-workers, and so on—is also less likely to be present in larger settle-ments. The wider housing market of a city makes it possible for such persons to be physically dispersed and yet to main-tain contact with each other (as in the earlier example of the Portland longshoremen, who were socially connected in many ways, although they were not especially likely to be neighbors; see also Frankenburg, 1965).

Third, the larger the community, the greater the indi-vidual freedom *not* to neighbor. That is, urbanites have more options as to whom they can interact with, and their more compatible associates may be outside the neighborhood. Park (1916) described it this way: "The easy means of commu-nication and of transportation [in the city], which enable indi-viduals to distribute their attention and to live at the same time in several different worlds, tend to destroy the perma-nency and intimacy of the neighborhood." Suzanne Keller

(1968: 48) put it crisply: "Village life makes neighboring mandatory. . . . In cities this type of neighboring . . . is mandatory
no longer."

An illustration of this point comes from a study conducted by Susan Freeman (1970) in a tiny Castilian hamlet,
one of the least urban places we will encounter in this book.
The several families living there were closely (though somewhat primly) bound together as neighbors, partly because
they depended on one another, partly because many were
kin, and partly because there was no other choice. The last
condition rankled many a resident. Freeman (1970: 199) concludes her study with a description of the ideal social life as
the average person in the hamlet imagined it:

> It is attained in a large and dense settlement where within
> the one town or barrio he can find all the companionship
> he needs, where he can select his own associates, and where
> the people he works with are not the only available friends.
> This idea is fully realized only by emigration [to a larger com-
> munity].

Urbanism reduces the likelihood that the conditions
needed to bring active group life to neighborhoods will jointly
occur. This general rule is dramatized by its exceptions. Many
urban neighborhoods do harbor active and intimate social
groups. However, they usually fit one or more of the following descriptions: being threatened from outside, being an
ethnic or occupational enclave, or being populated by people
with little physical mobility (for example, carless housewives).[23]

An example of an occupational enclave is our familiar
case of South Chicago. Residents there were heavily involved
in neighborhood life: they identified emotionally with the
neighborhoods, such as Irondale or Millgate, and they
strongly resisted incursions by outsiders. The reason for this
fierce localism in the midst of a huge metropolitan area was
that the residents shared an important and dominant involvement in the nearby steel mills. On top of the occupational similarity of the area was the ethnic homogeneity of the
specific neighborhoods. In exceptions such as this one,
neighborhoods can be cohesive in the most urban of areas;
they are, however, exceptions (Kornblum, 1974).

Urbanism, in general, makes concrete the abstract distinction presented earlier—the distinction between "just neigh-bors," a set of persons who live near one another, and the intimate social group that can develop from "just neighbors." Urbanism tends to reduce the role of neighbor toward its bare essence. That role seems to involve two essential norms or rules of behavior. The first is: Be ready to assist your neigh-bor at those times when physical proximity is important—either in an emergency, or when the assistance costs little and it would be silly for the other person to go long distances for it (for example, in the United States, a cup of sugar). The second norm is simple: Don't be offensive. Good neighbors don't disturb or offend the people next door (or lower the property value of their dwelling). These are the same norma-tive expectations generally held for any people in close physi-cal proximity, when they are standing in line, for example, or sitting on a bus.[24]

Even in the most urban and urbane of localities, it is, of course, true that neighbors will occasionally be more than just neighbors. In fact, all else being equal, the nearer two people reside, the more likely it is that they will have deeper and closer ties—including, for example, getting married (Ram-søy, 1966). The point is, the forces that overlay the neighbor-hood with primary ties are weakened in the city, thus re-vealing the neighborhood to be fundamentally a secondary impersonal group.

What implications for the individual urban resident fol-low from the conclusion that urbanism reduces the extent and intimacy of neighborhood relationships? One expecta-tion (consistent with determinist theory) is that the absence of local ties should reduce the sum total of the urbanite's personal bonds. But the evidence indicates that this is not the case. Instead, local relationships are only alternatives to extra-local ones.

Several studies support this conclusion. In one, eight hundred interviews were conducted in East York, an area of Toronto. Respondents were asked to name six persons to whom they "felt close" (very few could not name any). Only thirteen percent of the named "intimates" lived in the neigh-borhood. Most lived in Toronto, but elsewhere in the metro-politan region. Furthermore, when respondents were asked which of their intimates could be depended upon for assistance in time of need, the intimates living far away were selected as often as those closer by (Wellman et al., 1973).

Other studies report the same findings: Local ties form only a small portion of urbanites' social connections; and people with few neighborhood friends usually have intimates elsewhere.[25] By themselves, these facts cannot test the thesis that the total of personal relationships of city dwellers is reduced by the vitiating effects of urbanism on the neighborhood. But the relative unimportance of local ties indicated by these studies suggests that the fate of social relations in general is not dependent on the fate of neighborly relations. Although we need not go so far as to echo one researcher's rhetorical challenge "Who needs neighborhoods?" (Wellman, 1972)—some persons certainly do—many seem to do well without them.

Summary

In this chapter, we focused on the way secondary social groups are affected by urbanism. The largest group in a community, the community itself, becomes less cohesive the more populous it is. As local political affairs demonstrate, urban communities are more strife-ridden than rural ones, and tend to lose the attention of their residents to the national and international scenes. One reason for this is the emergence in urban places of meaningful social groups organized around occupations. People in large communities can more easily join in social worlds based on professional similarities and outlooks. They can also more easily join in special-interest groups, because there are more people at hand who share whatever the interest, hobby, or political orientation may be. One urban-rural difference that was expected but did not emerge was membership in formal associations—urbanites are no likelier to be members than ruralites. In any case, the determinist assumption that formal associations involve impersonal relations is not necessarily true; associations may instead be places to pursue quite personal relationships.

Finally, we examined the relative weakness of the urban neighborhood in some detail. Something about urbanism reduces the likelihood that personal, primary relationships will emerge among a set of neighbors. The determinist thesis is that the feebleness of neighborhood life in cities is part of general urban anomie. A better explanation, however, is that urbanism brings with it some "freedom from proximity." The ready availability outside the immediate vicinity of many potential associates allows people to construct social networks that extend beyond the neighborhood. What then develops are "localities of limited liability" (Janowitz, 1967; Greer, 1962)—neighborhoods where only a minimum is expected and demanded of neighbors, where the development of closer bonds is a matter of personal taste, and from which residents can leave with little emotional loss.

Conclusion

This chapter began and ended with groups—those partial social networks that are defined in terms of physical propinquity: the local community and the neighborhood. In both cases, urbanism tends to deflate their solidarity and intimacy and to reduce their personal importance to the individual. In between community and neighborhood we observed other types of social networks: formal and informal associations, class and occupational groups. In these cases, particularly those of occupations and special-interest groups, the evidence suggests the opposite conclusion: greater solidarity and importance. The larger the community, the more the population separates itself by profession and by life-style interests, and the more individuals find their social ties within such groups.

These trends were apparent to Louis Wirth and his associates at Chicago. Their influential interpretation of the facts is that they are evidence of urban anomie. Intimate groups that engage the full range of people's personalities are overridden in the city by partial, impersonal, and utilitarian social relationships in which people treat each other as means to some end. Persuasive as such an interpretation is, it is inconsistent with other facts: that there is no relatively greater involvement by urbanites in formal associations, nor any greater reliance by them on formalized ties, and that they obstinately personalize what seem to outsiders to be the impersonal connections of occupation or special interest. Furthermore, the assumption that the groups based on residence —the community and neighborhood—are in essence primary and personal is subject to great doubt.

Another possible interpretation of these findings is based partly on subcultural theory. According to this view, a residential group is not, in essence, primary in the sense that the family is. Residential groups are sets of people who live near one another, and who can therefore see each other more frequently and more easily than they can see others. Truly personal relationships can, and often do, emerge from such contacts, in both city and countryside.

What urbanism does is to place large numbers of other people within easy reach of the individual, and thereby to provide more bases of association than the locality alone. (Modern technology, through rapid transportation, does much the same.) In this larger population, there are likely to be many people—critical masses of them—who are more personally suitable for the individual than those who happen to be in his or her local area. Thus, it is easier for people in cities to build social networks and to live in social worlds that are distinguished by class, occupation, or interest. (Keller [1968: 61] calls it "a shift from a neighboring of *place* to a neighboring of *taste.*") Consequently, residential groups lose some, although hardly all, of their members' commitments to translocal associations (see Webber, 1968).

This interpretation suggests that there is greater freedom of association for urban than rural individuals, and probably a greater compatibility among urban associates. It also raises one of the thematic tensions discussed in Chapter 2: community versus individualism. Some have argued (for example, Nisbet, 1967) that groups based on freely chosen association cannot satisfactorily replace "natural," inherited groups in maintaining the "moral order" of a society, that such traditional groups better socialize, bind, and integrate the individual into the social whole.[26] This argument will be easier to evaluate once we have considered the nature and strength of the urban "moral order" in the chapters that follow. It is worth asking, however, whether associations based on common interests and personal similarities might not actually anchor individuals in society more securely than those based largely on proximity.

6

SOCIAL GROUPS IN THE CITY
PRIMARY GROUPS

Of the many social groups which the visitor to the city observes, either directly as they pass by his or her vantage point in the café, or indirectly through examination of the newspapers now piling up around the table, the psychologically and socially most significant are the smallest—those made up of a few people who know each other fully and intimately. These groups of relatives and close friends are the *primary groups* that help to shape our personalities, to influence our values and opinions, to encourage or restrain our actions, and to give us the most grace and the most grief. Our individual experiences of the world are transmitted through these primary groups, and largely interpreted according to the perspectives they have taught us.

Just as primary groups are vital to individuals, so they are vital to society. They form the basic units of which the whole is made, much as cells are the basic elements of the body. In traditional cultures, individuals are often not even recognized as autonomous beings, but are instead considered only as interchangeable parts or representatives of primary groups. When these groups are weakened, society as a whole is weakened. When individuals are not bound together in intimate units but instead drift off separately, society is disorganized, atomistic, and vulnerable to anomie.

The determinist theory of urban life argues that cities have debilitating effects on such intimate groups, and that urban societies consequently tend to be anomic. Cities produce structural differentiation and psychic overload, both of which cause personal ties to wither. Their decline is accelerated by the rise in urban settings of impersonal and instrumental institutions that usurp the functions of intimates. The ultimate consequence is social disintegration (see the detailed discussion in Chapter 2). We have already read the claim of one writer that "primary groups are doomed"; and "the awful fact is that modern urban society as a whole has

125

found no way of sustaining intimate contacts" (Alexander, 1967: 245). Although most determinists, such as Park and Wirth, would never have made such apocalyptic declarations, they would agree that urbanism inclines society in that direction.

Both compositional and subcultural theory maintain that intimate relationships are no less common in the city than in the countryside. Subcultural theory adds a significant twist: the fact that primary groups are alive and well in the city does not mean that they are unaffected by the urban experience. Both the composition of primary groups (that is, the kinds of people who become intimate with one another) and the character of close relationships are different in small and large communities. They differ because the urban setting provides individuals with a variety of associates with whom to be involved and a variety of subcultures from which they can obtain services. For instance, since the choice of potential spouses is ordinarily greater in an urban setting than a rural one, marital couples should be, on the average, somewhat more compatible in the former than the latter, according to this view. Similarly, relatives should be relied upon less often for assistance in larger than in smaller communities, because there are more alternative sources of aid in the city. However, from either perspective, compositional or subcultural, the urbanite is seen as embedded in intimate groups, and not as an isolated individual in "the lonely crowd."

In this chapter, we will examine the condition of primary groups in the city. Whether the discussion concerns ethnic groups, friends, or family, the two questions we will be asking are: Does urbanism reduce the vitality and social significance of these primary groups? Are they changed in any other respect?

Ethnic Groups

We have noted that people in the city are set off dramatically from people in smaller communities by their great variety of racial, regional, and religious types. Each type usually represents a social group distinguished by a shared ethnicity. Our concern here is with the consequences of the urban experience for such ethnic groups.

The people in any ethnic group share a distinguishable culture (tradition, values, customs, behavioral style) into which they were born or presumed to have been born. (It is because of the genealogical nature of ethnicity that it has been placed in this chapter on primary groups.) Beyond this simple definition, ethnicity is flexible. In some cases, it may be possible and warranted to make finer distinctions than in others. In small communities, for example, it might be enough merely to distinguish between Italian-Americans and non-Italians; in large communities, however, it might be appropriate to distinguish between Sicilians, Neapolitans, and Northern Italians. The bases for critical ethnic differentiation vary: nationality of origin in America, region in France, tribe in Africa, caste in India. But, essentially, we are dealing in all cases with descent-based cultural groups.[1]

The Chicago School held an ambivalent opinion about ethnic groups in the city. On the one hand, Park, Wirth, and their colleagues were clearly struck by the stubborn survival of ethnic enclaves in modern cities; those enclaves were significant pieces of the urban mosaic. But they also seemed convinced that ethnic cultures would ultimately be destroyed by the forces of "rationalization" in the city (see Wirth, 1928; Park and Miller, 1921: 296-308). According to this determinist thesis, urban ethnicity wanes in two specific ways. First, ethnic groups are less often a source of personal relationships and less often a basis for group activity in urban than in rural settings. Second, in the city, the cultures of ethnic groups— their values, norms, and life-styles—are less traditional, less distinctive, and less often a basis for individual behavior. Determinists therefore expect that ethnic identity will break down in the city. In contrast, compositional theory (Gans's in particular) considers ethnic groups to be the kind of small social units that are unaffected by ecological variables like urbanism. Subcultural theory provides a complex prediction. Urbanism generates various alternative bases of association: subcultures founded on occupation or life-style or special interest (Chapter 5). These subcultures attract individuals' allegiance and modify the values of ethnic groups. Yet at the same time the urban effect of larger numbers within ethnic groups and the subcultural opposition among them should have the same vitalizing effects for ethnic groups that they do for other subcultures. We should expect, therefore, to observe *both* processes—weakening and strengthening—and to see them working against each other. In some instances, for example in the case of small ethnic groups in a large city, defections and dilutions will predominate. In others, especially where the group is large, cohesion and cultural integrity should both be maintained, perhaps even deepened. Although the relative balance will vary according to specific circumstances, we should observe both subcultural vitality and ethnic diffusion as results of urbanism.[2]

Having set down the various predictions, we can turn to the research. What do the available studies indicate is the actual fate of ethnic groups in the city? The weight of the evidence is that they persist *and* they change.

Persistence in Ethnic Groups

Many descriptive anthropological studies have been conducted on urban populations around the globe—such groups as Italian-Americans in Boston; peasants from Andean villages living in Lima, Peru; Serbian migrants to Zagreb, Yugoslavia; tribesmen from the bush in cities all around Africa; rickshaw drivers in Dacca, Bangladesh; and Irish families in nineteenth-century London. Repeatedly, the researchers have discovered the persistence of ethnicity. They report that ethnic groups in cities consist of people who restrict their social ties largely to persons within the group, who identify themselves as members of the group, and who maintain the distinctive customs and traditional values of their particular culture.[3]

The maintenance of social ties within an ethnic group is manifested in various sorts of patterns: most friends are in a person's own ethnic group; marriages occur predominantly between fellow members (sometimes great efforts are made to recruit wives from home villages); and clubs and associations tend to have an exclusive ethnic membership.

When individuals identify themselves as ethnic group

members, it means that they think of themselves as Chinese in Bangkok, as Bretons in Paris, or as Armenians in New York. In South Chicago, for example, old animosities between Serbians and Croatians (regions of what is now Yugoslavia) still contribute to tensions between their American descendants (Kornblum, 1974). Urbanism can even *create* a new form of ethnic identity, in that self-identification may become more encompassing: for example, Neapolitans living in New York City come to identify themselves as "Italians." Some evidence for this persistence in ethnic identity is provided by studies of voting in American cities that indicate a continuing preference by electors for candidates of their own ethnicity into the third generation of immigrants (Wolfinger, 1965; Gordon, 1970; Glazer and Moynihan, 1970).

Maintaining the customs and values of an ethnic culture is a third way in which people demonstrate ethnic persistence. In South Chicago, some of the Slavic customs practiced by third-generation residents are so traditional that more recent immigrants from the "old country" find them bizarrely out of date (Kornblum, 1974). In most cases, however, cultural purity is not maintained in the city, not at least with regard to what might be termed "peripheral" cultural items. The customs, values, and artifacts of a culture can be scaled from "central"—those involving or reflecting the fundamental, almost preconscious, aspects of a culture (such as implicit understanding about the social world, ultimate life values and goals, and styles of interpersonal relations)—to "peripheral"—those that are relatively incidental, perhaps accidental, aspects of a culture (such as dress styles, specific rituals, and political attitudes, which are not integrally linked to its core ethos). Peripheral items are malleable and can change, in the sense that within a generation or two minority ethnic groups in a city adopt all or parts of such cultural patterns from the dominant group. (In colonial cities, the dominant group can be numerically small, yet economically and culturally powerful, such as the whites in South Africa.) However, the central cultural items seem to persist to a quite noticeable extent.[4]

These conclusions about urban ethnicity are based mainly on studies conducted only in large cities; in that way, they are limited. Such studies rarely contrast the nature of the ethnic group in the city with its counterpart in rural settings. There is usually evidence of ethnicity in most settings, but without urban-rural comparison, there is no way to conclude whether there is much or only little ethnic persistence. (This is the familiar problem: Is the glass half empty or half full?)[5] Comparative evidence also indicates that ethnicity is generally as significant in the city as in the countryside, and in some cases is more significant.

Consider four studies: Anthropologists studying migration to the rapidly growing cities of Africa have frequently described a process labeled "retribalization" or "supertribalization." Becoming an urbanite is often associated with increased awareness of, pride in, and self-conscious attachment to the individual's tribe. This attachment often manifests itself in tribal organizations and in tribal conflict.[6] The anthropologist Edward Bruner (1961; 1973a) studied a Christian tribe in Indonesia, called the Toba Batak, both in their home village and in the largely Moslem city of Medan. He found that attachment to traditional values and to traditional norms concerning family life was at least as strong in Medan as in the village. The third study involved a survey of third-generation Ukrainian-Canadians living in a small, exclusively "Ukrainian" town and of those living in a larger, ethnically heterogeneous city. The respondents residing in the larger, more differentiated community were more resistant to assimilation and more identified with their Ukrainianism than those in the smaller town (Borhek, 1970). Finally, three political scientists investigated the extent to which Polish-American voters in a Chicago ward and in a rural county of Illinois were inclined to select a candidate on the basis of ethnicity. The Chicago voters were markedly more likely to choose the candidate with the Polish name than were the rural voters (Lorinskas et al., 1969).

This and similar evidence (for example, Nelli, 1970; Cornelius, 1971) suggest that the vitality and integrity of ethnic groups is not necessarily sapped by urbanism, and is sometimes even strengthened by it. How might this be explained? It may be that the forces in the urban setting that Wirth thought weakened ethnic groups simply do not exist or

are not very powerful. This would be a compositional suggestion: ecological factors are of little consequence. Or, a subcultural suggestion, it may be that there are countervailing urban forces that work to bolster ethnicity. We will discuss two
such forces here, elaborating arguments first presented in
Chapter 2.

The first of these two forces is the by now familiar factor
of numbers and the achievement of critical mass. Larger
numbers make it possible for people to find friends and
spouses within their own group, and to bring more members
of the group to the city. For instance, the chance that a Catholic will marry within the faith increases with the size of the
Catholic population, so that it is more probable in large than
in small American cities (J. L. Thomas, 1951); the same is true
for Jews (Rosenthal, 1967). The larger the ethnic group, the
greater also is the possibility of supporting institutions that
reinforce ethnicity: churches, newspapers, stores, clubs, political organizations. These institutions link people to their
groups, exercise authority over the members, protect them
from outsiders, help attract fellow ethnics, and constantly
remind them of their identity. In Chapter 3, we cited a study
of immigrants to Montreal that showed that nationality
groups with such institutions were best able to maintain ethnic cohesion and boundaries. Having those institutions was
partly a function of simple numbers (Breton, 1964). Another
example of the same process comes from a study of American Indians in San Francisco. Powwows provide important
social and ritual functions in Indian communities, but until
1962 there were too few Indians in the Bay Area who could
perform the necessary rites. People had to drive back to the
reservations for the powwows. Now that the Indian population of the area has grown larger, powwows have been held
there, and have served to unite the Indian community (Hirabayashi, 1972: 82).[7] The conclusion is that the larger the city,
the larger—in general—are its various ethnic groups. And, in
turn, the larger an ethnic group, the more likely it is to preserve its culture and its social boundaries. It may even become possible to maintain an isolated ethnic world in the
midst of the city (Lopata, 1967; Mathiasson, 1974).[8]

In Chapter 4, we noted that while ethnic variety is not an

inevitable concomitant of urbanism, it is a common one. In Chapter 5, we suggested that urbanism also tends to generate subcultures founded on bases of association other than ethnicity. The analysis here indicates that contact among urban subcultures promotes ethnic distinctiveness, ethnic boundaries, and ethnic consciousness. Cross-cultural contacts can and often do result in violence. More commonly, they frequently lead to mutual revulsion, because members of each group view the others from their own cultural perspective. Repelled and disgusted, the members are more than ever convinced of the virtue of their own group.

As a case in point, African "supertribalization" results largely from tribal members seeing for the first time, in the city, people who look, act, and believe differently than they do. This urban experience raises their tribal consciousness. The Toba Batak, the Indonesian group, also exhibit this process. In the following passage, Bruner describes encounters between the Batak and the Sundanese majority in Bandung, Java:

> Most Sundanese have not had much experience with Batak although all are familiar with the Batak stereotype of a rough and aggressive person. The Sundanese and the Batak each approach the initial interaction guided by their own customs and emotional set, and at first they judge the other by their own standards. What the Sundanese define as being crude the Batak interpret as being honest, straight-forward, and strong. What the Sundanese regard as refined behavior the Batak regard as being evasive, insincere, and feminine. Each group feels morally superior to the other and at least initially the behavior of each tends to validate these stereotypic evaluations. Each group in doing what it thinks is right and proper behaves in ways that the other feels are morally deficient [Bruner, 1973a: 265].

There are many examples of such culture-clash in the American urban experience. Describing the Addams area of Chicago, Suttles (1968: 61-72) notes common misunderstandings between blacks and whites. Their styles of dress, of physical and verbal expression, and even modes of eye-contact differ. What one considers honest the other perceives as rude; what one considers polite the other perceives as hostile. One result is the conviction held by each group that the other is unworthy of trust and friendship (see also Nelli, 1970; Borhek, 1970; Gans, 1962b).

The ultimate outcome of intergroup suspicion and tension is overt ethnic conflict. Sometimes violent, such conflict is more likely to occur in large than in small communities. Racial violence during the 1960s in the United States, for example, was especially concentrated in the larger cities (Spilerman, 1971; Morgan and Clark, 1973; Danzger, 1975). Relatively large black populations in the metropolitan areas created more friction with whites, a greater sense of racial pride and unity, and a greater feeling of power—all of which made collective violence more likely.

Change in Ethnic Groups

Ethnicity both persists *and changes* under the influence of urbanism. As we have known since at least the time of Thomas and Znaniecki's *Polish Peasant* (1918), Poles in Chicago are not identical to their cousins in Polish villages. The changes that occur can be grouped into the same categories of social ties, identity, and customs that we used to discuss persistence. But before examining the ways in which urbanism modifies each, let us consider the forces that produce the changes.

Some of these forces are incidental to urbanism and not unique to living in cities: the disruption and separation resulting from migration, and the change in language and occupation that are the result of a move from one society to another. A study of rural migrants in Bombay, India, revealed that they had given up some religious rituals because their new jobs made the services more bothersome to perform than had been the case when they were farmers (Prabhu, 1956; see also Husain, 1956).

Besides such factors, which are connected with migration, there are two familiar ones that are peculiar to urbanism: the numbers of people and the heterogeneous contact between them. These are the very same forces that support ethnicity. Community size modifies ethnic groups because it supports the development of alternative subcultures based on other factors, such as occupation, life-style, and age. These subcultures tempt defections from the ethnic culture—as when young professionals turn their backs on the old ethnic neighborhood, for example. Furthermore, a large city in which there is a sizable, dominant population becomes a precarious environment for small minorities. Even when they are tolerated by the majority group, they must modify at least their public behavior. That was the fate of the Batak in Java, and of most minorities in white, Anglo-Saxon, Protestant America.

As we noted, contact between groups leads to repulsion and conflict, but it also leads simultaneously to diffusion—to the adoption of selected life-styles, beliefs, or objects from other groups. Usually, subordinate groups accept cultural items from dominant ones, but the influence can operate both ways, as in the case of urban black culture and its influence on whites.

The forces of diffusion modify the social ties of ethnic group members. People almost inevitably make connections across ethnic lines, with close involvements sometimes growing out of what began as impersonal relationships between members of different groups. Frequently, people drift away from the ethnic group, committing themselves instead to subcultures based on profession and life-style. Or sometimes they marry into another ethnic group, as is becoming increasingly common among middle-class, urban Africans (Little, 1973: 131). It is remarkable that this weakening of ethnic boundaries has occurred so little even in the United States, which is a difficult environment for pluralism.[9] Note that, in crossing ethnic boundaries, the "defectors" are not left drifting, isolated without any bonds; rather they have been drawn into an alternative group. Note as well that the defection leaves behind a more "purified" core of committed ethnic group members.

The same sorts of pressures alter ethnic identity. In particular, intergroup contact in cities creates an allegiance to larger ethnic categories. For example, in peasant China, people saw themselves as members of a village, sometimes as members of a region (say, Cantonese); in American cities, they are "Chinese," an identity rarely acknowledged back home. In the African bush, people see themselves essentially as members of specific family lineages; in the cities they are identified as, and identify themselves as, members of the tribe. Sometimes, in the larger cities, the process is reversed; size redivides ethnic definition. There come to be so many immigrant Chinese, for example, that the distinction of Cantonese versus Szechuan is again important (see Handlin, 1969; Hanna and Hanna, 1971; on pan-Indianism in the United States, see Price, 1975).

And ethnic culture—traditions, customs, institutions— changes. For instance, organizations develop that did not exist in the rural homeland: mutual-benefit societies, credit unions, ethnic newspapers, political clubs. These are partly cultural borrowings from other groups, and partly adaptations to new economic conditions and to hostility from other groups (the B'nai B'rith Anti-Defamation League is an example of the latter). In any case, they represent new ethnic institutions.

Customs and traditions are altered. Sometimes the alteration is toward more cultural distinctiveness, often as a response to threats from other groups. For example, one Indian caste, finding itself in competition with other migrant groups in the city of Madras, redefined traditional rules of its membership and changed its customs so as to encourage internal marriage. Both moves helped to consolidate its political and economic strength (Barnett, 1973). Another example is the trading tribe of West Africa, the Hausa, who reside in Nigerian cities dominated by the Yoruba tribe. Earlier in this century, Hausa leaders initiated a vigorous religious (Moslem) revival and the group became more orthodox. This was probably a political tactic designed to fight off potential trading competitors (A. Cohen, 1969).

The more common changes in ethnic cultures are probably those that blur the lines between groups. For example, the Toba Batak in Java learn, as they must in order to succeed in that society, to lower their voices, to display "refined behavior," and generally to adopt Sundanese ways. Batak children change even more, so much that they come to judge their own families by Sundanese standards (Bruner, 1973a).

The extent to which an ethnic group's structure and culture can be altered is dramatized in the African urban experience. In rural areas, the African tribe is the entire society, economy, polity, and culture; it is the whole of the individual's world. In urban centers, the tribe is an ethnic group: a category of people, an identity, a source of relatives and friends, an instructor in belief and behavior. In these ways, it distinguishes the individual from others with whom he or she shares a common society, economy, polity, and national culture. The tribe becomes one social world among many (see Epstein, 1967).

For all these changes, ethnic boundaries nevertheless remain, and a cultural core persists. What is altered most are the peripheral items, such as style of clothing or taste in food; least altered are basic understandings of the world. People identify themselves with, display the cultural traits of, and find their most intimate social ties within their ethnic groups. Cases of ethnic assimilation into the urban melting pot, of course, occur, as do cases of continued ethnic purity. Most ethnic groups are in between, their particular balance of change and constancy depending on their internal characteristics (such as size and degree of orthodoxy), the society around them, their distinctiveness from other groups, the distance from their homeland, their flow of migration, and other such factors.

In sum, the status of ethnic groups in the city is best described by the complex analysis of subcultural theory. The size and the cross-cultural contact that accompany urbanism bolster ethnic groups in various ways. These forces simultaneously stimulate competing subcultures that can influence ethnic groups and lure their members away. In most societies, urbanism produces in ethnic groups a combination of both constancy and change. At the same time that the people of a city dress, speak, work, and play in shared ways, they trust and relax with "their own," interact in a style peculiar to "their own," pursue goals particularly stressed by "their own," and urge their children to marry "their own."

Friends

A friend, states Webster's Collegiate Dictionary, is "one attached to another by affection and esteem." Friendship, to sociologists, is a complex social relationship. Unlike being neighbors or relatives or co-workers, being friends is not ascribed or structured from outside, but is instead a state freely chosen by the people involved. To be sure, most friends are simultaneously neighbors, co-workers, kin, or connected in some other way; rarely are they *just* friends (Shulman, 1972). We tend to select as friends people we know in some other context (see Fischer et al., 1977). These contexts are the "pools" from which we draw our friends. Our first question concerns what effects urbanism has on these pools and the process of selecting friends from them.

From the standpoint of arithmetic alone, the larger the community, the greater the number of people who can meet and befriend one another. It is obvious, for example, that an individual in a town of 10,000 has about ten times as many potential friends in his community as does a person in a town of 1,000. It is less obvious but no less important that the *combinations* of friends increase even more rapidly with increases in population. In the larger community there are a hundred times as many possible friendships (pairs of friends) as in the smaller one.[10] One apparent implication, then, is that the more urban the community, the greater the available choice in friendships, and, consequently, the more compatible are the friendships that actually result. Another implication seems to be that urban friendships are more likely to involve *just* friendship and no other relationship.

However, the actual differences between large and small communities are not nearly as great as these calculations imply. Both in urban and rural settings, people do not canvass their entire town for friends, but select them instead from relatively small pools or milieus—the work place, neighborhood, social club, and so on. These friendship pools are not likely to be so much more populous in cities than in small towns. In the absence of data, we could estimate that the average population size of such milieus increases slowly as community size increases sharply. But although the sheer numbers exaggerate the extent of the difference, it is still likely that urbanites can select friends from a wider range of choices than can ruralites. Urban friendship pools are probably somewhat larger, there are more of them, and their populations do not overlap as much in large communities as they do in small ones (see Barker and Gump, 1964). What difference does this make to the actual patterns of friendship of urban residents?

The determinist and compositional theories give contrary answers. As we previously noted, determinists argue that intimate relationships are eclipsed in the city by impersonal ties, so urbanites have fewer friends than ruralites. Although surrounded by and in ceaseless contact with people, city dwellers rarely interact at a personal level. Simmel (1905: 58) refers to "the brevity and scarcity of the inter-human contacts granted to the metropolitan man." Park (1916: 125) compares people in the city to people "in some great hotel, meeting but not knowing one another. The effect . . . is to substitute fortuitous and casual relationships for the more intimate and permanent associations of the smaller community." Should an urbanite claim to have friendships, they are in truth shallow and transient ones. The same authority who earlier proclaimed the death of primary groups described such "friendships" in these terms: "People who live in cities may think they have lots of friends; but the word friend has changed its meaning. Compared with friendships of the past, most of these new friendships are trivial" (Alexander, 1967: 241). In contrast, compositional theory asserts that friendships, like other intimate social groups, should be no less common or meaningful in cities than in the countryside. Subcultural theory agrees, and goes further: Urban friendships should be somewhat more intimate than rural friendships, because they are likelier to emerge from distinctive, homogeneous, and freely chosen subcultures (themselves partly a function of simple numbers).

For evidence, we turn first to the ethnographic studies that have been conducted in cities around the world. These studies repeatedly find that city dwellers are not isolated and do have a number of friends. There are, to be sure, specific cases that closely fit the image of the lonely urbanite: skid-row alcoholics whose "friendships" last only as long as the shared bottle (Bahr, 1973); unemployed men who hang out on ghetto street corners, whose "friends" pass out of their lives without exchanging last names (Liebow, 1967; Hannerz,

1969). But these are exceptions. The general rule is that city dwellers, apparently no less than country dwellers, have friends from whom they draw both emotional and material support.[11] By comparison, studies of small communities suggest that city dwellers might actually have more and deeper friendships. Reports of rural, particularly peasant, life are replete with accounts of hostility, suspicion, and feuds that estrange many people from most of their neighbors who are not also their immediate relatives.[12]

Survey studies affirm the same general conclusion. Few city residents report themselves to be without friends. For example, only one percent of men interviewed in San Francisco in the 1950s said that they "never" saw people informally; eight percent reported seeing friends and relatives only a few times a year; but half reported seeing such people more than once a week (Bell and Boat, 1957). Similarly, less than five percent of respondents to a survey conducted in Lansing, Michigan, said that they had no "best friends" (Smith et al., 1954).[13]

A number of reservations about these studies should be noted: for one, they are not comparative. Although the percentage of friendless people in the city may seem low, that proportion may still be higher than that in rural areas. Nor do these studies take into account factors that may mask urban-rural differences in friendships (for example, the fact that urban people tend to be younger than rural people). Finally, the surveys asked only superficial questions about friendships; surveys usually cannot distinguish between deep and trivial relationships when both are called "friendships."

Several comparative surveys have found that urbanites are just as involved in friendships as ruralites. One of the most exact studies was conducted in the Nashville, Tennessee, area by Albert Reiss, Jr. (1959b). Men in the city and in the rural hinterland—both on and off farms—were asked to provide "time budgets," that is, to recount exactly how and with whom they had spent the previous working day. As Figure 6 indicates, even with social class taken into account, there were essentially no differences between the city and rural aggregates in the average amount of time spent with kin. Furthermore, urban men allocated their time *more* heav-

FIGURE 6

AVERAGE TIME SPENT WITH FAMILY, FRIENDS, AND OTHERS
BY URBAN, RURAL NONFARM, AND FARM MEN
(NASHVILLE, MID-1950s)

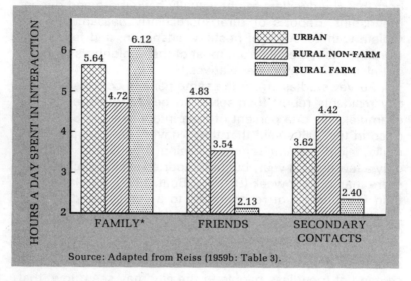

Source: Adapted from Reiss (1959b: Table 3).

Source: Adapted from Reiss (1959b: Table 3).
* Within each residential category, the results for high- and low-status respondents
were averaged. "Family" included both nuclear and extended family; "friends" included both those rated as close who were not derived from a work context, and close
friends met at work; "secondary contacts" included distant associates or acquaintances,
those cordially recognized, and purely client relationships.

ily in favor of friends, as against secondary associates, than
the rural men did. This study, and other comparative research, reinforces the conclusion that urbanism does not impair friendship.[14]

To conclude that urbanites are as involved with friends
as ruralites are is not to say that the nature of those friendships is untouched by urbanism. Friendships might in fact
differ between city and country—for one thing, a person's
friends are probably more geographically dispersed in urban
areas. In Chapter 5, during the discussion of neighborhoods,
we suggested that the relative unimportance of the locality as
a source of intimacy was explained in part by the availability

to city dwellers of many potential friends beyond the immediate vicinity of their homes. Urbanites' friends are probably drawn from a wider variety of pools than are ruralites' friends. If our earlier conclusion is correct—that urbanism gives rise to social worlds constructed on bases of association not found in rural places—then it is plausible that this multiplicity of sources would yield sets of friends who represent that variety.

There is a little, although admittedly quite limited, evidence in support of the latter conjecture. For instance, in a Japanese study, Takashi Koyama (1970) asked about three hundred families in a farming village and about three hundred in a Tokyo ward whom they would turn to when in need of various sorts of assistance. The answers showed that an equal proportion of urban and rural families would turn to personal sources of help. On the average, only eight percent of each group said they would have to turn to a welfare institution. Both groups would most often rely on relatives for virtually all types of aid. The major difference between the urban and rural people was in the importance assigned to neighbors, the Tokyo residents relying on them to a lesser extent than the farm families. In place of neighbors, the city people would turn to relatives, co-workers, or others.[15]

The suggestions that urban friendships are relatively dispersed and that they are relatively specialized—each involving separate aspects of people's lives—are only hypotheses. But we do have one fairly firm conclusion: the idea that urban people have fewer or less intimate friends than rural people is not supported by the evidence.

Family

Our study of social groups in the city has gradually moved from those that are physically most distant from the individual toward the most intimate group of all, the family. No one should underestimate the importance of the family, in this age as in any other. The family of origin—the family into which one is born—is the immediate shaper of one's life-chances and life-views; the family of procreation—spouse and children—is one's main investment and reward, sadness and joy. The family is also the basic unit of society, and a major instrument for teaching and social control. The fate of the family is therefore of central concern to urban sociologists.

In the traditional sociological view, as expressed by the Chicago School, urbanism weakens the family by producing institutions that have "deprived the family of some of its most characteristic historical functions" (Wirth, 1938: 161) and that tempt defections from its members. Community size and structural differentiation provide alternatives to the family for economic support, emergency help, leisure activities, and other services. So, too, in this view, other social groups in the city—such as work friends and club associates—draw people away from home. These losses of function and attention sap the authority of the family and render remaining family ties narrow, superficial, and unfulfilling. Consequently, society, which is dependent on the family for sustaining and restraining individuals, suffers disorganization and anomie.[16]

To this entire analysis, compositional theory answers simply that kinship persists in the city. Oscar Lewis (1965: 494) reported that in his studies of people in Mexico City, "family life remained quite stable and extended family ties increased rather than decreased." The family may be affected by economic differences between urban and rural communities (such as the available jobs), but such an intimate social unit is not seriously affected by population size as such. Subcultural theory takes seriously the challenge to family allegiance posed by other sources of attachment that arise in the city, such as commercial services and social groups. However, whether these alternatives actually weaken the family depends on other circumstances: whether one social bond precludes another to any significant degree; whether family relationships are weakened or strengthened by loss of certain functions; and so on. We will return to these considerations later.

The following discussion will largely ignore the distinction that is sometimes made between the nuclear and the extended family, in which "nuclear" refers to the immediate family of husband, wife, and children, and "extended" refers to remaining close relatives such as aunts, grandparents, and in-laws. Since most theoretical analyses and empirical data meld the two, we will do the same.

We begin with the basic demographic facts. First, the larger a community, the less likely it is that its residents live in families. Single adults living alone or in unrelated groups are more common in city than in countryside. In 1970, 20 percent of metropolitan households and 17 percent of nonmetropolitan households were formed of "primary individuals" (Bureau of the Census, 1971b: 78); the differences are somewhat greater when the largest metropolises are compared and when suburbs are excluded (Fischer, 1973a: note 3). Second, divorce and desertion rates tend to be greater in larger communities, although this is not universally the case. In America today, urbanism is modestly related to family dissolution. For example, in 1970, 9.6 percent of all nonmetropolitan American families were headed by females; that figure was 11.5 percent for metropolitan families, and 13.1 percent for those in metropolises of over three million (Bureau of the Census, 1971b: 9).[17] Third, families tend to be smaller in larger communities. For example, in 1970, 20 percent of young, married couples in nonmetropolitan areas had no children under eighteen at home; the figure for metropolitan couples was 24 percent (Bureau of the Census, 1971b: 20). And, fourth, members of extended families are less likely to share a common household in urban than in rural areas (Laslett, 1973; Goode, 1963).

These demographic patterns indicate that the larger a community, the smaller are its families. But there are many exceptions to the rule; and the differences are small, particularly in the United States. For instance, although households composed of extended families are the ideal in many societies, the actual statistical norm around the world in urban and in rural places is the nuclear-family household (Gulick, 1973). And the differences that appear in American statistics are largely a result of the traits of center cities; in the suburbs, households made up of families are at least as common as they are in small towns.

In short, there is a relationship between urbanism and family structure that calls for explanation. A determinist interpretation fits well: these differences are signs of the urban disintegration of the family. A compositional explanation would focus on self-selection: certain kinds of people—the young and unmarried, the upwardly mobile, the nontraditional—disproportionately reside in cities, and it is their presence that accounts for the observed differences. The research which would permit us to choose between the two explanations has yet to be done. In any case, these statistics do not speak to the essence of the question—the social-psychological nature of family ties. Single persons have relatives; divorced persons remarry; small families can be intimate. Demographics do not tell the whole tale.

Sociological studies of the family provide an even more complex story than do census data. They suggest that urban and rural families differ on two dimensions. Kin (mainly extended kin) are more dispersed geographically in large communities than in small. For example, in an American survey conducted in the late 1960s, families living outside metropolitan areas were about 12 percent more likely to report having relatives within walking distance than were metropolitan families.[18] This difference in distances leads to more frequent contact among relatives in nonmetropolitan than in metropolitan areas. A national study found that rural fathers and sons lived nearer each other and thus saw each other more frequently than urban fathers and sons (Klatzky, 1971). This dispersal of kin in cities occurs in various societies (see Schnaiberg, 1970; Bruner, 1973b; Koyama, 1970).

And as Wirth, Ogburn, and others have suggested, the family probably serves fewer functions in the city than it does in the countryside. Chapter 3 documented the wealth of facilities and services available in cities. This wealth implies that urbanites will more often than ruralites satisfy their needs (for a job, advice, recreation, a meal, etc.) outside the family. We have seen that there is probably less overlap among kin, friends, co-workers, and neighbors in the city than in the countryside. Consequently, urbanites should rely less often on relatives for personal relationships than ruralites. Bits of research tend to support these conclusions: city dwellers less often pursue leisure activities with their immediate family than country dwellers (Swedner, 1960; Leevy, 1950); and, urbanites distinguish among their personal associates when seeking services, turning, for example, to friends for job advice and to kin for aid during illness (Roberts, 1973; Litwak and Szelenyi, 1969). But research also cautions us that these urban-rural differences are not great. Even though they have outside alternatives, city dwellers turn first and most often to relatives for assistance (Wellman, et al., 1973; Goode, 1963: 70-76). Though urban services and urban friends permit people to look outside their family for satisfaction of their wants, they do not compel them to do so. (See general discussion in Hawley, 1971: 120ff., 302ff.)

Urbanism tends to disperse and to specialize the family. Does it also weaken the social importance and the emotional intensity of the family relationship? The evidence indicates that it does not. Over and over again, ethnographic reports from around the world tell us that kinship persists and even thrives in the city. A classic study in this vein, one which helped shape a consensus in sociology on this issue, was conducted in Bethnal Green, a dense and gritty working-class borough of London (Young and Wilmott, 1957). The investigators reported: "We were surprised to discover that the wider [extended] family, far from having disappeared, was very much alive in the middle of London." They discovered that young couples chose to stay near their parents, and, indeed, depended on their mothers to help them find flats nearby. Both husbands and wives saw their "mums" frequently, the women averaging four times a week, and family get-togethers at "mum's" were common. In all, Bethnal Green was an extended-family neighborhood, in which kinship dominated the residents' lives. Discoveries such as this one of familism in the city have become so common as to make the finding virtually a truism (See Gulick, 1973: 1003ff.).[19]

Survey studies conducted in many cities also find that residents maintain frequent contact with their kin and that urbanites both see and depend on their relatives more than on any other associates. Two California studies conducted in the 1950s serve as examples: half the Los Angeles housewives interviewed in one survey reported seeing relatives at least once a week; less than ten percent said they never saw kin (Greer, 1956). Forty percent of men interviewed in San Francisco reported seeing kin more than once a week; about 15 percent reported never seeing kin (Bell and Boat, 1957). These studies, and more recent ones, show that relatives are seen more often, cared about more, and relied on more for assistance than friends, co-workers, or neighbors.[20]

Both the ethnographic and the survey studies of kinship

in urban areas are subject to the now familiar reservation that they are not comparative. Since each study was conducted in a single location, it cannot tell us whether the amount of kinship contact in the city was greater or less than would have been the case if the study was extended to comparable rural populations. Some comparative studies have been done on family relations. A few have examined frequency of contact; others have looked at the number of kin living with, or accessible to, individuals. The results are quite mixed.

A few found essentially no differences by size of community in the extent of contact with kin (Key, 1968; Swedner, 1960; Koyama, 1970). An example is Figure 6, the Nashville time-budget study, in which city men averaged about as much time with their families as did men in the countryside. A few studies report that rural people saw their kin more often, or were emotionally closer to their kin than were urban people (Klatzky, 1971; Schnaiberg, 1970; Winch and Greer, 1968).[21] Two other studies report the opposite: more involvement with kin in urban than in rural areas (Bultena, 1969; Palmore et al., 1970). The few comparative ethnographic studies repeat these contradictions. For example, Bruner (1962) reports that the Toba Batak residing in Medan saw more relatives than did the Batak in the home village, but that the urban contacts were less frequent, less "personal, intimate, and familial than in the village." Other comparative ethnographic studies report stronger family ties in the city (Lewis, 1952, 1965; Butterworth, 1962; Shack, 1973). If there is a conclusion that can be drawn from these conflicting studies, it is that, in general, there are no major differences by size of community in the extent to which people are bound to their families.

The conclusion that urbanism is unrelated to family cohesion is buttressed by those few studies that are comparative and that also take into account the physical distances between kin. One, mentioned earlier, examined the frequency of contact between male relatives; once distance was controlled, there were no size-of-community differences (Klatzky, 1971). This study strongly suggests that there is nothing about urban life, other than distance, that lessens contact with kin. Another study compared elderly people living in a

medium-sized city to those living in small towns in the frequency with which they saw their children. In this study, the
city residents had more frequent contact, but the difference
was due to the fact that they lived closer to their offspring.
When distance was controlled, there were no residual differences between community sizes (Bultena, 1969; see also Palmore et al., 1970; and, Winch and Greer, 1968).

The connections between distance, contact, and intimacy
should be carefully considered. The farther people live from
their relatives, the less often they will see one another. As
noted earlier, urbanites usually live farther from their kin than
ruralites and are thus more often discouraged from visiting
relatives. However, the critical issue is the extent to which
either distance or frequency of contact determines the emotional intensity of personal relationships. Certainly, the more
easily people can make face-to-face contact, the more they
can nurture their relationship. But there is evidence that long
distances and infrequency of contact do not necessarily impair basic family ties. Relatives may be far away and rarely
seen, yet still be considered intimate, written to or telephoned
—at least in modern societies—cared about deeply, and turned
to first in time of need. (And the old saying, that separation
makes the heart grow fonder, is doubtless often true.) There
are relationships that survive not only the large city but
long distances as well.[22]

Just as distance should be taken into account when assessing urban-rural differences, so should other variables,
such as age, social class, and the question of whether people
were raised in their community of current residence. Only a
few studies have controlled for such factors. They have found
no substantial and independent urban-rural differences in
familial relationships (Reiss, 1959b; Schnaiberg, 1970; Palmore et al., 1970).[23]

Drawing together the bits of research reviewed here, we
can make a few general statements about urbanism and the
family. First, the larger the community, the less complete the
average family. City dwellers are slightly more likely to be
unmarried, or without children, or with fewer children, or
divorced or separated, than are people outside the cities.
Second, the larger a community, the more the extended

family tends to be geographically dispersed. However, the great urban-rural difference that once was thought to exist— exemplified in the mistaken idea that the typical rural house- hold contained three generations—does not. And third, the larger the community, the probably somewhat fewer func- tions the family serves. It tends to specialize in child-rearing, companionship, and the provision of emotional succorance; other institutions, groups, and people in the city can meet further needs of the individual.

These effects of urbanism are not sizable, and in any event seem not to impair the intimacy and depth of family ties. Such qualities of kinship do not decline as a conse- quence of increases in urbanism. Although the frequency of contact among kin may be affected, family ties seem as close and as psychologically important in the city as in the country- side. It is worth speculating briefly as to why urban family ties are not weakened, in view of the apparent reduction in the services city families provide their members. Perhaps, con- trary to the assumption of theories that expect the breakdown of urban families, economic, recreational, service, and other such ancillary functions are not the stuff of which family strength is made. That "stuff" is more personal, emotional, and psychological. Indeed, certain functions may actually in- terfere with intimacy (the sharing of a business, for example, may cause a falling out between brothers). Furthermore, the urban setting does not require that such functions be per- formed outside the family; it merely permits them to be. For instance, parents may still prefer to use relatives, even though commercial baby-sitting services are available in the city. The presence of alternatives often allows urban families to *choose* which functions will be performed within or out- side the household.

The findings described here have clear implications for the theoretical controversy this book is presenting. Determin- ist theory predicts the breakdown of the urban family; that prediction is not confirmed. Compositional theory predicts no independent effects of urbanism on the family; this predic- tion is closer to the facts. The urban-rural differences we discovered could be explained in terms of composition: ur- banites tend to be young, and young people tend to have few children, to move away from home, and to turn away from the family for companionship. The class distribution of urbanites is higher than that of ruralites: people of higher status depend less on relatives for aid, and can afford to live farther away from their kin. These factors may suffice to explain the modest urban-rural differences in family structure without recourse to subcultural theory, which is more complex. It makes much the same prediction as compositional theory, but it also stresses the presence of institutions and groups in the city that supplement family functions, and thereby render the family a somewhat more specialized primary group. In either case, an accurate theory of urbanism must incorporate the fact that, while the family may be changed by the city, it still persists.

Summary

The quality of individuals' lives depends greatly on whether they belong to intimate social groups—sets of people on whom they can rely, who provide both moral support and moral restraint. These personal networks are the indispensable ingredients for integrating the individual into society and for maintaining social cohesion.

Urban people belong to such groups to the same extent as do rural people. Whether by answering survey questions or by their other behavior, city dwellers demonstrate that they have people whom they can call on for friendship, advice, and assistance. Urbanites probably differ a little from ruralites in the extent to which each of their associates provides distinctive kinds of services. Friends might supply sociability, co-workers advice, relatives long-term assistance, and neighbors emergency aid. Compared with the ruralite, the urban person probably turns more often to different individuals for specialized relationships. This one knows a good lawyer; that one is fun at parties; the other is supportive when one is upset.

Specialization does not seem to reduce the meaningfulness and intrinsic value of social ties to people. But neither can we say that it increases them. In any case, the difference between city and countryside ought not to be exaggerated; for all sizes of community, kin rank nearest and dearest, and associates are largely drawn from within the ethnic group. City and countryside differ markedly in the extent to which people turn to those physically nearby. Urbanites usually can and do go beyond their immediate vicinity to gather the personal elements they need to construct a viable social world. (In Chapter 5 we mentioned the constraint felt by the residents of a Castilian hamlet because they could not do the same.)

What happens to primary groups under the influence of urbanism? They persist and they change. They persist in that urbanites are involved in intimate relationships to the same degree that ruralites are. And they persist in that each of them —the ethnic group, friends, the family—exists as a distinguishable and vital group in the city. As theorists of primary-group breakdown point out, the city provides a multitude of competitors, of alternative bases of association. These other social worlds often challenge and alter ethnic groups and the family. But two important points about that challenge should be remembered: First, to leave one social world for another does not mean the loss of primary ties, but only their transference. People who neglect their extended kin in favor of friends met in a professional context are not without intimate ties, it is just that they have formed different intimate ties. Second, and more important, the availability of other acquaintances, friends, and intimates in the urban setting does not rule out close ties with kin (or, indeed, neighbors). Urban relationships do not replace the kind found in rural areas, they add to them. This is also Bruner's conclusion about the social relationships of the Toba Batak in Medan:

> It is a process of addition, not substitution, and the quantity of social relations is not fixed. Those Batak who relate more to non-kin may be said to be more urbanized and modernized, but this does not mean that they become less Batak, or that they renounce their ethnic affiliation, or that they cut ties with their fellow villagers and clansmen. They are urban and Batak at the same time (Bruner, 1973b: 391).

Primary groups in the city also change. They change in that they are more dispersed over space, and they are somewhat more specialized in function. These changes are neither so great in extent nor so significant in effect as to weaken the social-psychological role of primary groups.

If a single lesson can be distilled from all this, it is that people both in city and in countryside lead their lives not on the huge scale of complex metropolises or of vast prairies but in small, intimate, private social worlds.

7

THE INDIVIDUAL IN THE CITY
STATES OF MIND

Our visitor to the city has now had plenty of time to observe the urban scene from the sidelines, and is committed to understanding the urban experience. He or she might leave the café, enter the passing throng, ask many questions, and, by interviewing and probing, seek a direct understanding of urbanites. What are city dwellers like psychologically? What are their characteristic states of mind and types of personality?

The theoretical controversy we have been examining reaches its climax in questions of this sort. According to determinist theory, city life poses a harsh dilemma for the individual—a hard choice between equally unsatisfactory alternatives. On the one hand, urbanism produces a great deal of psychological stress at the same time that it weakens the sources of social support that could help ease the strain. The probable outcome is psychological disorder—anxiety and irritability at best; severe malfunction at worst. On the other hand, urban individuals must adopt various ways of coping that, in effect, alter their personalities and styles of life; these include becoming aloof, cynical, superficial, or mercenary. Both compositional theory and subcultural theory deny that urban life poses this dilemma; they assert that neither effect occurs. In their view, the stresses probably do not exist; even if they did, however, the main sources of social support are active in the city and would buffer any pressures.

In Chapter 8, we will consider the second horn of the determinist dilemma—that the urban experience alters people's personalities and life-styles in a negative way. In this chapter, we address the first horn—that living in cities produces psychological stress. In our examination of urban states of mind, we first review a school of thought and research called "crowding studies." Authorities in this field often argue that urban densities violate intrinsic human needs for space, with seriously harmful consequences. Then, we focus directly on

153

the relationship between urbanism and psychological stress and disorder. Next, we examine "urban alienation." And, finally, we sum it all up by considering whether living in cities makes people unhappy.

As always, we must remember that the urban experience is pluralistic, varying according to the city-dwellers' personal traits, specific community, and specific location within the city. The importance of specific location has been underlined by studies of the mental pictures ("cognitive maps") people have of the cities in which they live. When asked to draw maps of their cities or to indicate locales with which they are familiar, people tend to exaggerate the size or detail of their own neighborhoods in relation to the rest of the urban area. On these maps, everything except the immediate neighborhood tends to resemble the vague *terra incognita* of medieval maps. The extent to which this distortion occurs is partly a function of how far individuals regularly travel in the metropolis—for example, employed women know more of their communities than homemakers—and partly a function of how often traversed the various locales are. Locations in Manhattan are usually recognized by New Yorkers from all the boroughs, but Queens is generally a mystery, even to residents of Queens (Milgram et al., 1972).[1]

Urban Crowding[2]

In recent years, a popular metaphor of city life has been one of packed, teeming cages of rats climbing over, fighting with, and devouring each other, with a few individual animals sunk in listlessness or engaged in rodent parallels to juvenile delinquency and homosexuality. This is the picture of population density among rats conveyed by the experiments of John B. Calhoun (1962). It is a great temptation, often yielded to, to draw conclusions about human crowding from these and similar studies. In a relatively typical statement, one psychoanalyst asserted that

> many people find life in cities irritating and exhausting [because] they are compelled to control aggressive impulses which arise solely as a result of overcrowding. It is also probable that it is because of wider spacing between individuals,

which is usual in the countryside, that rural folk are less tense,
more neighborly, and often better mannered than their urban
counterparts (Storr, 1968: 37).[3]

And a United States senator warns that population density
causes "the erosion of trust between people" (Sundquist,
1975: 21). What, then, is the current state of theory and fact
about human crowding, its consequences, and its relevance
to city life?

Crowding Theory

Many models of the experience and effects of cities can be
brought together under the heading of crowding theory. The
general argument of these models is this: Residence in a
large community means that individuals will find themselves
in specific settings that are relatively dense in terms of the
ratio of people to space. The denser those settings, the more
crowded people feel. This density and sense of crowding
create strains and tensions requiring relief. Relief must some-
how be found—for example, by aggression or withdrawal—
or the stress will result in mental or physical illness. Urban
crowding thus leads to antisocial adaptations or psychopathol-
ogy. A psychiatrist warns that overstimulation, in part an
effect of urban life, "is a social and public-health problem no
less grave than overpopulation, pollution, and the growing
scarcity of natural resources" (Lipowski, 1975: 219). A variety
of theories, or models, follow this general line of analysis,
and we will examine five of the more important ones (for
others, see Fischer et al., 1975).

   1. *High density creates problems of interference and of
distributing resources.* This theory is the simplest, and places
the least emphasis on psychological strains: The more persons in a limited area, the more likely they are to trip over
each other's feet, and the more subdivided the available
goods—whether food, tools, or fresh air—must be. Deleterious effects result from the ensuing competition and confusion (see R. E. Mitchell, 1974; Stokols, 1974; Wicker, 1973).
This model has the obvious and reassuring implication that
as long as interaction is organized and there are sufficient
goods for all, no ill consequences will result from density

alone. The other theories, however, are more dramatic and controversial, because their arguments are that problems arise from density for reasons other than simple interference.

2. *High density generates stress because, as part of their evolutionary heritage, human beings have a territorial instinct.* This territorial theory holds that the more people in a place, the more likely it is that any individual's (or group's) area will be invaded; natural reactions to such an invasion—aggression, physiological changes, and self-destructive impulses—will then be mobilized. ("Human aggression," writes one sociologist, "has . . . a biological basis in territoriality" [van den Berghe, 1974: 778].) A standard example is the youth gang defending its "turf." This theory has been popularized in recent years as "the territorial imperative," and, in effect, portrays urbanites as caged "killer apes."[4] ("We have caged ourselves in zoos of our own creation; and like caged animals, we have developed pathological forms of behavior" [van den Berghe, 1974: 787].) The basic implication of this theory is that the only nondestructive relief for crowding is to uncrowd.

Various reasons lead us to doubt that humans actually have such a territorial instinct. One is that instincts develop and persist because they provide an evolutionary advantage to a species. A territorial instinct might indeed be advantageous for certain species. For some, such as grazing animals, it would help distribute the members evenly across the available resources; for others, it may help protect nests. But it is not advantageous for humans, who instead survive best by living and working together, rather than by spreading thinly across the landscape. A second reason is that instinctive behavior is rigid. For example, the display of territorial defense among those animals that exhibit it at all is usually reserved for specific times and places, such as mating season and near nests. Such stereotypy is not characteristic of human behavior with regard to territory. Third, many animals—especially the apes, who are most closely related to humans—show few or no signs of a territorial instinct. Finally, the emphasis on instinctive behavior ignores humans' unique character as a culture-bearing species. It is precisely the triumph of brain over biology that distinguishes *homo sapiens.*[5]

3. *The presence of other members of a species in "unnaturally" high numbers and in close quarters produces physio-*

logical overstimulation. This model, related to the second, is also drawn from animal studies, but it is not as insistent on human aggressiveness. It holds that density among humans leads to "overstimulation," causing adrenal glands to enlarge, average physical size to diminish, disease resistance to wane, pregnancies to abort, and other behavioral abnormalities and stress-linked physiological changes to occur. Crowding produces these effects perhaps because of the strain of constant interaction with others (social pressure), perhaps because of increased competition for resources, or perhaps because of an instinctual device that operates to reduce population size; opinions differ as to the reason. The reduction of population size upon reaching high densities is often observed among animals; it serves to rebalance numbers and resources. (The rebalancing is not a result of starvation, but is instead a biological and social reaction to the density itself.) We have encountered a psychological version of this theory as "psychic overload" (Chapter 2). The physiological overstimulation theory is more general: too many people in too little space upsets psyches and stomachs. ("It would seem reasonable to expect that people would react to the incessant demands, stimulation, and lack of privacy resulting from overcrowding with irritability, weariness, and withdrawal" [Galle et al, 1972: 207].) This model, like the last theory, implies that separation and small numbers are biological necessities.[6] Criticism similar to that presented against the idea of territoriality can be applied as well to the overstimulation theory.

4. *High density generates stress because it leads to frequent violations of the "personal space" surrounding each human being.* This is a less biological and more social version of territorial theory. Personal space has been defined as "an area with invisible boundaries surrounding a person's body into which intruders may not come" (Somer, 1969: 26). Consider the familiar practice of maintaining a calculated distance from strangers in public settings, or of retreating from a conversational partner who has become overly excited, advanced too closely, and is spraying his *bons mots* into one's face. Common experiences such as these suggest that we each are surrounded by personal "bubbles" that cannot be invaded without producing distress.[7] Again, the only relief would appear to be separation, or uncrowding.

We will consider this theory in more detail below, but one

observation is in order here. Although the reactions described by the notion of an invasion of personal space are no doubt real, the proper interpretation may not be one involving "bubbles," but one based on the fact that people vary their interpersonal distances as a means of nonverbal communication. Our physical postures and distances convey messages to those around us. In this view, inappropriate distancing is poor etiquette. A stranger who stands too close conveys a message not unlike an indecent verbal proposal. This interpretation of personal space is more optimistic about avoiding the ill effects of crowding, for we take room-density into account when we interpret people's nonverbal communications (see Watson, 1972). This observation leads us to the final theory of crowding effects, a cultural rather than biological model.

5. *High density generates stress when the socially defined standards for what are appropriate distances between persons are violated.* These standards depend on the situation, the specific people involved, the place, and the society. (For example, American standards for housing assign ten times as much space to each individual as Japanese housing standards assign—R. E. Mitchell, 1975.) Expectations about the spaces between people are subject to a tacit etiquette, and tension occurs when anyone violates the rules of that etiquette. According to this view, typically dense situations should not cause psychological stress because, being typical, crowding is expected (see Stokols, 1972a; Baldassare and Feller, 1976). What New Yorker seriously expects much elbow room on the subway at rush hour?[8]

These five specifications of a general crowding theory are not incompatible, but each has its own implications: the second and third theories, the more biological ones, imply that density (almost) invariably means trouble; the last two theories, the more social ones, imply that people can handle a reasonable amount of density when their culture conditions them to expect it. The theories delineated, we turn to the data.

Crowding Research

Crowding-research studies fall into three groups: studies of animals, studies of people in dense situations, and, on a different plane, studies of the densities of physical areas.[9]

Scientists have analyzed the population patterns of a great variety of animals in the wild, and they have conducted experiments in which animals were permitted to multiply unchecked in laboratory pens, as in Calhoun's rat studies (1962), or in which animals were placed in cages and groups of different sizes. Despite some contradictory results, a few general conclusions about animal density appear justified. Clearly, there are natural mechanisms for population control in some species (deer, for example—Christian et al., 1960), which operate to keep their numbers down (even in cases where there is abundant food). These mechanisms involve biological changes: As population increases, so do rates of sterility, age of maturation, incidences of mortality. In certain species these mechanisms also involve changes in social behavior; rats, for instance, exhibited violence, withdrawal, and subgroup formation in Calhoun's studies.

It is uncertain that we can draw sound conclusions about the behavior of people in crowds from these animal studies. While physiological and behavioral changes do occur in some species as a result of crowding, it is also true that similar alterations sometimes occur during periods of isolation! The significant changes are usually observed in the most extremely dense conditions (as was the case in Calhoun's rat pens), while smaller variations in density show only slight changes. In any case, these animal studies seem to have little relevance for humans; as mentioned earlier, the human species probably lacks both the need for and the availability of instinctual devices for population control. Instead, the collective, social character of human subsistence patterns makes dense aggregation—with the exception of extreme cases such as over-filled refugee camps—generally beneficial, and nurtures man's special nature: culture.

Among the studies of humans are a long series on personal space, which have found that people manifest various forms of avoidance and protective responses when approached closely. In one of these studies, a classic, the target was a person sitting alone at a college library table. Depending on a randomly determined schedule, the experimenter's confederate selected a seat at varying distances from the target person. When the confederate ignored other available chairs and sat in one right next to the target, the latter tended to be disturbed, and either left or placed books in between

them (see Somer, 1969). In addition to experiments, researchers have conducted observational studies of the systematic
ways in which people maintain distances from one another.
For instance, investigators have noted that when one member of a conversing pair starts to inch forward, the other will
generally match these moves backward, and apparently do
so unwittingly. Such findings support the notion that people
have personal "bubbles" of space.

Personal-space studies have also documented the fact
that the size of the bubble varies tremendously—by person,
situation, and culture (for example, Tedesco and Fromme,
1974; Heshka and Nelson, 1972). It comes as no surprise that
the response of most males to the proximity of an attractive
female is not at all like their response to the proximity of a
beefy football player. So, too, different situations evoke different responses to interpersonal distances. A degree of proximity that we find intolerable on some occasions—say, mo-
ments of private contemplation, or in our private quarters—
we accept, even welcome, on other occasions—at parties,
rallies, discotheques. Finally, there are major cultural variations on the spatial theme: for example, Latin Americans
stand closer to one another than do North Americans, Arabs
closer than Scandinavians (Hall, 1966; Baldassare and Feller,
1976).

Such variability in spatial behavior suggests that a bubble metaphor is less appropriate than a body-language metaphor. Just as cultures use different symbols for verbal communication, so they use different symbols in nonverbal
communication. Space is a mode of nonverbal communication, and varying distances are signals in that mode. That is
why a person, when unavoidably pressed against another
person in an elevator or subway, often uses other nonverbal
cues, such as looking away, to say in effect: "Don't misunderstand; this is *not* an intimate message." The implication of all
this is plain: If spatial relations provide a language or are
governed by an etiquette, they can be readily modified for
crowded situations—presumably with no pathological consequences. That is, when people are "too close" to us in situations understood as necessarily crowded, we also understand
that they are not broadcasting messages that should disturb
or anger us.

Another and rapidly expanding body of experimental re
search attacks the issue of crowding most directly by placing
people in dense situations and observing the consequences.
In a common type of study, groups of volunteers—usually
those overworked guinea pigs, undergraduates—are brought
at random into one of two rooms: one that is considered an
appropriate size for a group of that number, or one that is
quite cramped for such a group. For an hour or two, the
groups discuss assigned topics, play games, perform tasks,
and, of course, fill out questionnaires. Thus far, the results
show that, although people in smaller rooms report feeling
crowded, they generally do no worse on their tasks, and are
not any more hostile, anxious, or aggressive than those who
spent their time in more spacious quarters. [10]

The situations in these crowding experiments can be
criticized for being of too short duration to permit density to
exert its full impact. But it is not altogether obvious what
longer sessions would show. Perhaps the negative consequences of density build up over time and would eventually
become apparent; or perhaps negative effects occur only
initially, when people are first placed in this rather extreme
position—often forced to sit face-to-face in a small cubicle,
knees practically knocking—and, over time, adjustments
would be made that would reduce any ill effects.

The third category of crowding research consists of
studies in which the densities of physical areas are related to
their rates of social pathologies. These include housing
studies—the areas are rooms or dwelling units—and neighborhood or census-tract comparisons within cities. (Some
have even foolishly extended such comparisons to states or
nations.) The general result is a familiar one: The more dense
the housing or the census tract, the higher the rates of crime,
disease, social breakdown, aggression, and so on.

However, as usual, we must consider what other factors
common to both density and pathology might be creating a
spurious correlation. Some are evident: Since space in and
around the home is almost universally desired, the people
who lack it are, in general, those usually unable to obtain the
good things in life—the poor; the minorities; and the socially,
physically, and psychologically handicapped. When statistical controls for factors such as these are introduced, the

association of density and pathology becomes tenuous. It is more nearly the case that suffering people come to live densely than that density causes suffering.

The research on housing suggests that density is disliked, often uncomfortable, and awkward. However, even relatively high densities—as much as an entire family to one bedroom in the case of overseas Chinese (Anderson, 1972)— can be handled without pathological consequences as long as family functions are properly organized (for example, scheduling the use of rooms conveniently). Ill effects show up only in extreme circumstances, for instance when several children must share a bed (see the discussion on housing in Chapter 3). "There is no body of convincing evidence that crowding in a dwelling unit contributes materially to mental disorder or emotional instability" (Wilner and Baer, cited by R. E. Mitchell, 1971; see also Cassel, 1972; Michelson, 1970).[11] What is "extreme," or even "high," is not quite clear, but the range of densities found in the great majority of urban settings probably does *not* reach such extremes. (Examples of extremes might include the quarters of the 1840s cellar-dweller described in Chapter 3, and a few areas of Calcutta today.) The conclusion that crowding below extreme levels does not cause negative consequences is reinforced by the findings of a study recently completed in Toronto. The researchers measured 560 families on many attributes, including physical health, mental health, family relations, aggression, and social involvement. Neither crowding in the home nor density in the neighborhood was found to have a substantial effect on these variables (Booth, 1975).

Crowding Theory Reconsidered

Having looked at a variety of research studies, we can now reconsider the state of crowding theory. Its most general proposition is that the more dense a situation, the more likely people are to feel crowded, thus stressful, and to be forced into often inadequate adaptations. The upshot is a conclusion like that of anthropologist Edward Hall (1966: 165): "The implosion of the world population into cities is everywhere creating a series of behavioral sinks [the pathological condition of Calhoun's rats] more lethal than the hydrogen bomb." The evidence gathered to date provides little basis for accepting this theory, since density has generally not been found to have such effects.

When high density does have effects—when people complain of lack of space, or act to avoid intrusions into their personal space—the most appropriate specific models seem to be those of resource distribution and cultural standards. That is, when density is so high or poorly managed as to prevent children from sleeping, problems can occur. Or when density violates a cultural standard of proper distance—what is fine at a party is too close in an airport lounge—people come to *feel* crowded, to view the circumstances as inappropriate and, consequently, to be upset—though not necessarily deranged. (Indeed, to the extent that owning space is a value per se, as it is in North America, the lack of space will itself create feelings of deprivation.) These nonbiological interpretations of crowding have less pessimistic implications than instinct theories about our ability to deal with the particularly dense occasions of urban life—and they are probably more correct.

Beyond these considerations about urban crowding is a much more general one: How relevant is the entire topic of crowding to an understanding of the urban experience? Many researchers and commentators assume, seemingly without serious reflection, that by understanding crowding they understand city life. Those who write about territoriality and interpersonal spacing suggest that they have explained why cities have high crime rates (for example, van der Berghe, 1974; Lorenz, 1966). A reviewer of the literature on crowding includes in his book a chapter entitled "In praise of cities" (Freedman, 1975). Researchers often casually move from reporting the results of a crowding experiment or small-scale study to making speculations about urban life (for example, Freedman and Ehrlich, 1971; Sherrod and Downs, 1974; Griffit and Veitch, 1971). This connection is not all certain (Baldassare and Fischer, 1976). It would be foolish to say that a city is analogous to a crowded room, such as those used in the experiments. It is only somewhat more plausible to say that city life involves more frequent experiences of crowding. How many urban occasions *are* actually dense? How much of urban life *is* crowded? In Chapter 3, we saw that urbanites are no more crowded in their homes than ruralites are in theirs. Focusing on stereotypic crowd scenes, during rush hours for example, may lead to gross overestimates of the average daily experience of the people in these crowds. Even assuming that interpersonal crowding in small spaces is at all relevant to understanding the urban experience, the resources and cultural models imply that high densities need not lead to pathologies. No matter how small the amount of physical space per person, when resources are well distributed (as in small but efficient apartments) and people's expectations are in line, social life can proceed quite well. For instance, an efficient mass-transit system could move large numbers of people in dense vehicles comfortably, perhaps pleasantly.

Studying the consequences of density in micro-environments is important for various aspects of living in cities—for instance, as an aid in designing housing units or planning neighborhoods. But it seems to have little utility for understanding the nature of the urban experience itself, the consequences of living in cities. Of even less utility are those theories that seek to explain urban ways of life by analogies to rat cages. If rat cages and laboratory rooms do not contain the answers to our questions about urbanism and mental states, perhaps direct studies of urban psychology do.

Psychological Stress and Disorder

As we have seen, crowding theory argues that urban life creates psychological pathologies—cities are viewed as tight "cages" and their residents as somewhat crazed animals. This idea is carried over into general determinist urban theory. Wirth (1938: 156) wrote: "The necessary frequent movement of great numbers of individuals in a congested habitat causes friction and irritation. Nervous tensions which derive from such personal frustrations are increased by the rapid tempo . . . under which life in dense areas must be lived." Thus crowding theory is similar to the "psychic overload" of determinist theory (see Chapter 2). But psychological alterations supposedly occur to urbanites for other reasons, as well: the breakdown of primary groups and of the moral order. The functional integration which arises in their stead "does not . . . insure the consistency and integrity of personalities. . . . Personal disorganization, mental breakdown, suicide, delinquency, crime, corruption, and disorder might be expected under these circumstances to be more prevalent in the urban than in the rural community" (Wirth, 1938: 162). Determinist theory, however, also presents an alternative to psychological distress—the adoption of a particularly urban type of personality, cool and calculating. In contrast to that viewpoint, neither compositional nor subcultural theory expects that such a choice—between disorder and estrangement—need be faced, because intimate social groups encapsulate human psyches in the city as well as they do elsewhere.

The question here is: Does the experience of living in cities produce psychological stress or psychological disorder? (Or, as the jacket cover of one book asks rhetorically, "Can the city drive you crazy?") While "stress"—nervous tension, anxiety—is invisible as such, there is scientific consensus on the symptoms it produces in people: irritability, physical weakness, fear, hypertension (high blood pressure), insomnia, and the like. Using this symptomatology, do we find that urban people have these symptoms more often or to a greater degree than nonurban people?

The ethnographic studies cited in earlier chapters yield a mixed answer to the query. From most reports, for instance, those on residents of London's East End or Boston's North End, there is little indication that urbanites suffer especially from stress. Other studies, particularly of rural migrants recently arrived in the city, do describe serious tensions. The newcomers occasionally feel lost, anxious, and overwhelmed —at least at first (see discussion on migrants in Chapter 4). This distress would appear to be a result more of the problems of adjusting to a new home than to the fact that it is an urban home. Furthermore, as we saw earlier, most studies of migrants indicate that apparently satisfactory adjustments come pretty quickly.

Survey studies of the incidence of stress symptoms tend to be either mixed or do not support the hypothesis that urbanism causes tension. The United States National Health Survey cited in Chapter 3 shows that stress-related health problems are not regularly associated with community size. For example, there are generally small differences between

urban and rural people in rates of hypertension and hypertensive heart disease. The only major contrast is among black
males, who suffer much more hypertension in rural areas—
perhaps as a result of diet (N.C.H.S., 1973—unfortunately, the
N.C.H.S. analyses control only for age, race, sex, and occasionally region, but not for other social factors such as diet
or education.) One general survey of the American population found that urbanites were more likely to report that they
"worried" than did ruralites, but the researchers concluded
that the differences were "minimal" (Gurin et al., 1960). As
part of a major study conducted on modernization, a "psychosomatic symptoms test" was administered to carefully
selected and matched samples of men in six developing nations. The test asked questions such as whether the respondent suffered from insomnia or "nerves." The investigators
concluded that there was no substantial relationship between
such symptoms and the amount of their urban experience
(Inkeles, 1969). In sum, the data available to date does not
support the urbanism-tension hypothesis.[12]

Various indicators have been employed to measure rates
of psychological disorder ("mental illness"). Admissions to
mental hospitals have often been used, and rates of such
admissions generally tend to be higher in cities than in rural
areas (Clinard, 1964; Mann, 1964; but not Szabo, 1960). But
several considerations keep us from concluding from this
finding that urbanism leads to disorder. We know from Chapter 3 that facilities for detecting and treating psychological
problems are more readily available in urban areas and this
could account for their higher rates of hospitalization. Since
urbanites tend to hold more liberal social views (Chapter 8),
it is likely that attitudes toward mental illness differ between
city and countryside, and that city dwellers would be more
able to diagnose, and more willing to admit and seek a cure
for psychological problems. From Chapter 4 we also know
that migrants to cities occasionally move there with rural-
grown psychiatric problems. Finally, we should note that
what conventional citizens consider "crazy" is often simply
the unconventional behavior of members of "deviant" subcultures, not the symptoms of deranged minds (see also Srole,
1972).

Suicide and alcoholism are perhaps less ambiguous

signs of psychological disorder than are hospital admissions. In the nineteenth century, suicide rates were almost always higher in cities than in the countryside (Gibbs, 1971; Dublin, 1963; Durkheim, 1897); today there is no consistent difference (Gibbs, 1971).[13] The pattern prevailing in the last century might have been the result of unique difficulties in the rapidly changing early industrial city. The absence of differences in this century might reflect a "leveling" of urban-rural distinctions. Or the data might be faulty: urban-rural differences in the earlier era may have simply reflected the greater efficiency of record-keeping in cities. Rural suicides may have more often gone uncounted. (For example, in Catholic countries, fewer deaths may have been categorized as suicides in rural than in urban areas because of the Church's relative strength in the countryside and its condemnation of suicide.) In any case, suicide statistics today do not suggest that urbanites are more disordered than ruralites.

In the United States, alcoholism is more common in urban than in rural places (Trice, 1966). In France, the opposite is true (Szabo, 1960). The by now familiar difficulties in the data confound a comparison on alcoholism just as they do on suicide: The behavior may be more visible or better recorded in cities; and rural people with problems move to the city—to drink or to die.

Rather than muddle through alternative interpretations of institutional statistics, some investigators have elected to go into the field to measure psychological disorders more directly. Most researchers have been equipped with paper-and-pencil tests designed to measure levels of "adjustment." These have usually been administered to children, and the rural-urban comparisons have varied greatly: farm versus village, village versus town, or single city versus its hinterland. Of seventeen such studies, three found that personality problems were more common in the larger places, five found them more common in the smaller communities, and nine found no differences. In most of the studies, however, the differences were quite small, and in most, there were no statistical controls for possible confounding variables such as social class.[14]

A few investigators have used brief diagnostic instruments in surveys of general populations. The most compre-

FIGURE 7

PSYCHOLOGICAL DISTRESS SYMPTOM SCORES, BY
COMMUNITY SIZE, FOR 6,672 U. S. WHITE ADULTS, 1960-62

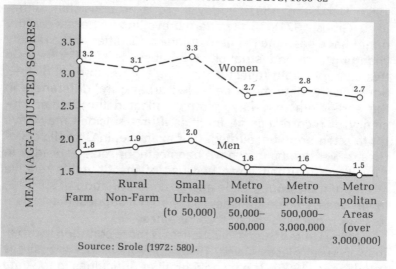

Source: Srole (1972: 580).

hensive effort along this line was, once again, that of the
National Health Survey. In 1960-62, the N.C.H.S. medically
examined and interviewed almost 7,000 adults. They were
asked to report whether they suffered from any of eleven
symptoms of "psychological distress," including having had,
or sensing the onset of, a nervous breakdown. The sociologist Leo Srole (1972) obtained a compilation of the results
broken down by community size (see Figure 7). Besides the
fact that women report more symptoms of distress than do
men, the data show that residents of larger communities
report fewer, not more, symptoms than residents of smaller
communities. We cannot conclude from this that city dwellers
are mentally healthier than ruralites, however, because the
analysis of the data is not complete. Although age, race, and
sex are controlled, socio-economic status is not. But we can
conclude that the survey does not confirm the proposition
that urbanism leads to psychological disorder (see also
Schwab et al., 1972).[15]

From this review of the evidence, it is obvious that several difficulties impede our ability to draw firm conclusions

about urban-rural differences in rate and kind of psychological disorders. Such differences can be spurious—the result of statistical procedures, the "drift" to cities of the disturbed, the greater availability in cities of efficient detection, and, in some cases, the labeling as disorder of what is merely unconventionality. On the basis of the evidence currently available, it cannot be said that the urban experience tends to drive disproportionate numbers of people to the brink of madness. Nor can it be said that urban subcultures nurture particularly healthy psyches.

The conclusion is important enough to reiterate. Despite widespread notions that city life inflicts psychological damage, we have no evidence that it is so. It probably is not so.

Alienation

The concept of "alienation" is heavily weighed down with confusing connotations from sources as varied as philosophical treatises and political slogans. Despite the pummeling it has suffered, the term retains a core meaning that can serve us in our examination of urban psychology. As used here, *alienation* can be defined as an individual's sense of separation from the society around him or her (see Fischer, 1976). There are various forms of alienation, depending on the part or parts of the society an individual feels unrelated to.[16] We will consider how such alienation may be affected by urban life, and we will evaluate statements such as the following found in a research report to the United States Government: "All contemporary trends associated with the emergence of alienation are directly or indirectly tied to the growth of very large urban environments" (Elgin et al., 1974: 64; see Seeman, 1971, and White and White, 1962, for reviews of theories of the "urban alienations").

Powerlessness

The most intensively studied variety of alienation is powerlessness, the sense some individuals have that they cannot determine, and so are unrelated to, the outcomes of their actions. Fatalists who believe that no matter what they do, the gods or Lady Luck or City Hall will decide their lives suffer from powerlessness. This variable, as measured by the responses people give to questions probing their feelings of efficacy, has proved to be reliable, valid, and significant. People who do not think they can succeed do not make much effort to do so, and when they do make an effort they frequently fail. The factors that determine powerlessness are varied but largely reduce to the actual lack of power, such as being black or poor (Seeman, 1972, 1975; Rotter, 1966).

Urban life has been considered a condition that is bound to create feelings of powerlessness. Wirth, for example, refers to "masses of men in the city being subject to manipulation" (1938: 163). Lewis Mumford (1961: 547) writes of the modern metropolis as

> a world where the great masses of people, unable to achieve a more full-bodied and satisfying existence, take life vicariously . . . , [live] remote from the nature that is outside them, and no less the nature that is within . . . [and] are progressively reduced to a bundle of reflexes, without self-starting impulses or autonomous goals. . . .

The sheer mass of people, the complex structure of society, the disintegration of general social expectations and of personal social groups, the formality of institutions—all these elements emphasized by determinist theory should leave individuals convinced of their powerlessness. Careful survey research has failed to support such expectations. In the United States, at least, there is no association between size of community and expressions of powerlessness, even when controlling for variables such as class (Fischer, 1973a; Schooler, 1972; Photiadis, 1967). Ethnographies of peasants in some other nations tend to portray these *rural* residents as quite fatalistic (for example, Foster, 1960; Banfield, 1958). Studies of urban migrants do not show them as generally defeated or discouraged by the city environment (see Chapter 4). More often, we read of cases such as the peasant migrants to Mexico City who experienced a "loss of fear" along with their move—the fading away of the general anxiety they had in the village that strong and malevolent forces plagued their lives (Butterworth, 1962).

In sum, the extent to which people believe that they can act successfully to achieve their goals is not reduced by urbanism; in some nations, it may even be greater in urban than in rural settings.[17]

Normlessness

Normlessness refers to the sense of detachment some individuals feel from social norms or rules, rules they feel no reason or obligation to obey. The person who thinks that "anything goes," or that "the ends justify the means" is normless (see Durkheim, 1893; Merton 1938a; Clinard, 1964). If the urban condition is particularly anomic, city dwellers should exhibit a tendency to dismiss the enfeebled norms ("Everyone cheats; why shouldn't I?"). However, if urbanism vitalizes subcultures, we should expect as much if not more attachment to group norms in cities as in the countryside.

This comment about subcultures points to a crucial distinction: Whose norms? If the concern is for the rules of the majority, then there is strong support for the prediction of urban normlessness, for official rules are broken far more often in cities than in rural places (see Chapters 4 and 8). But our interest here is psychological: the question of people's attachment to any norms at all. Thus the proper concern is whether urbanism weakens or strengthens people's beliefs in the rules of their own particular groups. Do urbanites tend to operate outside of *any* moral system?

A classic portrait of city life is that of the son of the immigrant peasant family who leaves home, turning his back on the "old country" ways, to "make it" in the big urban world. We should not be misled into considering this to be a typical case of normlessness. The Italian boy from Boston's North End who cuts his ties to Little Italy as he enters college is, except perhaps during the transition period, not normless. He has been attracted by an alternative subculture and its norms. As people abandon one group, they usually enter another, rather than hang suspended in a moral void. The review in Chapters 5 and 6 of social groups in the city indicated that not only do the traditional normative systems of ethnic groups persist in the city, but that urbanism stimulates the emergence of new sources of normative regulation, such as occupational and special-interest groups.

The implication is that urbanites are not more apt to be

normless than ruralites, not at least in terms of their own subcultures. We can go further: To the extent that urban groups are more specifically tailored to their members' interests than rural ones, city dwellers will be *more* attached to their groups' norms than will country people. This urban norm*ful*ness would support a subcultural rather than a determinist model. In any case, there is little evidence of distinctly urban norm*less*ness.[18]

Social Isolation

Social isolation refers to a sense of loneliness or of rejection by others. Here we wrestle with one of the most prevalent ideas about city life—that the urbanite feels alone in the midst of the crowd (Riesman, 1952). One urban planner writes: "The people who live in cities are often contactless and alienated. A few of them are physically lonely: almost all of them live in a state of endless inner loneliness" (Alexander, 1967: 239). In the last chapter, we reviewed evidence indicating that the urbanite was not in fact socially alone. But the possibility remains that the experience of cities—its masses of strangers, for example—might yet create a subjective sense of separation from others.

Ethnographies of urban life usually describe feelings of social involvement, not of isolation. At the same time, some ethnographies of *rural* communities, at least in peasant societies, describe intense suspicion and hostility. Representative of these rural portraits is the famous description of a French village by the observant anthropologist-scholar Laurence Wylie. He reports having been constantly warned about *ils*—"the others"—the ones who could not be trusted:

> Most people believe that it is wise to keep important things to oneself, to avoid involvement with "the others" insofar as it is possible. At the same time, contact with other people is important for them. . . . [So] when they are with other people they are cordial, friendly, hospitable, even jovial, but this behavior is superficial (Wylie, 1964: 204-205).[19]

Comparative surveys of the distribution of feelings of isolation are rare. Among the more frequently used indicators are questions measuring general distrust—for example, "Do you think that most people would take advantage of you if they got a chance or would they try to be fair?" A 1972 survey of Americans revealed a small but noteworthy difference on this item: 33 percent of rural people thought that they would be taken advantage of, while 41 percent of people in cities of over 250,000 thought so.[20] In one study, questions such as this were combined into "distrust" scales for four national surveys (three American, one British). The results of the analysis were similar in all four surveys: When confounding factors such as social class are taken into account, the correlation of community size with distrust increases; it appears that urbanism is independently—although slightly—associated with feelings of suspicion about other people (Fischer, 1973a).

Given the evidence that urbanites are not particularly isolated, why do they, in these surveys, seem to be a bit more estranged, or at least distrustful? A subcultural explanation is plausible: Urbanites do not feel estranged from fellow members of their own subcultures, but they do feel that "out there" beyond their own group are other, very different people, the "strangers," those who would "take advantage." An even more direct explanation is that, given the higher rates of crime in cities, some distrust is expectable and probably sensible. Combining this interpretation with the data on actual isolation (and recognizing the absence of much other evidence), the conclusion is that any association between urbanism and social isolation remains to be demonstrated.

Taking powerlessness, normlessness, and social isolation as three important varieties of alienation, we conclude from this review that urban people are *not* especially alienated.[21] This conclusion was foreshadowed by the evidence examined in Chapters 5 and 6. Individual personality is created and maintained by the intimate groups of society, particularly family and friends. The finding that these groups persist in the urban setting should lead us to expect the findings in this section. But we note one important qualification with regard to normlessness: Just as the specific parts of the society to which people maintain commitment differ, so their social norms can differ radically from the ethos central to the society. Thus people can be both unconventional in terms of those central norms *and* unalienated.

Happiness

If urban life really does produce such ill effects as personal isolation and psychic tension, the result should be a general sense of malaise among urban residents. If, however, the benefits of city life outweigh its costs, that too should be reflected in their feelings. So our question in this section is: Do urban and rural residents vary in their reports of feelings about their lives? Occasionally, the argument is advanced that people may *think* (and report) that they are happy when they "really" are not. But no one can describe a person's state of mind as well as the person whose mind it is. Do urban people report being less happy than do rural people?

In Chapter 2, we reviewed the evidence that people, especially North Americans, tend to express dissatisfaction with large communities. Urbanites say that they generally prefer to live in more rural places, and more often than ruralites they report that their community has an unsatisfactory "quality of life." This popular assessment partly reflects the pastoral ideal of rural life; it also reflects grievances about specific features of American cities. Residents of large communities tend to report less satisfaction than residents of small communities with various important attributes of their towns, such as schools, housing, taxes, and safety (and they report *more* satisfaction on far fewer items—Fischer, 1973b; Hawley and Zimmer, 1971). These concrete sources of discontent explain a great deal of the negative evaluation of cities by their residents (Marans and Rodgers, 1975).

People's feelings about their communities are important in trying to understand the relationship between community size and happiness. More directly to the point, however, are people's feelings about their own lives, their personal contentment or despair. Does urbanism generate some deep, chronic malaise? The evidence suggests not. The Gallup Poll periodically asks Americans, "In general, how happy would you say you are—very happy, fairly happy, or not very happy?" In an analysis of such Gallup surveys of 1952, 1957, and 1963, and a similar one conducted in France in 1967, no regular or significant relationship was found between the size of community and self-reported happiness (Fischer, 1973b). This lack of relationship is generally seen in economically advanced Western nations (Cantril, 1965; COFREMCA, 1974;

Swedner, 1960). Developing nations, however, exhibit notable differences, with city dwellers *more* generally content than rural ones (re-analysis of Cantril, 1965, in Fischer, 1973b). Another notable result in these studies as a whole is that in most nations, developed or not, city residents are slightly more optimistic than rural residents about their futures.

These results are, however, only descriptive; they do not take into account the fact that urbanites have several advantages—youth, wealth, and so on. Without these, the depressants of the city—crime, pollution, perhaps just its size and heterogeneity—would perhaps take their toll. The survey analysis just mentioned indicated that this is probably the case, but only to a very slight extent and only in economically advanced societies. That is, when such third factors as age and income are controlled in analyzing surveys from these countries, there is left a quite small but noticeable *negative* association between urbanism and happiness. (In developing nations, a *positive* association remains after class is controlled.) The small negative impact of urbanism appears, at least in the United States and France, almost exclusively in the very large metropolises, those with populations over 3,000,000. Further analysis suggests that the mild depressant is explainable partly by the real urban problems of such cities as New York and Paris, and partly by the general taste, at least in North America, for small communities. The fact that this dip in morale appears only at the extreme implies that it is not a general and inherent feature of urban life (Fischer, 1973b; also, Marans and Rodgers, 1975).

We have seen that this dip is balanced out so that city dwellers in economically advanced nations appear no less happy on the average than do country residents (although they may be "reluctant urbanites"). And in developing nations, the drawbacks are more than balanced out. We cannot conclude that urban life is a source of personal malaise.[22]

Even this reserved conclusion needs to be qualified, at least for the case of the United States, by attending to recent fluctuations in American morale. As of late 1975, the national sense of well-being has, for the last few years, undergone an unusual decline (Lindsey, 1975). This plunge in morale has been sharpest among city dwellers: From 1963 to 1973, residents of communities larger than 500,000 dropped nine points in satisfaction with their "standard of living" (from 74 percent satisfied to 65 percent), while rural residents dropped five points (from 79 percent to 74 percent); the same metropolitans lost thirteen points in optimism about their future (64 percent to 51 percent), while the ruralites lost only four (60 percent to 56 percent). (See G.O.I., 1973, #102; also, Hynson, 1975; COFREMCA, 1974). Consequently, the most recent polls indicate that contentment is somewhat lower among Americans in large metropolitan areas than among those in small communities. The reasons for this development are not certain, but two explanations seem most likely. One, during this last decade, the social problems of American cities have, if not worsened, at least become much more apparent and directly relevant to individuals. (For example, the difference between the satisfaction of urbanites in the largest areas and those in small towns with their children's education more than doubled between 1963 and 1973, the city dwellers becoming much more dissatisfied. This could well be a result of recent changes in city school systems.) A second explanation is that the unusual decline in morale is a national phenomenon, a result of factors such as recession, Watergate, and setbacks in foreign policy. Urbanites are leading this change in national attitude—just as they lead most changes in public opinion (see next chapter). This second interpretation implies that the current pattern is a temporary fluctuation. Whether this recent development is only a passing ripple on a stable level of urban and rural happiness, or whether it presages a fundamental tilt in the association of urbanism and morale, it is too soon to tell.

Summary

This chapter has examined the condition of the urban psyche. Do city dwellers, unable to adapt completely to the social and individual experiences of urban life, suffer psychologically? Or do urban social groups nurture psyches as healthy as rural ones? We reviewed a popular theory that interpersonal crowding violates human nature and generates serious pathology, and found this thesis more myth than matter (and perhaps just immaterial). On a more general level, we found little evidence that urbanites are more stressed, disordered, alienated, or unhappy than ruralites. Certain subtle effects of urbanism were noted: Cities probably attract and record behaviors labeled as "sick" more than rural places do; parochialism within urban subcultures (as well as urban crime) probably creates some suspicion of and anxiety about "others"; large modern metropolises may be exacting some small cost in happiness from their residents in return for the economic advantages they provide (if for no other reason than that large cities do not represent the pastoral ideal). Yet, in all, the urban state of mind seems none the worse for its urban experience.

In terms of the theoretical controversy we have been pursuing, these conclusions seriously challenge the determinist position. The psychological disorganization determinists predicted to accompany the social disorganization of urban life has not been confirmed (neither, for that matter, has the social disorganization). Thus, compositional and subcultural theory are once more supported by the available evidence. However, we have considered in this chapter only one horn of the determinist dilemma—that the urban environment causes psychological distress. In Chapter 8, we will consider the other horn—that urbanites maintain their psychological balance through specific personality alterations that produce a distinctively urban type of individual.

8

THE INDIVIDUAL IN THE CITY
PERSONALITY AND SOCIAL ACTION

Despite opinions to the contrary, we have found that urban individuals are on the whole just as mentally healthy as their rural counterparts. How has this psychological balance been kept? Determinist theory argues that cities pose a dilemma for their residents: Urbanites who want to avoid psychic stress and disorder must adapt themselves to the special psychological and social demands of city life. These adapta-

tions—for instance, indifference to strangers' pleas for assistance, or nonchalance amidst bizarre events and people—have brought about a uniquely urban type of personality. In the first part of this chapter, we examine several styles of behavior thought to be especially characteristic of urbanites' dealings with one another. Do city dwellers develop patterns of social interaction that help to insulate them from excessive demands, while simultaneously estranging them from other people?

In the second part of this chapter, we will expand our focus to include general social attitudes and behaviors; we will ask in particular whether urbanism induces people to be unconventional and deviant.

Styles of Interaction

Folk wisdom has it that the country boy who journeys to the big city must be on his guard in dealing with the natives there. Should he seek a casual, friendly conversation—say while waiting for a bus—he will find to his dismay that the city dwellers are too busy rushing from one transaction to another to be casual, and too suspicious and insincere to be friendly. Worse still, they may attempt to exploit the rural innocent.

As we have often found to be the case, determinist theory and popular image are in this instance quite similar. The folk tale highlights three key aspects of what is ostensibly the urban personality: urbanites juggle different social roles with separate people, so that they are always "managing" several distinct identities; they are impersonal and even exploitative with others; and they are indifferent to the needs of others, because they do not want to "get involved." The determinist argument contends that these habits arise as necessary adaptations to the contingencies of urban public life, but become so customary that they permeate urbanites' entire personal style, not only with strangers but with intimates as well. One urban critic writes: "Withdrawal soon becomes a habit. People reach a point where they are permanently withdrawn, they lose the habit of showing themselves to others as they really are, and become unable and unwilling to let other people into their own world" (Alexander, 1967: 253).

The contrary point of view, held by both compositional and subcultural theory, is that the determinist dilemma of psychic stress versus personality change is nonexistent, because social groups that protect psychological stability persist in the city. Subcultural theory makes a further observation: At those times and places when urban people from different subcultures meet, we would expect to see public styles of behavior—hostility, for example—that are less commonly found in smaller communities only because there are fewer and less intense subcultures.

Multiple Identities

The first determinist thesis we will examine holds that city dwellers live in several and separate social worlds, and that they adopt a different personality in each. "By virtue of his different interests arising out of different aspects of social life, the individual acquires membership in widely divergent groups, each of which functions only with reference to a certain segment of his personality" (Wirth, 1938: 156). And this "makes it possible for individuals to pass quickly and easily from one moral milieu to another, and encourages the fascinating but dangerous experiment of living at the same time in several different . . . widely separated worlds" (Park, 1916: 126; see also Frankenburg, 1965; Craven and Wellman, 1973).

As an employer at work, the city dweller may be a tyrant; as a husband at home, a mouse; to his poker pals, a hail-fellow-well-met; and so on. In each role, with each group, he is a different "self." The psychologist William James wrote, "A man has as many different selves as there are distinct groups of persons about whose opinion he cares" (quoted by Gergen, 1972: 31; see also Mead, 1934: 142). According to this analysis, urbanites, compared with ruralites, are adept personality-manipulators, changing their identities with the ease of changing hats.

Two variations exist on the argument that urbanism promotes multiple identities. The first states that there are simply many more roles available in cities than in rural communities, so that urbanites regularly move through a greater number of them than ruralites do (Meier, 1962: 8). The structural differentiation of cities—their varied jobs, services, and special-interest groups, indicate that urban communities offer a relatively great number of social roles.

However, the extent to which this difference between communities applies to individuals is far from clear. For any given resident, there may not be significantly more roles in large places than in small. His or her job, for example, though perhaps more specialized, is still only the one job. The village may have a single school teacher for all grades, while the city has dozens of teachers and administrators, but each person still holds only one job. Indeed, to pursue the analysis, we may come to the opposite conclusion—that *rural* people do more role-changing. Small social systems commonly lack enough people to fill all their positions, so that many individuals are pressed into double- or triple-service. The proprietor of the country store may also run the post office and be drafted to act as mayor. In a larger community, there is a full-time professional in each role (see Barker and Gump, 1964; Wicker, 1973).

More important yet is the distinction between possibility and actuality. Perhaps a peripatetic person can hold three jobs, be a member of ten clubs, have twenty close friends, and play four sports on the side, and do so more easily in city than countryside. But few of us can make use of *all* of our opportunities. What evidence we have from time-budgets on daily activities does not indicate that urbanites engage in hyperactive role-changing (Brail and Chapin, 1973; Reiss, 1959b). The urban-rural difference may reside not in the *number* of roles individuals have, but in the *choice* of roles that they have. The advantage urban dwellers have may be the wider range of options they can take or leave, as their taste dictates. Usually they leave them.

The second, more common, argument—that urbanism promotes multiple identities—derives not from the number of roles but from the separation of roles. "People in rural society tend to play different roles to the same person [while] . . . people in urban society tend to play different roles to different people" (Frankenburg, 1965: 287). In smaller communities, people are more likely to "play" neighbor, co-worker, fellow club member to the same audience; in larger communities they play these same roles to different audiences (see also Craven and Wellman, 1973; Southall, 1973b). Once again, the implication is that ruralites are compelled to maintain a generally consistent identity for they are constantly with the same people; urbanites need not be consistent—perhaps cannot be consistent—and are more likely to have two (or three, or four) identities. Determinists argue that, at the least, urbanites will suffer psychologically from the strain of balancing disparate expectations from different people (for example, P. Berger et al., 1973).

The discussion of social groups in Chapters 5 and 6 lends some credence to the argument. Such groups are more functionally specialized in urban than in rural places; various primary and secondary relationships probably overlap somewhat less often in large than in small communities. For example, a survey of poor families in Guatemala City showed that in most cases the associates of the respondents were either kin or neighbors or co-workers or friends, but were usually no more than one of those. This segregation of social relationships increased with length of residence in the city (Roberts, 1973; see also Pons, 1969: 259).

This evidence is necessary, but it is not enough to demonstrate that urbanites actually maintain multiple identities, that they change personalities as they go from group to group. City dwellers can distinguish the rules and expectations appropriate to each of their role relationships (Roberts, 1973; Plotnicov, 1967), but apparently so can country dwellers (Foster, 1961). For instance, rural people discriminate between the expectations appropriate to neighbors as neighbors and to the same people as relatives (see Arensberg, 1968a; Freeman, 1970). There is apparently no direct evidence that urbanites display different personalities to their various associates; nor is there indirect evidence in the form of psychic stress resulting from urbanites' efforts to manage their multiple selves (see Chapter 7). Indeed, multiple and segregated relationships need not result in psychic or social difficulties (Fischer et al., 1977). Individuals who have chosen and maintained such multiple roles probably do so because both the material and psychological rewards from those relationships outweigh the logistical problems of managing them (Sieber, 1974; Gergen, 1972).

Unfortunately, the topic of multiple identities is another in which the speculation outweighs the evidence. The best current guess is that urbanites could maintain separate personalities more easily than could ruralites. But except for certain dramatic examples, say, the stably-married man who is a "closet" homosexual, urbanites do not appear especially likely to engage in identity manipulation.

Impersonality and Exploitation

In Chapter 2 we mentioned the determinist view that an important way urbanites adjust to city life is to adopt an impersonal orientation to other people—to perceive and deal with them only with respect to the functions they perform and not as unique individuals. Simmel (1905: 49) referred to the urbanite as "calculating"; "the metropolitan man reckons . . . often even with those persons with whom he is obliged to have social intercourse." Park (1916: 109) wrote that urban "human relations are likely to be impersonal and rational, defined in terms of interest and in terms of cash." Bus drivers are just drivers of a bus; their family life, political attitudes, and personal troubles are irrelevant. And so with store clerks, employees, and most other people. Indeed, each of these persons is interchangeable with any other so far as it comes to having the function performed. As a description of public interaction with strangers, impersonality is neither surprising nor terribly interesting; we can hardly be intimate with everyone we encounter on a busy street. The significance of the topic lies in impersonality as an individual orientation, when people are impersonal even when they need not be, and even with people they know relatively well.[1] Do urbanites have a more pervasively impersonal style of behavior than ruralites?

There is no easy way to measure impersonality, and therefore no easy answer to the question. The available bits of evidence suggest that the answer is no. Sensitive ethnographers have provided many descriptions of urban people who are highly personal and particularistic in their attitudes and behaviors, at least toward members of their own social worlds. Groups we have already encountered—steelworkers in South Chicago, Italian-Americans in Boston, the working class in the East End of London—and many others like them belie the image of great urban impersonality. At the same time, ethnographers have found clear instances of impersonality in small communities. One investigator described people in a small Appalachian mining town as impersonal, isolated, cynical, and suspicious (Lantz, 1971: 246), and reported that "the general impersonality found in Coal Town permeated relationships in the family" (p. 149). There is too little evidence in the ethnographic literature to allow us to answer the question in the affirmative.

And there is practically no relevant survey evidence. One study attempted to measure the degree to which workers in six developing nations held "modern" attitudes, attitudes that reflected some degree of impersonality, such as feeling that nepotism is wrong. The investigators found no independent effects of urbanism (Aksoy, 1969).[2]

Beyond impersonality there is exploitativeness—not just using people, but abusing them. In the determinist city, where the moral order is weak and "anything goes," rapaciousness is expectable, perhaps even sensible ("It's a jungle," goes the saying). Wirth (1938: 156) argued: "The close living together and working together of individuals who have no sentimental and emotional ties foster a spirit of competition, aggrandizement, and mutual exploitation." We should therefore find that residents of large communities are more exploitative than residents of small ones. Subcultural theory also anticipates more exploitation in urban than in rural communities. However, there is a significant difference in the two sets of expectations. For subcultural theory, the increase in incidents of exploitation results not from urbanites' grasping personalities, but from greater contact between very different subcultures. Taking advantage of people from one's own group is considered morally reprehensible, but doing the same to one of "them" is often considered legitimate.

Descriptions of selective (therefore condoned) exploitation come from a variety of places. In Indonesia, among both the urban and rural Toba Batak, it was considered acceptable behavior to fleece the outsider in a business transaction. But transactions with non-Batak were much more common in the city than in the countryside and, thus, so were incidents of cheating (Bruner, 1973b: 380). In a slum area of Chicago, some blacks considered it right to "rip off" white storeowners who were themselves viewed as exploiting the neighborhood (Suttles, 1968; see also Molotch, 1969). And, in Ghana, members of other tribes and Europeans were often considered fair game for petty theft (Clinard and Abbott, 1973: 87). In short, some exploitation is to be expected as a consequence of intergroup contact in the city. Also to be expected in the city is some extra degree of suspicion of other groups.

This analysis makes it plausible that there would be relatively more instances of exploitation in large than in small
communities. But the determinist thesis goes on to suggest
that the very character of urbanites is exploitative. This thesis
has little empirical support. The ethnographic studies we have
reviewed do not lend much evidence for the notion of an
exploitative urban type. And neither do surveys. Psychologists have identified a personality disposition called "Machiavellianism"—an inclination to use others amorally as objects to one's ends—but a national survey in the United States
found an equal proportion of Machiavellians in large and
small communities (Christie and Geis, 1970: 318-320).[3]

We have little reason to believe, then, that urban people
are any more or any less impersonal and exploitative than
rural people. In the clash of subcultures that does occur in
cities, individuals often misunderstand and even take advantage of one another. People can therefore to themselves and
to their own be true, but to others they can appear—and can
even *be*—devious.

"Not Getting Involved"

The stabbing murder in 1964 of Kitty Genovese in Kew Gar-
dens, New York City, sent a great wave of despair across the
United States. Ms. Genovese's screams had been heard by
over thirty neighbors, none of whom tried to help her or even
to phone the police. Popular oracles and mass-media savants
saw in this sad event a sign of the nadir of humanity in city
life. The murder became the archsymbol of callousness and
indifference, a theme developed in the many newspaper stories that followed in rapid succession.

(The press treatment of this and other cases illustrates
the hazards of resting sociological conclusions on news
events. The wave of "aloof witnesses" stories was followed
a few years later by a wave of "vigilante witnesses" stories,
in which bystanders pursued and often attacked would-be
assailants, as well as stories in which ghetto residents freed
arrestees from police custody. Obviously, little is settled by
counting press clippings.)

Determinist theory expects that unwillingness to "get
involved" is a particularly urban trait, because being aloof
and callous is a basic adaptation to the stressful demands of

the urban setting. In describing this phenomenon, Simmel (1905: 50-53) used words such as "reserve," "aversion," "indifference," and "blasé." Milgram (1970: 1412) wrote explicitly: "The ultimate adaptation to an over-loaded social environment [the city] is to totally disregard the needs, interests, and demands of those whom one does not define as relevant to the satisfaction of personal needs. ... " There are other grounds, as well, for expecting that indifference might be especially common among city dwellers: fear of crime (a result of the reality of crime), and misunderstanding or indifference between people of different subcultures. Are urbanites more likely than ruralites to avoid getting involved?

Social psychologists responded to the Genovese case and the subsequent public furor by conducting studies grouped under the label of "bystander intervention." Researchers investigated the conditions which facilitate or impede intervention in a crisis. Experiments were conducted simulating emergencies under controlled conditions, both in laboratories and in "real world" settings (see, for example, Berkowitz and McCauly, 1972). For example, a study was conducted on New York's Lexington Avenue subway to see, among other things, whether people would be more likely to help a striken individual if he appeared to be a heart-attack victim than if he appeared to be drunk. The answer was yes (Piliavin et al., 1969; these researchers also found that New Yorkers in this case were almost universally quick to help people in need!).

Why do people often *not* help? Early studies found that individuals were less likely to help someone in a simulated emergency if the observers were in a group than if they were watching the crisis alone (Latané and Darley, 1969). Later research suggested that this group inhibition on helping is not a result of collective indifference on the part of the bystanders, but instead is an outcome of difficulties in collective decision-making: of trying first to determine whether the situation is actually an emergency, so that one does not foolishly interfere in others' personal affairs (for example, do yells in the apartment next door indicate that a crime is in progress, or simply a family quarrel?); and then of deciding who should act. When a crisis is obvious, people in groups seem as willing to act as individuals alone (see, for example, Darley et al., 1973). The thrust of this and other research on bystander intervention is that the failure to act is probably not in most instances a product of callousness.

Only preliminary tests have so far been made of the association between urbanism and the willingness of individuals to assist others in need.[4] We can, however, engage in some informed speculation. For a given victim, the chances of receiving any assistance at all probably increase with community size. In larger towns, there are likely to be more people around, including a Good Samaritan or two.[5] For any particular bystander, the chances of being called upon to help someone and actually doing so probably *decrease* with larger community size. In more urban places, there are likely to be other people who either act in one's stead, or who contribute to a false sense that there is actually no emergency. (Often, in bystander studies, each person's studied composure in the face of crisis misleads the others into believing that there is no crisis after all.) Also, in urban settings an officially responsible person, such as a policeman, is more likely to be nearby.

But these are actuarial calculations, which have nothing to do with the individual's *willingness* to help. At least two considerations suggest that, on the average, urbanites would be less willing to intervene in an emergency than ruralites. One is fear of crime, a quite rational fear for city dwellers. Robbers have even been known to pose as poll-takers in order to gain entry into a house.[6] Second, chances are greater in rural than urban areas that the victim will be known to the observer or, at least, will be a similar sort of person who can thus arouse the witness's sympathy. In cities, fear and suspicion across subcultural boundaries probably dampen sympathy for people who are quite different from the bystander. Still, our concern here is with *personality,* and so the basic question is: Under the same circumstances, would urbanites be as willing to intervene in a crisis as ruralites, or has urban life made city dwellers so callous that they are by character indifferent? Alas, we do not have any answer to this question. Newspaper stories one way or another will not suffice; for each account of city dwellers rebuffing a needy stranger, there are similar stories of villagers doing the same. Until harder evidence is presented, we can only assume that city people are—no less or no more than country people—their brothers' keepers.

In this chapter and the last, we considered the determinist proposition that the urban experience offers people a harsh choice: either succumb to the psychological strains of living in cities, or adopt a personality that estranges them from other people. Indeed, both are expected to occur to some degree. In contrast, both compositional and subcultural theory argue that, because intimate social groups survive in the city, so do healthy psyches and supportive emotional relationships. The determinist dilemma is therefore a false one. In the previous chapter, we concluded that there was little support for the notion that city dwellers suffer particularly from psychological stress. In this chapter, we have reviewed a few suggestions concerning the alterations in behavioral style that city dwellers are said to make as means of buffering this stress. There is very little evidence to support these suggestions, either. Given the present state of knowledge, the compositional and subcultural positions on this alleged dilemma appear most defensible. This conclusion does not foreclose new research that may refute it, but it does present the current "best guess."

Urbanites in Public

Yet a nagging question remains: If this conclusion is true, why is the impression so strong among ruralites and urbanites alike that the latter are cold, indifferent, and perversely individualistic? One possible answer is the general anti-urban prejudice that exists in Western culture. Another is that the impression results from encounters with special sorts of people who are disproportionately found in cities—merchants and bureaucrats, for example. More interesting than either of these is the possibility that city living systematically promotes the impression that urban residents are impersonal and distant. Consider two ways in which this might happen.

Social behavior is a function of both situation and individual personality, and there are many times when urbanites find themselves in situations that *call* for impersonal behavior —behavior which, when we observe it in others, we attribute to personality.[7] Buying milk at the supermarket, riding a bus, waiting at a corner for the "walk" sign to flash, standing in the ticket line at a movie—in many such situations urbanites are in the presence of strangers. The proper etiquette in these circumstances is to be politely impersonal, not to intrude, not to annoy. Each individual may actually feel very personal— eager to talk, sexually attracted, hostile, curious, and so on— but usually will not act on those feelings. Consequently, while individuals sense themselves as involved and sensuous persons, they see around them what seem to be cold and aloof people. (Sometimes, some special circumstance—getting stuck in an elevator, for instance—breaks down the etiquette, and people are surprised to discover how warm others can be; see Goffman, 1971). Similarly, if individuals witness someone in danger, they may feel surges of concern and sympathy, but still refrain from intervening for reasons we have seen earlier. Each of them might then conclude that he or she is the only concerned person in a crowd of apathetics. In this manner, urbanites might form the impression that all their fellows are callous and distant, even if none of them are!

Lyn Lofland (1973: 178) makes a similar observation: The city dweller "did not lose the capacity for knowing others personally. But he gained the capacity for knowing others only categorically. [He] did not lose the capacity for the deep, long-lasting, multifaceted relationship. But he gained the capacity for the surface, fleeting, restricted relationship." A study conducted in Malaysia illustrates the point. The social life of two neighborhoods in the city of Kuala Lampur was compared with that of a village nineteen miles away. Malay culture has two styles of interaction (in terms of address, for example)—one formal, the other informal and used with intimate associates. The formal style was much more evident in the city than in the village. This difference was not a result of the city-dwellers having become formal types of people, but instead a result of their more frequent encounters with strangers. At home, urbanites, as well as villagers, were informal; there was no difference in the ability to have or the actuality of familiar, personal relationships (Provencher, 1972).

A second probable reason for the impression that urban residents are impersonal is their frequent encounters with people from different subcultures. People are more open and familiar with, and less exploitative of, those like themselves than those who are distinctively different. In small communities, meetings will occur relatively more often among people who are from the same social world, and in large communities more often across cultural lines. Consequently, people in cities may well experience coldness or abuse more frequently from people who are hardly cold or abusive in other circumstances, in their own social circles. Probably even more common than actual abuse is simple miscommunication and misunderstanding between people of different backgrounds which leave each one feeling abused by the others.

Confrontations between blacks and Jews in many large American cities illustrate the tension and distrust that can arise from intergroup encounters. Blacks often follow Jews into neighborhoods and jobs, replacing the Jews who have moved on to better homes and positions. During the turnover, members of the two groups frequently meet in inauspicious circumstances, as, for example, landlord and tenant, shopkeeper and customer, supervisor and worker. Blacks often feel—sometimes rightly—that they are being discriminated against and exploited; frustration and hostility follow. Jews often feel—sometimes rightly—that middle-class blacks will be followed by "bad elements" who will depress land values, increase the crime rate, and drive the remaining Jews out; fear and suspicion follow. One Jewish woman living in a transitional neighborhood put it this way: "I'm not prejudiced; I'm just scared" (Ginsberg, 1975: 144; Gans, 1969; Cuomo, 1974).[8]

These two analyses help explain how cities may have the appearance and, indeed, the reality of impersonal encounters, when, in fact, city dwellers are not actually particularly aloof. There are many circumstances in urban life when people must interact with strangers. Friendly intimacy is not to be expected in such meetings. But simply because they find themselves in such circumstances more often than ruralites, urbanites need not be any less warm and engaging as individuals. The impersonality lies in the situation, not in the people. We have no clear evidence that the experience of living in cities alters individuals' personalities or basic styles of interaction.

Thus far in this book we have undermined a large number of popular images about urban people. We come to one more: the city dweller as unconventional, offbeat, and deviant. This image, however, is not undermined by the evidence; it is supported.

The Unconventional Urbanite

In Western culture, the conviction that cities breed nontraditional and deviant ways of life is central to any urban theme, whether the theme is a paean to urban progress or a denouncement of urban decadence. For sociological theory, also, the unconventionality of urban behavior is a central concern. The basic goal of Wirth's theory was to provide an explanation for the pervasive phenomena observed by the Chicago School—crime, vice, delinquency, family breakdown, and bohemianism and other new life-styles—phenomena which were labeled "pathologies" and "social disorganization." Is this keystone proposition of determinist theory—that urban dwellers are disproportionately "deviant"—valid? Yes.

But let us be clear about what "deviant" means in this context. At one end of the continuum of values and beliefs are those we term "traditional" or "conventional," those held by a majority or plurality of the society. They tend to be the older values, the ones celebrated on ritual occasions—God, Country, and Motherhood, for example. At the other end of the continuum are the "unconventional" or "different" values and beliefs that lead to behaviors, postures, and practices the general society considers criminal, immoral, crazy, innovative, or just odd. Sometimes applauded but more often castigated, these life-styles are deviant in the sense used in this discussion.

As a general rule, the larger the size of their community, the more likely it is that individuals will hold unconventional values and beliefs, and display unconventional, deviant behavior. This appears to be almost universally true—across different cultures, periods of history, and different realms of life. Of course, what is unconventional in one era often becomes traditional in the next. But in two respects this historical process also demonstrates the relationship of urbanism and unorthodoxy. First, new ways spread through the cities and then to the countryside on their path to orthodoxy; thus, rural people are generally the last to surrender the old ways.[9]

Second, even as the urban-bred deviance of yesterday becomes the national tradition of today, further deviations from *that* norm emerge in the cities, so that the process does not cease. For example, as the consumption of alcohol became an unremarkable habit almost everywhere in the United States, the use of marijuana arose in and began to disseminate from the larger cities.

Let us be specific about urban unconventionality: Some types of behavior in the cities are so seriously unconventional that they are considered to be major crimes. We saw in Chapter 4 that cities have a perverse "advantage" in rates of crime. At least with respect to property and vice crimes, the association between urbanism and criminality is found in most nations in most times.

More distressing yet from the perspective of the "powers that be" is the tendency for cities to harbor the politically radical and to be the arenas of rebellion. Karl Marx once lamented that peasants could not lead the revolution because they were too dispersed to organize, a problem that did not hinder the urban proletariat.[10] Though not completely prescient, Marx was describing an empirical uniformity: French political turmoil in the nineteenth century was particularly urban (Tilly, 1974; Lodhi and Tilly, 1973), as were American racial uprisings in the twentieth (Spilerman, 1971; Danzger, 1970, 1975; Morgan and Clark, 1973). A survey of American males conducted in 1969 revealed that the larger a man's community, the less likely he was to support the use of violence to protect the status quo (for example, police repression), and the more likely he was to endorse violence for social change (Blumenthal et al., 1972; on French urbanites' resistance to authority, see COFREMCA, 1974). In belief and in action, urban dwellers tend to be more politically deviant than rural dwellers (see Figure 8; see also Lipset, 1963: 264–67).[11]

Less threatening to the "system" but only slightly less threatening to many people is what might be termed moral deviance—behaving and believing in ways that, if not illegal, are at least considered wrong or distasteful by the central groups in the society. Deviance of this kind includes indifference or hostility to religion, sexual irregularity, divorce, bizarre physical appearance, drug use, nontraditional family

FIGURE 8

PERCENTAGE OF THE U. S. POPULATION ENDORSING
OR ENGAGING IN NONTRADITIONAL BEHAVIOR,
BY COMMUNITY SIZE

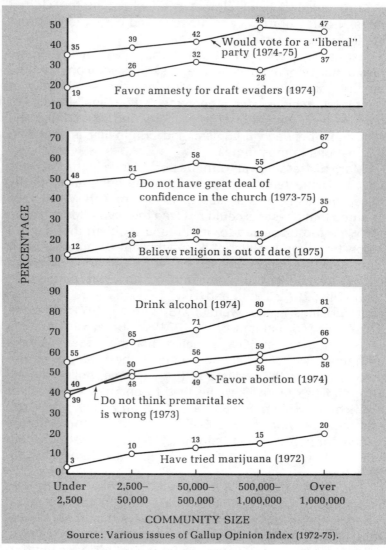

Source: Various issues of Gallup Opinion Index (1972-75).

roles, and the like. Although it is not always the case, urbanites are usually more "immoral" by conventional standards than ruralites in most nations, most times, and on most issues. Figure 8 presents, in the bottom two panels, a sample of these differences as they exist in the United States today. The percentages show a generally regular, though not dramatic, increment in the willingness of respondents to endorse nontraditional behaviors as the size of a community increases. We referred to one interesting pattern earlier: As ruralites became the last hold-outs against the consumption of alcohol, urbanites turned to (turned *on* to?) something newer still, marijuana. The topics sampled in Figure 8, ranging from religion to sex, represent a broad domain of "social morality." We can examine three specific areas in this domain more closely.

Attachment to religious institutions and beliefs—and, specifically, attachment to a society's traditional religion—decreases with greater community size. In survey studies, this pattern is evident with regard to the degree of religious orthodoxy, although sometimes less clear with regard to attendance at church services (which partly serves a social-participation function—see Fischer, 1975c). Cities both harbor and tolerate deviant religious sects, as well as atheists. Even the minimal religion which urbanites hold tends toward the less fundamentalist and more dissenting. These urban-rural differences appear across most (though not all) societies and historical periods.[12]

Sexual attitudes and behavior, to the extent that we can tell, follow the same pattern. In social surveys of Americans' views concerning premarital sex, birth control, abortion, nudity, pornography, and the like, the larger the community, the more common are endorsements of the nontraditional opinion (see also I. Reiss, 1967). And in France, for example, city dwellers would let young women date unchaperoned at an earlier age than would rural parents (Goode, 1963: 31). In terms of behavior, illegitimacy rates usually increase with urbanism (N.C.H.S., 1968; Shorter, 1971: 251; Clinard, 1964); and homosexuality flourishes in cities (Hoffman, 1968: 38). This is another realm of mores in which urbanites are relatively deviant. (Excluded from consideration here are those "primitive" societies in which sexual behavior considered liberal in the West is traditional.)

A third area of social morality encompasses family structure and family life. In Chapter 6, we pointed out the ways in which they differ in rural and urban places. In cities, families are less often formed, as people remain single longer; they are more often broken by divorce; and they tend to be smaller. These differences can be attributed to various factors, including urban-rural differences in age composition and economic opportunities. But one of these factors is values; urban dwellers are more willing to accept alternative family structures than rural dwellers. Residents of cities tend to want slightly fewer children than do people in the countryside (G.O.I., 1974, #107: 28), to exercise less patriarchal authority over their children (Douvan and Adelson, 1966: 310-315), to be more egalitarian in decision-making (Fischer, 1975c), and so on. In these three realms, as well as others, urbanism is associated with less traditional social morality.

Another facet of "unconventional" behavior is innovation, including the invention of gadgets, the production of new fads, the adoption of alternative life-styles, and artistic creation. In all these endeavors, cities are usually first and foremost, and have almost always been so. Images of rural tinkers notwithstanding, science and engineering are particularly urban. Art, music, literature—their relation to the city is a commonplace. And it is also a commonplace that most innovations diffuse from cities to their hinterlands. Cities produce the material and cultural advances of their societies, in addition to producing a high proportion of their societies' crime and immorality.[13]

It is often argued that these urban-rural differences are rapidly disappearing (Greer, 1962; Stein, 1960; see analysis in Sjoberg, 1964; 1965a). As the world enters the age of instantaneous communications, hundred-mile jaunts by jet, and cross-national allegiances, urban and rural increasingly become one. In the United States, city- and small-town persons alike read *Time,* watch Monday Night Football, see Hollywood movies, hum the same top-40 tunes, work for national corporations, belong to the Lions Club, and buy at J. C. Penney's. In this synchronized society, how can tastes, values, or life-styles differ greatly from urban to rural?

These developments in communications and transportation have certainly lessened cultural differences between city and countryside. Both passing fads and lasting faiths no doubt diffuse far faster today than they did in the nineteenth century, with the automobile, television, and telephone having turned many rural areas into metropolitan suburbs. All this granted, still the homogenized society has not yet arrived. The material we have reviewed here—on crime, insurrection, social values, innovation, and the like—shows consistent urban-rural differences in the United States in the last half of the twentieth century. We have no evidence that the gaps have substantially narrowed with respect to these topic areas, and a little evidence that indicates some have not narrowed at all (Willitis et al., 1973; Glenn and Alston, 1967).

Basic social orientations—unlike clothing styles or television preferences—do not change rapidly. As we suggested earlier, rural people alter their attitudes later than do urbanites. And, as we also suggested earlier, while the ruralites are adopting the new attitudes, still newer deviances are arising among the city dwellers (see Friedl, 1964). Perhaps divorcees are no longer pariahs even in rural hamlets—but then arises the challenge of purposefully unwed mothers. Specific issues may pass, but there will always be issues. And, in general, urbanites will be disproportionally found on the unconventional side of those issues.

We come now to a critical juncture in this book. While many of the popular descriptions of urbanites have turned out to be inaccurate, this one, that urbanites are unconventional, is indeed accurate. The larger their community, the more likely people are to believe in unconventional values and act in unconventional ways. Why?

The Theoretical Confrontation

Each of the main theories of urban life must explain the greater unconventionality of city dwellers, and it must do so in a way that is consistent with the other known facts about urban life.

Determinist theory is certainly appropriate, for the ideas of the Chicago School were, in great measure, attempts to account for the rapid social change and the new social forms so evident in that city. This theory explains urban deviance, in a compelling fashion, as a result of urban anomie, the shredding of the moral order and the fraying of individuals' bonds with that order. This social disintegration releases the inhibitions to crime, deviance, and innovation.

We can surely support the Wirthian analysis with specific cases: hobos on Skid Row, immigrants suffering from cultural shock, community conflicts, and so on. These familiar features of urban life dramatically illustrate the determinist thesis. Yet the conclusion to be drawn from the last few chapters must be that this analysis does not work. In the great majority of tests, predictions about city life derived from the theory of urban anomie—that primary ties are replaced by secondary ones, intimate relationships decline, rules of morality weaken, individual personalities are disordered or transformed—do not hold. In the determinist model, these changes are supposed to explain how urbanism creates deviance. If the predictions of alienation and anomie do not stand the test, neither does the theory.

Compositional theory has a simpler explanation: Urban-rural differences in belief and behavior are produced by differences in social composition. Relatively more often than rural-ites, city dwellers are young, without family responsibilities, highly educated, and members of minority groups. These are characteristics usually associated with unconventional life-styles and they thereby explain the urban-rural contrasts in deviance. Furthermore, the rural migrants who swell the city population are a group distinguished in part precisely by their willingness to change their way of life. These factors are sufficient to explain urban unconventionality; size and density are unnecessary. Compositional analysis, therefore, goes far toward providing an explanation.

But, while age differences help account for urban mores, occupational differences for political views, ethnic differences for religious beliefs, and so on, these factors do not suffice. The great historical and cross-cultural consistency in the association between urbanism and unconventionality, the wide variety of ways this unconventionality is manifested, and the frequently large gaps between urban and rural cultures—all these challenge the adequacy of an explanation that relies on the somewhat less consistent and often smaller urban-rural differences in social composition. Furthermore, although the drift by deviants to the cities is also part of the explanation for urban-rural behavioral differences, why do these individuals choose to move to cities? Finally, a few studies of unconventionality have statistically controlled the variation in social composition between large and small communities. They tend to find that a small, but consistent, effect of urbanism remains that cannot be explained away by the background characteristics of the residents.[14] In sum, the relationship of urbanism to unconventionality is too large to be completely explained by compositional theory.

And so we come to subcultural theory, which argues that, while population composition does explain urban unconventionality in part, size and density are also relevant. These two factors facilitate the congregation of people with common interests in numbers sufficient to form viable social worlds. Urban concentration affects the minority, the unconventional, and the deviant most. The average citizen can find comradeship almost anywhere; the more unusual people are, however, the larger the population they require in order to find their like. It is the availability of these deviant congregations in cities that explains urban unconventionality.

Criminals are found everywhere, but cities permit them a full-time specialization and provide them with helpful associates. Thus, cities produce underworlds. Discontented citizens are found everywhere, but cities permit the militant ones to meet, to organize, to mobilize. Thus, cities produce insurrectionary movements. People with eccentric tastes and habits are found everywhere, but cities concentrate enough of them to allow each variety to sustain a way of life and to systematize its philosophy. Thus, cities produce distinctive life-styles. Creative people are also found everywhere, but cities permit them to find collaborators and audiences. Thus, cities are centers of art and science. (Robert Park once wrote: "The small community often tolerates eccentricity. The city, on the contrary, rewards it. Neither the criminal, the defective, nor the genius has the same opportunity to develop his innate disposition in a small town that he invariably finds in a great city" [Park, 1916: 126]).

The city's special conduciveness to unconventionality results not only from the growth of sizable and viable social worlds, but from their interaction as well. These culturally dissimilar worlds of the urban mosaic occasionally touch, rub, and scrape. In the process, new ideas and new ways are adopted by members of more conventional groups. Construction workers and junior executives grow beards and long hair; middle-class matrons defend civil liberties for homosexuals; working-class people are slowly convinced of liberal, sociological explanations of the causes of crime; white teenagers slap palms and yell the latest catchwords from the black ghetto. Everywhere, in city and in countryside, the national culture exercises social influence as heavy and as constant as atmospheric pressure. In the cities, however, subcultures that are ethnic, exotic, avant-garde, or deviant exert some counterinfluence, one consequence of which is the further intensification of urban unconventionality.

The theoretical debate comes down to this: Urbanites are relatively unconventional. Determinists explain this fact by a theory of urban alienation and anomie for which there is little evidence. Compositionalists explain it in terms of population traits, but this is only a partial explanation. There is a way in which urbanism itself generates deviance, but does so without generating anomie. This way is the nurturance of varied social worlds—vibrant and cohesive and frequently unconventional. Subcultural theory best fits the facts of urban life as we know them now.

Summary

In Chapter 7, we considered one horn of the dilemma posed to urbanites by traditional determinist theory—that their price for residing in the city is psychological stress, alienation, and unhappiness. We concluded that there was slight evidence of such stress. In this chapter, we consider the other horn—that urbanites avoid the stresses of the city by developing a special personality and style that ultimately estrange them from other people. Little evidence could be marshaled to substantiate this prediction, either. Instances of seeming impersonality, exploitation, and callousness probably occur relatively more often in urban than in rural communities, even though urban *people* are no more impersonal, exploitative, or callous than rural people. These experiences occur when strangers are together (for instance, in bus stations), or when there is contact between members of different subcultures (for instance, in changing neighborhoods). Cities are more often the locales of these *situations* than are small towns, but not necessarily homes to different *personalities.*

Perhaps the psychic or social pains of city life are too subtle, too camouflaged, or too spiritual in character to be measured by the crude instruments of social science. Plausible arguments along this line can be constructed. But plausibility is promiscuous, and will couple readily with most theories that come by, no matter how incompatible the theories are with one another. So reasonable arguments about hidden psychic costs of rural life could also be made, based on the dangers of monotony, overly intertwined social ties, or absence of recreational outlets. A debate between these arguments cannot be resolved except by recourse to whatever instruments social scientists can command, no matter how crude. To date, there is little reason on the basis of scientific measurement to believe that cities exact such hidden personal costs.

But there *are* reasons to believe that urban residents are particularly wont to subscribe to unconventional views and to behave in unconventional ways, in realms of life ranging from crime and politics to sex and religion. The best explanation for this fact and others is subcultural theory. The congregation of large numbers of people permits the minorities and deviants to establish active and supportive subcultures, and to influence the majorities around them.

The profusion of vital and varied social worlds characteristic of cities has implications, as well, for mental states and behavioral styles. As suggested previously, we might indeed expect some traces of worry or some untoward incidents to occur because of interaction across cultural lines. So, for example, urbanites tend to distrust the vague category of "most people" slightly more often than ruralites do. In the urban setting, these "most people" frequently include those who are clearly foreign and perhaps deviant—those who may be threatening or upsetting to the individual.

Worry and hostility might be expected to arise in such

unconventional surroundings. Determinists and subcultural theory provide very different interpretations of these feelings. According to the first, urbanism alters individual psychology in various ways, including the stimulation of anxiety and perhaps anger. Then individuals with "disorganized" personalities commit deviant acts. According to subcultural theory, urbanism stimulates unconventionality in the community, and subsequently that unconventionality—in the form of crime, bizarre life-styles, and the like—creates fear and resentment among other residents. The available data conform best to the latter interpretation. Furthermore, the fact that these psychological states differ very little, if at all, between large and small communities suggests that urban subcultures may be quite insulated from one another and that there may exist a quite effective public etiquette that is used in urban encounters.

Conclusion

The portrait of urbanites that has emerged in the last few chapters is this: The urban community is one of plural, social worlds; urbanites' relationships are specialized in function and spatially dispersed, but even so their circles of acquaintance and attachment mark out only a small portion of the city's people; most of their personally important experiences occur within a single subculture or two, which are distinguished by occupation, ethnicity, life-style, or some combination thereof. This small circle, occasionally supplemented by outside ties, provides urbanites with the social affiliation and the psychic support they need to help them meet their life goals. These small social milieus fulfill the same functions in the city or the countryside, but the more unconventional ones can fulfill those functions better in the city.

The plurality of subcultures in the city fractionates any community-wide moral order into many parochial varieties. The individual who lives in a more unusual subculture generated or enhanced by urbanism will exhibit values and behaviors that deviate from the common norms. But almost all urbanites, conventional or not, seem able to use the wider urban resources, while still maintaining a base in a cohesive home milieu, and are thus able to conduct their lives in no more stressful, alienated, isolated, or dehumanized fashion than rural persons do. Healthy personalities, of whatever social persuasion, are bred in intimate, personal groups. Those groups flourish in small and large communities alike.

9

INSIDE THE METROPOLIS

THE SUBURBAN EXPERIENCE

To understand urban life fully, we need to do more than just compare people who live in the large, urbanized area of the metropolis with people who live in small towns and rural areas. As the metropolis has grown larger, it has become more and more diverse. In particular, the people and action of the modern metropolis are increasingly to be found in suburbia, outside the large core municipality of the center

city. For sociologists at least, the most significant ecological distinction in an urban region is that between the center city and its suburbs. So we turn our attention from packed downtowns to the great suburban expanses of broad streets bordered by well-kept single-family houses, places such as Los Angeles' San Fernando Valley and New York's Nassau County.

In this chapter, then, we change our locale and focus: Instead of comparing the milieu and nature of metropolitan people with those of rural or small-town people, we will be making comparisons *within* the metropolis and among metropolitans. In the previous chapters we tried to answer this question: What are the effects of urbanism on a person's social life and psychological traits? In this chapter, our question is: What are the effects of suburbanism on those factors? We will follow the same procedure in answering the second question as we did in answering the first: comparing and contrasting suburbanites to city dwellers with regard to their milieus, social groups, and personalities. (In this chapter, the term "city" refers specifically to the *center city* and not, as it did in the previous chapters, to the metropolis in general.) After reviewing the differences between city life and suburban life, we will consider the implications of those differences for the three theories of urbanism. Although these theories were formulated largely as efforts to understand the differences between urban and rural life, their general utility can be assessed by seeing how well they help us understand the differences between city and suburban life.

Suburbs are not phenomena unique to the modern era, although they have grown tremendously as a result of modern technology. Ancient and medieval cities had suburbs of sorts—clusters of dwellings just outside the city walls, often lived in by low-caste groups or by merchants who managed long-distance trade. And the elite often owned country estates located at a distance from the city that we would now call suburban. The great expansion of suburbs started in the late nineteenth century as a result of technological innovations in short-distance transportation: the commuter train, the omnibus, and then, and most especially, the automobile. These inventions and advancing industrialization created a new type of urban structure in which the work place was separated from the home; thus the commuter was created, and the "bedroom" suburb. Before the automobile a commuter could go, at best, six miles in sixty minutes, so that urban development was effectively restricted to a hundred square miles. The car and later the freeway increased the sixty-minute radius to 35 miles and thereby opened up two thousand square miles for settlement. In seventy years, the potential size of urban areas has multiplied forty-fold (Hawley, 1971; see also Zimmer, 1975; Warner, 1962).

Suburbs have expanded rapidly in the United States, especially since World War II, and by now more Americans live in suburbs than in either center cities or nonmetropolitan areas (see Figure 9).[1] The nation's factories, businesses, and services are moving outward with the population, so that each year fewer suburbanites need visit the city for work, shopping, or play. For example, most of New York City's suburban residents who work do so at jobs in the suburbs (Hoover and Vernon, 1959; Hacker, 1973); over a third of Detroit's suburbanites *never* visit downtown for reasons other than work (Lansing and Hendricks, 1967; see also Zikmund, 1971; Schwartz, 1976). Suburbanization elsewhere in the world, although trailing behind the pace of the United States, is accelerating (Hoyt, 1969; Hawley, 1971).

Before we can consider the social-psychological consequences of suburbanization, we must pause to define "suburb." In spite of all the contemporary interest in the suburbs and suburbia, there is no commonly accepted interpretation of those terms. The U.S. Census defines a suburb roughly as the part of a metropolitan area that lies outside the political boundaries of the center city. For example, The Bronx is part of New York City, so it is part of the center city; but since Westchester County is across the city line, it is suburbia. This political definition is the one used in the statistics presented in Figure 9.

A political definition of suburb has some uses. For example, city lines are quite important in metropolitan politics and school systems. But sociologically it is a limited definition; there is little reason to believe that social life changes abruptly from one side of the city line to the other. When we defined "urban," we argued that the simplest definition—population size—was the best. Here as well, the simplest is the best—distance: A suburb is a locality within a metropolis relatively distant from the center of population. Just as "urban" was defined as a matter of degree, degree of size, so "suburban" is defined as a matter of degree, degree of distance. In the previous chapters, "urban" and "city" were used as shorthand terms for relatively large communities; in this chapter, "suburb" is used as a shorthand term for relatively

FIGURE 9

U.S. SUBURBAN POPULATION GROWTH (1900–1970)*

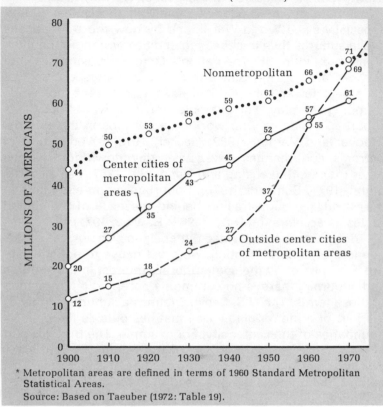

* Metropolitan areas are defined in terms of 1960 Standard Metropolitan
Statistical Areas.
Source: Based on Taeuber (1972: Table 19).

distant localities, and "city" for relatively central localities. As
before, when specific data and research are considered, we
will have to accept the definitions used by the researchers;
fortunately, these criteria will usually be strongly related to
distance.[2]

The Idea of Suburbia

Informed opinion on the suburban experience has fluctuated
sharply in this century. Early in the century, suburban residence was praised mightily for combining the cultural and

economic benefits of city life with the physical and spiritual wholesomeness of rural life (see Chapter 2). Ebenezer Howard, father of the "new town" concept, proclaimed: "Town and country *must be married,* and out of the joyous union will spring a new hope, a new life, a new civilization" (Donaldson, 1969: 23; Tarr, 1973). By the middle of the century, social critics saw the suburbs differently, as the home of mass society's "organization men"—conformers, status-seekers, anti-intellectuals, and neurotics (e.g., Riesman, 1958; Whyte, 1956). This critique of suburbia has eased in recent years, but other critiques have replaced it. In particular, housing restrictions in the suburbs are currently viewed as locking low-income and minority families into decaying center cities (for example, Downs, 1973), and suburban "sprawl" is seen as a wasteful consumption of open space and natural resources (for example, Whyte, 1968; Canter, 1974).[3]

Whatever the vagaries of intellectual opinion, popular opinion on suburbia is strongly favorable. As we discussed in Chapter 2, most Americans would prefer to live in a small town near a metropolis—in other words, a suburb. A few surveys have asked respondents whether they preferred to live closer to or farther from the metropolitan center than they currently do. Usually, most persons (sixty to seventy percent) prefer their present distance, whatever it is; the remainder, however, select "farther" much more often then "closer," by three or four to one (Lansing and Mueller, 1964; Lansing and Hendricks, 1967; Butler et al., 1968).

Actual migration patterns are consistent with these expressed preferences. Many more people are moving out to the suburbs than in toward the cities. Suburban ideology may have some effect on this movement by encouraging people to seek "a country home in the city." However, these ideals are probably not as significant today as they were early in the century, at the time of the largely upper-middle-class migration to the suburbs (see Tarr, 1973; Warner, 1962). Research indicates that most people move from one home to another for concrete reasons—most importantly, space for growing families; and also good schools, safety, the physical condition of the neighborhood, and convenience (see Rossi, 1956; Butler et al., 1968; Michelson et al., 1973). Americans do indulge their special taste for the single-family house (see

Chapter 3), which is usually justified as being beneficial for raising children. Thus, the great suburban expansion of the last generation should probably be attributed minimally to suburban ideals and maximally to suburban practicalities. When people seek spaciousness, indoors and out, at prices less-than-rich families can afford, they largely find it in the suburbs. The economics of housing has had more to do with suburban growth than either intellectual or popular ideology.[4]

No sociological theories of suburbanism as a way of life have yet been developed that are as comprehensive, powerful, and influential as the Chicago School's determinist theory of urbanism. At most, there have been fragments of theories stating that deleterious consequences result from this or that aspect of suburbia. For example, the physical layout and homogeneity of the suburbs have been charged with producing conformism (Whyte, 1956). The most thorough statement about suburbanism as a way of life is the compositional one: There are no independent effects of distance from the center of population other than purposeful ones—for example, the opportunity to garden or make other use of open space (see Gans, 1962a, 1967; B. Berger, 1960).

We can, however, apply determinist theory to suburbanism in the following way: To the extent that suburbs lack the psychological intensity and the accompanying threat of "psychic overload" that are found in the center city, then they should stand in relation to the city as rural areas do to the metropolis, with parallel differences in ways of life and personality. Subcultural theory can be similarly applied to suburbanism: To the extent that distance from the center of population inhibits the ability of people to get together, particularly in unconventional subcultures, then suburbs should resemble small communities in contrast to the city. Both determinist and subcultural theory imply that suburb-city differences should be similar to rural-urban differences. Of course, the two theories do not agree on what those differences are.

The Contexts of Suburban Life

Just as cities vary greatly, so do suburbs. One important distinction among suburbs is their developmental histories.

Some suburbs have grown gradually as a result of population "spill-over" from the city (for example, Warner, 1962). Others are the product of commercial development—"instant communities" that spring up virtually overnight in what was yesterday open land (for example, Levittown—Gans, 1967). In a third category are "engulfed towns"—communities that were once autonomous villages or small cities but have since been inundated by the metropolis and turned into bedroom suburbs (for example, Dobriner, 1963: 127-141) or satellite industrial suburbs (Schnore, 1957). Somewhat different social patterns are likely to arise in each type. Because of marketing decisions made by its constructor, the "instant" suburb, for example, is likely to be more homogeneous in the ages and incomes of its residents than most neighborhoods. The engulfed suburb often becomes the scene of a great deal of "oldtimer"-"newcomer" conflict.

Suburbs are heterogeneous in other ways as well, ways similar to those that differentiate city neighborhoods: social class—there are blue-collar, white-collar, as well as affluent suburbs; age—both of the suburbs and of their residents; religion and race—there are Protestant, Catholic, Jewish, and a few black suburbs (Ogburn, 1937: Ch. 10; Walter and Wirt, 1972). These distinctions are significant, for the life-styles of blue-collar suburbanites resemble those of blue-collar city dwellers more than they do those of white-collar suburbanites. In general, differences among suburbs are greater than the average differences between cities and suburbs. This great variability should be constantly kept in mind, even as we endeavor to draw general conclusions about cities and suburbs.

The physical environment of suburbia is, as we noted earlier, a significant public attraction. In general, the farther from the center of a metropolis, the fewer the irritants produced by congestion: crowds, noise, dirt, and pollution.[5] This difference between city and suburbs is clearly perceived by the public. City residents cite irritants as major drawbacks to their neighborhoods, and suburban residents note their absence as positive features of their locales. This contrast appears to explain in part why suburbanites are more satisfied with their residences than city dwellers are with theirs (Hawley and Zimmer, 1971; Marans and Rodgers, 1975).

Probably more significant in producing this satisfaction is

the city-suburb difference in housing. Each mile farther from the metropolitan center adds exponentially to the land available for building. And, in general, the more distant from the center a plot of land is, the less valuable it is commercially, and consequently the less costly it is for home-building. Thus, the construction of single-family houses is cheaper in the suburbs than in the center city. And, as a general rule, the more distant a neighborhood is from the center city, the higher its rate of detached houses to apartment buildings (see Evans, 1973; Treadway, 1969). A glance back at Figure 2 (page 55) reminds us that suburban housing is on the average more spacious, valuable, and generally desirable than center-city or nonmetropolitan dwellings.

Several consequences flow from the relative concentration of single-family houses in the suburbs. The house encourages suburbanites to spend more leisure time at home (tending the lawn, making repairs, and so on), and to be more interested in the neighborhood and more involved with their neighbors (Michelson, 1973a; Gans, 1967; Berger, 1960). The lower density associated with single-unit housing means that stores and services are beyond walking distance, and thus the purchase of a second or even a third car for wives and teen-age children is more likely (Foley, 1975).[6] And, given the general preference for such housing, lower density means that suburbanites are usually more satisfied with their locations than city residents are (see, for example, Stueve et al., 1975).[7]

The price suburbanites pay for a pleasant environment (in addition to the cost of a house) is difficulty and time in reaching services and facilities. This is being quickly alleviated, at least in North American suburbs, as jobs, stores, and entertainment places spring up there (Kasarda, 1976; Zimmer, 1975). Though residents on the city's rim are disadvantaged by their dispersed residential patterns in attracting services, these suburbanites have the counterbalancing advantage of relatively large disposable incomes. A preeminent symbol of suburban facilities is the grand shopping mall, which in some areas has taken on the aspect of a suburban downtown, complete with loitering adolescents and crime (King, 1971; Muller, 1974). Nevertheless, suburbanites must travel farther for services, and live more often without them.

This is particularly true with regard to the more specialized services, and for persons with more specialized needs or whose mobility is restricted, such as the elderly.[8]

This trade-off—the physical setting and house versus ease of access—is consciously perceived by most people when they decide where to move. The majority choose, when they are in the position to choose, a nice house in a less accessible location (Lansing, 1966; Butler et al., 1968). Thus, a great many choose the suburbs.

In doing so, they choose a residential environment marked not only by a particular physical context, but by a particular social context as well. One dramatic difference between city and suburb in the United States is racial composition. In large metropolitan areas, about 24 percent of the center-city population is black, in contrast to about 6 percent of the suburban population (Bureau of the Census, 1969). Furthermore, the black population defined by the census as suburban is largely confined to ghetto areas that have overflowed city lines and to small ghettos in satellite cities. In fact, the entire growth of suburbs in the United States has served to increase racial residential segregation (Farley, 1976; Muller, 1974; Berry et al., 1976).[9]

Cities and suburbs also differ consistently on the dimension of life cycle. Young adults in the pre-family stage and elderly people whose children have grown up tend to live in cities. Married adults between the ages of 25 and 44 and their children under 18 tend to live in the suburbs. In general, the farther from downtown a neighborhood is, the higher the proportion of child-rearing families (Anderson and Egeland, 1961; Guest, 1971). Current mobility patterns in metropolitan areas are reinforcing these differences: Young adults are moving inward; slightly older, married, and child-rearing adults are moving outward (Long and Glick, 1976).

City and suburb also differ in social class. Although suburbanites tend to be more educated and to hold more prestigious jobs than city people do, the two groups differ most in income. In 1969, the median income of suburban families in the United States was 18 percent greater than that of city families—$11,210 as against $9,510 (Bureau of Census, 1973: 11). Median suburban income exceeded median city income in all but one of the 29 largest metropolises (Farley, 1976).[10]

Residential moves are still augmenting these differences, as high-income families move outward and low-income families inward (Hawley and Zimmer, 1971; Farley, 1976). The moves by poor families are probably a result of being priced out of developing suburban housing markets. Although it is foolish to imagine that suburbanites are uniformly wealthy—a good many are working-class—it is true that they are on the average wealthier than city dwellers.[11]

Although this description of suburban affluence is probably familiar to any casual observer of the American scene, it is actually a rather new and unusual pattern. As we pointed out in Chapter 3, preindustrial cities had largely an opposite structure. That is, the rich people of Moscow in 1897, for example, lived near the center, while it was the poor who were on the outskirts (Abbott, 1974). This was also the pattern for urban areas in the United States in the mid-nineteenth century (D. Ward, 1971; Conzen, 1975). And this continues to be the pattern for metropolises in the industrializing nations, for others which matured before their nations had industrialized (Schnore, 1965; Hoyt, 1969); and even for many metropolises in the southern part of the United States today (Schnore, 1972; Schlitz and Moffitt, 1971). Nevertheless, the "North American" form, with greater affluence in the outskirts than the center, deserves close attention, because most major metropolises not yet in that pattern are evolving toward it. The growing middle classes are moving out of the cities to the peripheries and becoming suburbanites (Hoyt, 1969; Hawley, 1971; Schnore, 1965).[12]

The differences in racial and class composition between cities and suburbs in the United States is one of the few contributors to the American "urban crisis" that is truly *urban* in nature. That is, the demographic structure of the metropolis is a major part of the problem. The ability of the affluent to segregate themselves and their tax moneys behind suburban political walls has left the center cities with immense social services to support (including those such as museums and police protection for suburbanites "on the town"—Kasarda, 1972a) and decaying physical plants to renew, but without the financial or human resources to succeed at those tasks. It is ironic that the individual who can manage the price (and color) of admission to many suburbs—that is, purchasing an expensive house—can also enjoy "rebates" in the form of better services at lower tax rates.

American suburbanites and city dwellers also differ with regard to migration histories. Movers from city to suburb outnumber those going in the opposite direction by about three to one. And suburbs are absorbing most of the migration into metropolitan areas from smaller communities (Farley, 1976). Consequently, suburbanites are relatively more often newcomers to their neighborhoods, not yet firmly rooted, but in the process of planting those roots. Suburban communities often possess short histories, and, as a result, unsteady social and political structures (Gans, 1967; 1951).

The last aspect of social composition which we shall consider is homogeneity. There is some evidence that, as many have suspected, suburban neighborhoods tend to be more homogeneous in class, race, and religion than city neighborhoods. The difference is, however, modest.[13] The consequences of slightly greater homogeneity could be (though need not necessarily be) slightly more conformity, cohesion, conventionality, and consensus in suburban than in city neighborhoods.

The social context of suburbia is also defined by the typical activities of the people who live there. American suburbs have usually been thought of as the sites of home activities, child-rearing, and leisure, while cities were the work sites. Never completely true, this becomes less true every year. There always were factories and businesses in the suburbs, and their number has increased rapidly in recent years, so that the critical issues are not just the amount of work done in city and suburb, but also the type of work done. On the first count, it remains as a general, though weakened, rule that commercial and industrial land use declines with distance from the center, while residential land use increases. Cities still house more work activities than do suburbs. On the second count, center cities are increasingly specializing in professional, administrative, and general white-collar work, while blue-collar, manufacturing jobs shift to the suburbs where lower land costs permit cheaper factory construction. These changes are producing a daily criss-cross commute in American metropolises: Some white-collar workers travel from suburban low-rise homes to city high-rise offices; some blue-collar workers who have the means travel from high-rise city apartments to low-rise suburban factories (Guest, 1975). Above and beyond this difference in *type* of work, there is a general move of all sorts of jobs toward the suburbs (W.R. Thompson, 1973; Kasarda, 1976; 1972b).

City dwellers and suburbanites also differ in their leisure activities. Residents closer to downtown tend to use public facilities, such as theaters, relatively often, while suburbanites tend to be relatively involved in home activities, such as gardening and entertaining friends (Gruenberg, 1974; von Rosenbladt, 1972). This difference reflects in part the residential choices of people with different tastes (Zelan, 1968), but studies of individuals who have moved from city to suburb indicate that they changed their leisure pursuits, often without having intended to (Michelson, 1973a; Gans, 1967; Clark, 1966). House ownership and child-rearing, both more common among suburbanites, also "root" leisure activities. Nonetheless, there seems to be an effect of suburbanism itself (Gruenberg, 1974; Wallden, 1975). The effect probably involves simple distance: Theaters, restaurants, and the like tend to be inconveniently far away for suburbanites (see von Rosenbladt, 1972) so that home activities are stressed instead (Zikmund, 1971; Lansing and Hendricks, 1967).

Criminal activities show sharp city-suburban differences, largely as a function of differences in social class. In preindustrial urban developments, deprived groups reside on the outskirts, and so do the criminals; crime therefore increases with distance from the center (Herbert, 1972: 217-221; Abbott, 1974). In modern cities, such as American ones, crime is found in the city, where the low-income groups are, and it decreases with distance (Herbert, 1972: 199ff.). This difference, like many others, is in flux: Suburban crime rates in the United States are rising more rapidly than are city rates (McCausland, 1972; Malcolm, 1974). Nevertheless, people in the suburbs are safer from crime than are people in the city. FBI statistics for 1973 indicate, for example, that suburbanites ran less than half the risk of being murdered or having their cars stolen than city dwellers (Kelley, 1974: Tables 1, 6). Suburbanites also feel safer: In one survey, while only twenty percent of the suburbanites interviewed said that they thought it was unsafe for them to walk outside at night, over fifty percent of city residents felt it was unsafe (Marans and Rodgers, 1975: Table 18).

Most of the differences in social context between American cities and suburbs are not very great. (And they are differences in *averages*, which mask much internal variation.) Also, these differences are often reversed in other nations. But they form a consistent pattern, and one which is increasingly typical elsewhere. This brief overview of the physical structure and social formation of American suburbs suggests that, on the average, they are in some ways like affluent small towns within the metropolis. If that is indeed what they are, then they are meeting the aspirations of most of their residents, as we will see in the pages that follow.

Suburban Social Groups

Any attempt to contrast the lives and behavior of suburbanites to those of city dwellers runs into two major obstacles. One, both sets of people are urbanites. Socially and economically, they are both part of the greater metropolitan population, working, shopping, and playing at many of the same places and with the same people. Thus, suburbanites are not likely to act in markedly distinct ways (except insofar as their personal traits, such as class and age, incline them to do so). Second, though there has been much popular interest in suburban life-styles (Donaldson, 1969), the amount of careful, comparative research is quite limited. Consequently, we shall have to tread lightly and speculatively over a number of questions in this field. Of the secondary social groups in suburbia, we shall consider three: the community, the neighborhood, and the special-interest group.[14]

The Community

Attention to the community as a social group highlights once more the features of metropolitan life that are unique to the United States. This nation's home-rule tradition disperses power to local territorial units. Suburban areas are autonomous political entities that exercise a good deal of power over such important aspects of their residents' lives as taxes, schools, police, and zoning. This is unlike the situation in other nations where most or many of these functions are performed by the national or metropolitan government. Suburban political boundaries thus have significant substantive meaning. To move across the line from center city to suburb, or from one suburb to another, is often to find a drastic change in types of schools, tax rates, the quality of public services, and the like. Consequently, interest in the suburban community is more than an act of dutiful citizenship; it often means, in a much more significant way than in the city, the protection of low taxes, high-quality (and segregated) schools, and property values. The significance of these suburban political lines becomes dramatized when the autonomy of the community is threatened, as in the case of attempts to bus children from the center city to suburban schools, or efforts to create metropolitan-wide governments. Suburbanites fight these moves strenuously.[15] In addition, the small size of the suburban polities should make each resident's opinion count more than it would in the city, and accordingly he or she should feel politically efficacious.

These characteristics of suburbs in the United States should promote political involvement, thus making more cohesive "groups" of those communities. However, a number of suburban characteristics lessen involvement. Many residents are relatively new to the community (see Alford and Scoble, 1968); many, if not most, workers hold jobs outside the community (W.T. Martin, 1959; Verba and Nie, 1972: Table 13-2); and suburban political figures and issues are likely to be rendered invisible by the more publicized ones of the center city (Fischer, 1975d). So, for example, suburbanites, though more educated than city residents, are less likely to know their local political leaders (Hawley and Zimmer, 1971: 67ff.; Verba and Nie, 1972: Ch. 13), and less or, at most, equally likely to vote in local elections (Greer, 1962: 40; Hawley and Zimmer, 1971).

Perhaps the best description of suburban political opinion is that it is an apathetic but arousable consensus. Most constituencies are socially and ideologically homogeneous. Consequently, there is usually widespread, if implicit, agreement on political philosophy, and few issues arise to generate excitement in local government. Semiprofessional office-holders are commonly allowed to act as trustees of the general accord so long as they care to do so. Therefore, in the normal course of events, suburbanites do not show much involvement in the community affiars (Prewitt and Eulau, 1969). However, this appearance is misleading. When the consensus is threatened by a challenge from without or a schism from within, suburbanites become very active community citizens (Black, 1974). Metropolitanization, school busing, zoning changes—these are the kinds of issues that arouse the latent community "group." We can conclude that, in the suburbs, all else equal, the political community *is* a more significant social group than it is in the city.[16]

The Neighborhood

Another territorial unit, the neighborhood, is also more cohesive in the suburbs than it is in the city. Research in the United States and abroad is virtually unanimous on this point. Whether involvement in the neighborhood is measured by visits with neighbors, concern for the local area, the proportion of local personal activities, or almost any equivalent indicator, suburbanites score somewhat higher than city dwellers (but still lower than rural residents). Suburbanization is not always associated with increased neighboring; some people—those with special tastes, or members of minority groups—actually become more isolated in suburbia. We shall return to these people, later. Yet, for the bulk of the population, suburban life is associated with more neighborliness.[17]

Though there is consensus on city-suburban differences in neighboring, there is none on the explanation for it (Fischer and Jackson, 1976). Some point to the personal characteristics of suburbanites, such as their young children and high income. Although these provide a partial explanation, they do not account for all of the differences. A few studies have found that suburbanites are more neighborly than city dwellers even when such factors are held constant (for example, Tomeh, 1964; Fava, 1959; Tallman and Morgner, 1970). And another few studies have followed the same individuals from city to suburb and have found that they tend to increase their neighboring after the move (for example, Michelson, 1973a; Clark, 1966; Berger, 1960). These latter investigations cast doubt as well on the theory that neighborly personalities are drawn to suburban life, and that self-selection explains the city-suburban difference (Bell, 1959; Fava, 1959). While some self-selection no doubt occurs—people who love to neighbor might find the neighboring in suburbia an extra incentive to move—this change is not a significant purpose of suburban migration, and there seems to be little self-selection on the basis of sociability (Baldassare and Fischer, 1975; Michelson, 1973a; Michelson et al., 1973; there is some self-selection on the basis of preferred leisure activities, for example, gardening versus attending the theater—Zelan, 1968). Other explanations of suburbanites' proclivities for neighboring include the argument that the detached house is conducive to local social life (Gans, 1967; Dobriner, 1963), that neighboring is a result of pioneer eagerness in brand-new communities (Marshall, 1973), and that local involvement is a result of suburban homogeneity (Donaldson, 1969; Gans, 1967).

One more explanation should be considered: distance. Suburban neighborhoods are often inconveniently distant from the bulk of the population, and from metropolitan attractions. Consequently, friends and activities outside the neighborhood are relatively costly to see, and so suburbanites tend to settle for local relationships. This explanation is especially consistent with longitudinal studies of people who moved to the suburbs, which indicate that new suburbanites must make a major effort to maintain contact with their associates in the city. Quite commonly, those associates are dropped in favor of closer, local ones (for example, Clark, 1966; Michelson, 1973a). This analysis explains the cohesion of the suburban neighborhood by the definitional nature of suburbia: its peripheral location in the metropolis (Fischer and Jackson, 1976).

Whichever explanation(s) future research confirms, the difference is clear: suburbanites tend to be more involved in their neighborhoods than are city dwellers. Fitting this fact together with others—the significance of the community, leisure time spent at home, house ownership, and child-rearing —suggests a general style of life we might call "localism." People's activity and attention are directed toward the immediate locality and its residents. To be sure, some forces pull suburbanites *away* from their localities, including associates in the city, jobs outside the area, the necessity to travel far for services, and the easy mobility of middle-class families with two or more cars. Nevertheless, the countervailing tugs of the suburban neighborhood—the home, children, congenial neighbors, perhaps suburbanism itself (that is, distance)—appear to be stronger, with the net result being a somewhat more localized way of life.[18] Additional evidence of suburban localism comes from the relative weakness in suburbia of nonlocal special-interest groups.

Special-Interest Groups

Suburban communities certainly have their share, or more, of fraternal associations, PTA's, garden clubs, and the like. These are general and usually localized special-interest groups. Less common are the groups that cater to the slightly atypical resident. Members of ethnic minorities, single people, individuals with unusual tastes—compatible groups are scarce for them, even while their "Middle American" neighbors are surrounded by congenial groups. The small size of each unique population leads to a poverty of specialized services and facilities for them, and thus further deprivation. Consider two examples. Widely dispersed across the town, frequently carless, and lacking places to go and things to do, adolescents are commonly disgruntled in suburbia. This problem was illustrated recently by confrontations between police and teenagers in Foster City, California, a suburb on the San Franciscan peninsula. Police explained that the troubles were due to "boredom" among the youth. (On their part, the teenagers said that the troubles were due to "boredom" among the police.) A second example is provided by Herbert Gans, in *The Levittowners*. The population of suburban newcomers he studied included a number of Jewish women who were interested in cultural activities. They found, to their frustration, that they were too few, and too far from places and people in Philadelphia, the nearest city, to satisfy their desires. It is people like these, outside the mainstream, who are impaired in their efforts to form special-interest groups. Gans concludes:

The smallness and homogeneity of the population made it difficult for the culturally and socially deviant to find companions. Levittown benefitted the majority but punished the minority with exclusion, . . . [with] "the misery of the deviate" (1967:239).

The feebleness of translocal special-interest groups thus helps reinforce the suburban pattern of social life centered on the community and the neighborhood.

Primary Groups

The effects of suburbanism on *primary* groups are quite modest, but are still consistent with the tendency toward localism. With respect to ethnic groups, the vision of suburbia popular in the 1950s was that ethnic differences were largely dissolved in its melting pot. While not many studies have been conducted on suburban ethnicity, a few notable ones have been done on Jews. These studies found that Jewish suburbanites continued to identify themselves as Jews and, more importantly, that their intimate social relationships were almost exclusively with other Jews, even when they resided in overwhelmingly gentile communities. The subjects of the studies reported simply feeling more "comfortable" and "at home" with their coreligionists. However, the studies also revealed notable decreases in adherence to Jewish religious ritual and belief when compared to the practices of their parents. (This change was mostly a result of generational differences, or of upward social mobility, and minimally of suburbanism.) Nevertheless, Jews remain a distinct and meaningful ethnic group in suburbia (Sklare and Greenblum, 1967; Goldstein and Goldscheider, 1968; Gans, 1951, 1957, 1967). If this case can be generalized to unstudied groups, it implies that there is nothing inherently inimical to ethnicity in suburban life (see also Lieberson, 1962).

However, one major qualification should be noted: So long as members of an ethnic group remain few in number or widely dispersed, they face the harsh choice of isolation or assimilation. In these studies, the Jewish families who were early settlers in their communities anxiously awaited the arrival of others so that they could establish both formal and informal associations. Where they remained scattered, religious identity was weakened (Goldstein and Goldscheider, 1968). And some ethnic groups did not fare as well as the Jews. Gans notes in *The Levittowners* that "groups without a strong subcommunity were isolated, notably a handful of Japanese, Chinese, and Greek families" (1967:162). The persistence of ethnicity partly depends on the presence of sufficient numbers in the group.

Another proposition in what has been termed the "suburban myth" (Donaldson, 1969; Berger, 1960) holds that suburban residence promotes a peculiar sort of "hypersociability": People are involved with a great number of friends, but those friendships are superficial. From the evidence at hand, it appears that suburbanism is associated neither with a greater number of friendships nor with shallower ones than city residence.[19] However, two modest differences, already alluded to between city and suburban friendships are indicated by the research.

First, suburban friendships tend to be somewhat more localized than those of city residents. Suburbanites are a bit likelier to draw their friends from among their neighbors. For many new settlers on the urban fringe, there is a gradual fraying of bonds with friends who were left in the city, and the braiding of substitutes with neighbors.[20] In Chapter 6 we suggested that one difference between rural and metropolitan friendships was that the latter were more geographically dispersed. Within the metropolis, suburban neighborhoods seem to recreate a rural pattern of local ties.

Second, suburban neighbors cannot replace other friends for those who are too young or too old, who are members of ethnic, racial, or class minorities in their neighborhoods, or who are adherents to atypical life-styles. These people cannot satisfy their friendship needs in the locality (and they find it difficult to form special-interest groups). Consequently, those who can travel long distances to maintain alternative social bonds do so, but those who cannot or will not travel that far are often isolated in their suburban houses (Gans, 1967; Tomeh, 1964).

The elderly provide a case in point. Because of physical and financial problems, they tend to be relatively immobile, and therefore suffer more acutely from problems of access than do younger people. A study of the elderly conducted in San Antonio, Texas, found that the farther from the center they lived, the fewer friends they reported, the less active socially and the lonelier they were (Carp, 1975; see also Bourg, 1975; Cantor, 1975).

Other than the localization of friendships and the relative isolation of atypical people, there appears to be no difference between the friendship patterns of city and suburban residents—or, at least, no difference unattributable to the facts that suburbanites tend to be more affluent, more often in the process of child-rearing, and in other personal traits different from city dwellers.

Much of journalistic speculation about suburban life has focused on the damage suburban residence might do to family life (see Donaldson, 1969). Scholars, too, have been concerned, worrying, for example, that the long commuting times spent by fathers would lead to mother-centered families (for example, Burgess and Locke, 1953: Ch. 4). This concern is ironic, in light of the general public opinion that suburbs are ideal for family life, and the fact that families often move there "for the children." The indoor space of a suburban house provides individual privacy; a yard and a quiet street allow children to play in safety; the grounds and the structure promote leisure activities at home; and the house itself serves as an investment and symbol of achievement. Most movers from the cities to the suburbs desire and expect such changes and they are usually accurate in their expectations (Gans, 1967; Michelson, 1973a). This is not to say that suburban families are more cohesive or "healthy" than comparable ones in the city; there is little evidence for such an assertion. But people are generally convinced that suburbs are good places to raise children, and we have little empirical reason to dispute that belief.

However, when we view the status of the extended family as well as that of the nuclear family, one blemish in this portrait of suburban familism becomes evident. Movers to the suburbs tend to underestimate how inconvenient it will be for them to see their kin—parents, in-laws, siblings—after their move: At first, they try to stay in touch, but over time the frequency of interaction often declines, with local friends eventually replacing the relatives in many suburbanites' social lives (Tallman, 1969; Gans, 1967; Clark, 1966; Michelson, 1973a). This does not appear to bother husbands very much, but it does seriously disturb many wives.

A well-known case of family separation occurred when young families moved from Bethnal Green, the working-class district of London described in Chapter 6, to Greenleigh, a recently built housing estate on the outskirts of London (Young and Willmott, 1957). Contact between the suburban-ites and their parents was quite difficult and the resulting feeling of separation was quite strong, especially among the women. Though they tried to stay in touch—"When I first came I felt I had done a crime," said one woman, "It was so bare. I felt terrible and I used to pop back to see Mum two or three times a week" (p. 133)—almost inevitably they were isolated. When the researchers returned to Greenleigh a few years later, after it had become more populated, they found that neighborhood social life had grown and significantly eased the women's isolation (Willmott, 1963).

In sum, the effects of suburbanism on primary groups are apparently quite modest. Movers to the suburbs are much like movers within the city; those who have a choice choose homes and neighborhoods to match their life-styles and to promote their private lives. Insofar as people correctly antici-pate the changes that result from their moves, they presum-ably protect their primary ties, or alter them in desired ways. Hence, we should expect suburbanism itself to produce few differences between city and suburb in the character of social relations. However, anticipated or not, one modest effect does occur: a relative constriction of social networks, on two dimensions. There is a slight spatial constriction that results in more localized activities and relationships than occur in the city. And there is a modest constriction in variety, with people who are relatively atypical in the suburban population finding themselves more isolated from their fellows than would be the case in the city. (Even these differences are, we must repeat, small.)

Unfortunately, these conclusions are based largely on studies of *moves* to suburbia, rather than on suburban resi-dence alone. Most researchers have focused, often by ne-cessity, on recent arrivals to the suburbs; and studies of long-time suburbanites are relatively rare (see Hawley and

Zimmer, 1971; Zelan, 1968). Thus, we face the uncertainty of whether city-suburban differences, or even lack of differences, are a result of the *residence* or the *move*. Until further studies are completed, any conclusions we draw must be accepted with this qualification in mind.

The Individual in Suburbia

There is little reason to expect the mental state or personality of the suburbanite to differ from that of an otherwise comparable city dweller. Members of a common metropolitan social structure, suburbanites and city dwellers alike have presumably chosen, within the constraints of the family budget, a residence that maximizes their preferred balance of amenities and accessibility. We should find differences between suburban and city people of similar backgrounds if one or both of two conditions hold: if certain personalities are selectively drawn to suburbia; and/or if suburban residence has unanticipated consequences.

Some early speculations suggested that either or both of these conditions would produce a difference in the types of personalities, levels of stress, rates of mental illness, and overall morale of city and suburban residents—to the disadvantage of the latter. One sociologist asserts, for example: "We can clearly see the most grievous human loss that life in the suburb entails. Dedication to a status-dominated life style forces individuals into a rigid mold from within which they can see only limited aspects of human reality. . . . Emotional growth stops at [a] 'juvenile' phase" (Stein, 1960: 286; see review in Donaldson, 1969).

The available data fail to support such speculations. There are differences in *tastes* between those who prefer suburbs and those who prefer cities; the gardeners move outward, the gourmets move inward (Zelan, 1968; Fugitt and Zuiches, 1973; Michelson, 1973a). But there is as yet little evidence that suburbanism, in general, attracts or produces people who are stressed, disordered, or alienated (Pahl, 1970: 125-127; Berger, 1960; Baldassare and Fischer, 1975). Indeed, the most likely psychological change when the average American moves to the suburbs is an increase in happiness. Perhaps because of the specific amenities of the suburban home, and perhaps because of the achievement it represents in American society, suburbanites are usually happy with their moves (Gans, 1968; Berger, 1960) and slightly happier with their communities and their lives—other factors held equal— than city dwellers (Marans and Rodgers, 1975; Fischer, 1973b).

This conclusion does not hold, however, for notable sets of suburbanites who are *not* average, and for whom suburbia tends to cause anguish. These people, whom we have singled out before, are those whose age, social class, ethnicity, or lifestyle make them "cultural deviates" in their suburban neighborhoods, where they usually live because of error or lack of choice. In the suburbs, these people tend to be isolated from congenial associates and activities. In the city, they are more likely to reside in appropriate neighborhoods; but even if they do not, it matters less, for they have easier access to people and places outside the neighborhood. For those in the American "mainstream"—middle-class, middle-browed, raising children, and so forth—the difference between city and suburb on this score is largely moot. They can find their like almost anywhere (and in a suburb most of all). When members of the cultural minorities can, they hold on to social ties outside their suburbs through the active use of the car and telephone. When they cannot, or when traveling wearies, they are in danger of suffering loneliness, boredom, and unhappiness.

A number of studies have been conducted on the members of one particularly vulnerable group—women in general, and housewives in particular. These studies have found that housewives are more critical of suburbs, more displeased with moving there, and more likely to suffer psychologically from the move than their husbands. Employed men daily travel away from home and to a milieu usually more interesting than the one they left; they return to a house and a neighborhood which provide quiet relaxation and pride of achievement. For many housewives, however, the house and neighborhood represent hours of housekeeping drudgery, boredom if they step outdoors, and a lack of other involvements. Gans (1967: 226) reports the complaint of a working-class woman in Levittown: "It's too quiet here, nothing to do.

In the city you can go downtown shopping, see all the people, or go visit mother." To be sure, most women adjust, finding friends and diversions nearby, and supplementing those with trips and phone calls. Nevertheless, many in this group suffer in suburbia.[21]

Various efforts have been made to pinpoint the source of this housewife malaise. The suggestions include the hard labor of "keeping" a house, or the move itself and the tearing up of old roots (men maintain job associates, and do not seem to care much about losing touch with relatives), or the particular mix of persons in suburban neighborhoods. These hypotheses may all be accurate. If so, they do not indict suburbia, since none of them is unique to the suburbs or to moving there. There is some evidence, however, that the peripheral location of suburbs also contributes to women's unhappiness: William Michelson (1973a) conducted a very exact study in the Toronto area in which families were interviewed before and repeatedly after moves to residences of varying types. Few unanticipated major changes took place with these families, but one that did was the isolation and boredom of a number of suburban housewives. These ills were relieved only partly by neighboring. Many women continued to complain of problems resulting from the distance to the city, for example, or from the absence of things to do other than housework. (Ironically, those who spend the most time in the suburbs, housewives, are least benefited by it— in terms of happiness—while those who benefit the most from it, husbands, are least often there.)

The available evidence on city-suburban differences in social behaviors and attitudes is quite limited.[22] Bits of research suggest that most or all such differences can be explained by associated characteristics of suburbanites, their education, stage in the life-cycle, home ownership, and the like. "Unconventional" or deviant behavior—crime, for example—occurs relatively less often in the suburbs than in the city. This is largely a result of unconventional persons shunning the suburbs, or being shunned by them, rather than of suburbanism suppressing deviance. We might speculate that the physical isolation of cultural deviates described earlier also contributes to the conventionality of suburban life, but there seems to be as yet no firm evidence of such an effect.

It was once thought that people who moved to suburbia subsequently changed their political allegiance from Democratic to Republican, but that notion has been largely discredited (Wirt et al., 1972; Wattell, 1959; Gans, 1967). Suburbanites are relatively more involved in their local churches than city dwellers, but that activity appears to be part of their greater local participation, rather than an indicator of reawakened faith.[23]

Other theories about suburban life-style find even less support. The thesis that suburbanism promotes conformity (Whyte, 1956; Dobriner, 1963: Ch. 1) remains a speculation (see Gans, 1967). The argument that suburbs attract or produce consumption-oriented people (Bell, 1959) still lacks substantiation. The suburban house is certainly a major consumption item, but the difference between the ones who have it and those who don't is more a matter of income than of personality. And the suggestion that suburbia debases cultural tastes (Riesman, 1958) probably mistakes correlation for causality. People who prefer "high culture" tend to prefer the city (Zelan, 1968; Michelson, 1973a) and tend to feel isolated in the suburbs, but suburbanism itself probably does not reduce intellects to a low common denominator. Speculations such as these are often, in essence, (city-dwelling) intellectuals' critiques of middle-class American life-styles, critiques in which places are blamed for the ways of life people bring to them (see Donaldson, 1969; Gans, 1967).

Reflections on Theories

Earlier in the chapter, we suggested that, in the absence of any comprehensive theories of suburban social psychology, we could try to apply the three original theories of urbanism to this topic. The exercise would also permit us to assess the generalizability and power of each perspective.

Determinist theory implies that suburbanism affects the cohesion of intimate groups, psychological states, and behavioral styles.[24] Since suburbs are less dense and heterogeneous than center cities, they should resemble rural areas in these respects—producing stronger primary groups, less psychic stress, more personal behavioral styles, and less deviance than cities do. There is little evidence currently available to support any of these predictions, except perhaps the last. And the lower rates of criminal deviance in the suburbs are satisfactorily explained by the differences between the people who live in the cities and those who live in the suburbs, particularly their class status.

There are a number of sensory experiences found in the suburbs that most people deeply appreciate—the quiet, the spaciousness, the greenery, and the freshness. So far as we can tell, however, suburbia does not *determine* fundamental psychological states or processes.

The compositional stance on city-suburban differences is consistent with its position on urban-rural differences: any social-psychological variations result from the characteristics of the individuals who can and want to live in those communities, and not to ecological factors like density or distance. Herbert Gans's conclusion, drawn from his classic study of Levittown, New Jersey, is worth quoting at length:

> The findings on changes and their sources suggest that the distinction between urban and suburban ways of living postulated by the critics (and by some sociologists as well) is more imaginary than real. Few changes can be traced to the suburban qualities of Levittown, and the sources that did cause change, like the house, the population mix, and newness, are not distinctively suburban. Moreover, when one looks at similar populations in city and suburb, their ways of life are remarkably alike. . . .
>
> The crucial difference between cities and suburbs, then, is that they are often home for different kinds of people. If one is to understand their behavior, these differences are much more important than whether they reside inside or outside the city limits. Inner-city residential areas are home to the rich, the poor, and the nonwhite, as well as the unmarried and the childless middle class. Their ways of life differ from those of suburbanites and people in the outer city, but because they are *not* young working or lower and upper middle class families. If populations and residential areas were described by age and class characteristics, and by racial, ethnic, and religious ones, our understanding of human settlements would be much improved. Using such concepts as "urban" and "suburban" as casual variables adds little, on the other hand, except for ecological and demographic analyses of communities as a whole and for studies of political behavior (Gans, 1967: 288-289; see also Gans, 1962a; Berger, 1960).

This point of view appears to be the most accurate so far. We have seen the extent of selectivity involved in suburban residence: singles move away, families move in; whites are permitted to enter, blacks are not. These and other selectivity factors certainly explain far more than distance from downtown does. However, there remain some effects of suburbanism, some modest differences between city and suburb that are regular and patterned, and are not fully explained by self-selection. In particular, there is the localization of social life and the relative absence of unconventionality in suburbia. These differences bring us to our third theory.

Subcultural theory, like determinist theory, was designed to answer questions about differences between metropolitan and rural communities, and not about differences within the metropolis. However, the analysis can be extended: The critical factor is the ability of specific sets of people to come together in numbers sufficient to support an active subculture and its institutions. Having those numbers in a community is only part of the process. The viability of a subculture also depends on the access (in terms of travel time and cost) that those people have to one another and their institutions. Here, then, is a variable we did not explicitly consider in earlier chapters and one applicable to the issue at hand: *distance*. The farther apart people reside, the more costly it is for them to come together, and the less likely it is that they will do so.

Because of their peripheral location, suburbs are less densely populated than cities, and this in turn hampers the ability of suburbanites to get together. And distance from the center of the metropolitan population reduces the access of suburbanites to people and places in the center or other side of the area. City dwellers, conversely, are in the midst of the center's density and roughly equidistant to the various suburbs. Other things being equal, suburban residents would consequently have less opportunity to form or participate in viable subcultures than would city dwellers.

However, at least two factors mitigate this effect. One is the automobile. Cars and freeways permit suburbanites to travel great distances very rapidly, and thus to participate in groups throughout the metropolis. The second is self-selection. Those persons who most need population concentration—members of cultural minorities, for example—tend not to move to the suburbs; and those who do move are the ones who are best able to travel far and who are best able to accept "Middle American" culture. Thus, the distance of suburbia has only modest effects.

Nevertheless, it has effects: an emphasis on local, rather than metropolitan, activities and relationships; the isolation of people, such as many housewives, who underestimated suburban distances and are unable to overcome them easily (see Michelson, 1973a; Clark, 1966); and, for those persons out of the "mainstream" culture, the paucity of satisfactory social networks and supportive subcultures.

These consequences result from the relative difficulty suburbanites have in getting together with people other than their immediate neighbors. In this way at least, suburban neighborhoods have, in contrast to city localities, a "rural" flavor. According to subcultural theory, they should—and, indeed, they seem to—recapitulate features of nonurban areas: less subcultural vitality, variety, and intensity; less deviance; more localism, but no fundamental psychological differences. Scott Greer (1972: 63) has observed that "the culture of the suburb is remarkably similar to that of the country towns in an earlier America." And that is just what many suburban settlers wanted!

Summary

Suburbs are metropolitan neighborhoods lying some distance from the center of population concentration. Residents sort themselves out within the metropolis on the basis of their personal characteristics—largely their needs for space, their travel times from work, and their abilities to pay. Distance is fundamental to these calculations and the consequent sorting out, so that the suburbs become home to a somewhat distinctive population. In the United States and increasingly elsewhere, suburban residents, compared with city dwellers, are well-to-do, are raising children, and are members of the dominant ethnic stock. They have come to the suburbs mainly for a house, outdoor space, and physical amenities, available at prices they can afford.

An understanding of suburban life and social psychology must begin with these two related observations: The kinds of people found in suburbia differ in their backgrounds from those found in cities, and suburbanites have moved to the suburbs for particular reasons. Suburbanites may act differently from others, but the difference is probably a result of traits they brought with them (for example, being hardy consumers because they are affluent), or of personal tastes they have been able to satisfy by moving to the suburbs (puttering around the house instead of attending ballet), and not an effect of suburbanism as such.

Yet there is a pattern of differences between people in the suburbs and people in the cities that might reasonably be attributed to suburbanism (peripheral location) itself. Extrapolating from the evidence to some extent, the pattern is that social life is localized, occurring in and focused on the locality; and minority or unconventional subcultures are relatively rare, a fact that is largely a result, but also partly a cause of the relative scarcity of unconventional people. The psychology of suburbia reflects these social relationships.

There is no substantial *net* effect of suburban residence on mental states. However, this net balance is composed of two divergent trends. Most people who have moved to the suburbs enjoy their homes, pleasant environment, and congenial (that is, homogeneous) neighborhoods—all of which are reasons for being committed to the locality. However, other people (such as adolescents, elderly people, housewives, ethnic minorities) often find suburban life too localized, and themselves too isolated from compatible associates and activities. These people, who are often in the suburbs because of lack of choice or foresight, are vulnerable to boredom, loneliness, and discontent.

The latter group is outnumbered in the great suburban migration by those who find the move an improvement in their lives. And, in general, the unintended consequences of suburbanism arc few and modest—just as the effects of urbanism are mainly few and modest. These two factors share another commonality. We have argued in this book that urbanism fosters the growth of distinctive subcultures. Suburbanism, we have argued in this chapter, seems to produce at least a small decline in cultural differentiation; in some sense, it is, as David Riesman (1959) has implied, a form of "deurbanization."

10

THE URBAN FUTURE

CONCLUSIONS, PROJECTIONS, AND POLICIES

> The central problem of the sociologist of the city is to discover the forms of social action and organization that typically emerge in relatively permanent, compact settlements of large numbers of heterogeneous individuals. Only by means of [a workable theory of urbanism] will the sociologist escape the futile practice of voicing in the name of sociological science a variety of unsupportable judgments concerning such problems as poverty, housing, city-planning, sanitation, policing, marketing, transportation and other technical issues. While the sociologist cannot solve any of these practical problems—at least not by himself—he may, if he discovers his proper function, have an important contribution to make to their comprehension and solution. The prospects for doing this are brightest through a general, theoretical, rather than through an *ad hoc* approach.
> —Louis Wirth, 1938

The noted sociologist George Caspar Homans once began the end of a book by asserting a worthy principle: "According to my lights, a last chapter should resemble a primitive orgy after a harvest," in which the toiler "is no longer bound by logic and evidence but free to speculate about what he has done" (Homans, 1974: 356). Lacking that full measure of Homansian bravura, I will not in this chapter engage in any orgy of speculation, but only carouse a bit. I will attempt to draw some general conclusions about the urban experience; then I will consider what the urban experience promises to be like in the coming decades; and, finally, I will employ what we know about city life to enter into current debates over urban policies and policies affecting urban people (a distinction that will become clear later).

Conclusions

Considering the research reviewed in the last seven chapters, what can we conclude about the competing theories of urban sociology and social psychology, and about themes found in Western culture about urban ways of life?

We begin with determinist theory, which holds that urbanism—the population size of a community—produces structural differentiation and psychic "overload," each of which in turn weakens intimate social groups and isolates individuals, leaving them psychologically vulnerable and morally uncertain. Eventually, urbanism produces social disorganization.

Some of the research supports this theory: Urban social structure is differentiated and specialized; certain social groups, those defined by a territory, show signs of being eroded in cities; and other groups, such as the family, are altered in various ways. Most importantly, urbanism is associated with high rates of deviant behavior, as dramatized by the rate of violent crime in modern American cities. The precarious state of the urban "moral order" is also evident in bitter dissension within the community over rules and mores.

But most of the critical sociological research does *not* support the theory of urban anomie. Instead, it suggests that intimate social groups persist in the urban environment; that urbanites are connected firmly to others, to networks of social support, and to moral systems; and that urbanites do not suffer disproportionately from psychological stress and malfunction. Our inability to confirm determinist propositions in these specific ways is especially significant because it calls into question the essential processes by which urbanism was held to produce deviance and conflict—the weakening of intimate, supportive social relationships, and consequent "personality disorganization."

As for the compositional position, it is the antithesis to the determinist thesis. It maintains that there are no significant social-psychological consequences of urbanism. There are, to be sure, differences among communities in ways of life, but these variations result from the personal characteristics of residents—their age, job, income, ethnicity—or from the specific economic and historical features of the communities. They do *not* result from urbanism, or population concentration, itself. The small social milieus—the home, work place, friendships—that determine individual social behavior are not seriously affected by such gross ecological factors as population size.

The same research findings that cast doubt upon the theory of urban anomie serve as the major evidence in support of the compositional view. Intimate social circles survive, and often thrive, in large cities; individuals are integrated into meaningful social networks; social, behavioral, and psychological phenomena tend not to be related to community size, and when they are, the associations are usually a consequence of personal variables, such as age and income, not ecological variables, such as population size. Yet the compositional description of urban life is not entirely correct; many features emphasized by Wirth and his associates are indeed especially common in urban locations: structural differentiation, deviance, and "social disorder." In addition, there are other aspects of the urban experience that seem to distinguish it from the nonurban one: the decline of local social groups, the differentiation of social relationships, the availability of specialized services, and intergroup conflict. In sum, the compositional thesis seems to account for more of these phenomena than the determinist thesis does, but it is not wholly adequate.

The subcultural theory of urbanism in some ways synthesizes the two theories, and results in a model more fully consistent with the facts. The concentration of population does have social-psychological consequences, but not of the sort Wirth described. It divides a community into distinctive and intensive subcultures, causing new ones to emerge and old ones to be strengthened. The subcultures in turn generate the urban phenomena that concerned Wirth and his colleagues the most, the same ones that compositionalists have the greatest difficulty explaining: deviance, social turmoil, intergroup conflict, and the splintering of the moral order in the community. These result not from alienation, anomie, and normlessness, but from the growth of many diverse and divergent subcultures, each with its own, occasionally deviant moral order. At the same time, subcultural theory, along with compositional theory, predicts that intimate social relationships and psychic balance will persist in the urban setting. In short, subcultural theory subsumes the empirically correct predictions of the determinist and compositional theories while avoiding their errors.

It does more. It accounts for other distinctive features of the urban experience. Locality-based groups—the community and neighborhood—are relatively unimportant, because population concentration permits allegiances to subcultures based on significant social traits rather than on proximity alone. Social relationships can be specialized in content, without having damaging psychological consequences, because each is located within a supportive subculture. Intergroup suspicion and conflict can arise in cities even in the absence of hostile and exploitative personalities, because tensions result from the mingling of different moral systems in the city. And the subcultural model contributes to an understanding of what is unique about the *sub*urban experience.

To conclude that subcultural theory most fully explains urban social psychology is not to conclude that it has been demonstrated as true. Hardly. Many research issues remain gapingly open and still others are raised by the theory itself. Many of the empirical generalizations presented in this book are based upon limited research. Among the topics in need of deeper investigation are the relationship of urbanism to personality types and problems; the specific features of primary relationships that are altered by urbanism; the sorts of unconventional behaviors that typify large communities and the kinds of people who engage in them; and the relative importance of personal versus impersonal sources of support for individuals as this varies across communities. Few of the key propositions considered in this book have been fully investigated.

The subcultural approach stimulates questions like these: Along what lines do subcultures vary? What size critical mass is necessary for which features of subcultures? What kinds of individuals are tied to more than one subculture and how do they manage their separate social worlds? How much do communication and transportation technologies mitigate the need for population concentration? And, quite important, what means emerge in metropolitan communities to maintain a minimum, common moral order among their divergent subcultures (for example, which etiquettes reduce conflict among individuals, and which negotiation procedures are used to resolve disagreements over policy)? These queries only illustrate the common observation that, in the sciences, every answer raises yet more questions.[1]

Sociology is only one mode of apprehending the world. Another is collective folk experience, often expressed in cultural stereotypes. In Chapter 2, we considered four themes in Western culture dealing with urban life. On the evidence reviewed here, it would seem that those beliefs tend to be valid on the level of description of folk experience. But they tend to be misleading on the analytical level designed to explain those experiences.

The first theme involves the polarity of nature versus art: the countryside is "natural"; the city is ordered, civilized, rational, and artificial. With respect to the physical and cultural aspects of this theme, the description seems roughly accurate. Cities do disrupt many natural processes, as in the pollution they produce; and they also generate the social and economic support necessary for the artifacts of civilization. The social-psychological elements in the theme are more problematic. Urbanites may be more rational than ruralites, but, if so, the difference probably results from their greater educational experience rather than greater urban experience. Urbanites may appear guileful, but that impression probably results from contacts between subcultures, rather than from real differences in personality types or pervasive behavioral styles.

The second theme, familiarity versus strangeness, attributes to rural life the coziness and constancy of home, and attributes to urban life encounters with strangers, opportunities, and exciting adventures. As we have seen, the evidence supports this description in broad terms but amends it significantly. The important feature of urban encounters with strangers is that they involve meetings of different subcultures, with all that implies for uncomfortable or antagonistic interactions. Also, the strangeness of urban life—unknown persons, opportunities, thrills—does not supplant familiarity but *supplements* it. Some city people go beyond their small social circles to join in the wider, stranger urban scene; others, for instance, those Gans has called "urban villagers," rarely encounter those "foreign" worlds directly. Virtually all urbanites, however, have private milieus, so that their urban experience involves strangeness as well as familiarity.

Given the focus of this study, the most significant theme is that of community versus individualism. The rural person is seen as integrated into a cohesive and supportive "community"—an intimate social group (which may also be a local one). In the urban setting, by contrast, "community" is shattered. Although people may enjoy the freedom their isolation brings, they suffer estrangement and alienation in exchange. At first glance, certain features of urban life seem to confirm this belief: for example, the locality is less cohesive in urban than in rural areas while social ties are physically dispersed and functionally specialized. However, closer study reveals that this stereotype is in error; urbanites are involved in meaningful social worlds, in fact, in a great variety of them. This theme would be more accurate if phrased as the unity of rural community versus the multiplicity of urban communities. The individualism of urban life, such as it is, is not one of solitary freedom and despairing alienation, but rather one involving the personal choice of communities and the singular expressions of those social worlds.[2]

The fourth and final theme is tradition versus change. The city is seen as the site of creativity as well as of iniquity and as the source of turmoil as well as of new life-styles. This belief is, in great measure, accurate. To be sure, tradition frequently persists in the heart of urban areas, as in ethnic enclaves, and change does occur in rural areas, as in agrarian uprisings; thus it is an exaggerated stereotype. Nevertheless, deviance, nontraditionalism, and change are disproportionately spawned in urban environments. The sociological evidence, however, casts doubt on the popular explanation that it results from urban social and psychological disorganization. And our investigation tempers the theme by suggesting that beneficial innovation and detrimental deviance may be two sides of the same urban coin: they are produced by the same forces. Despite our best efforts, there may remain an irreducible amount of "bad" changes that accompany the "good" ones generated in cities, and vice versa.

Thus, it appears that the cultural themes about urban life are at least superficially true. The rural youth journeying to the great metropolis would, in general, experience a more artificial environment, "a world of strangers" and strangeness, a milieu of seemingly estranged and normless individuals, and frequent encounters with novel and perhaps threatening behavior. These urban experiences are predicted by folk sociology, which thus serves its purpose well. That is, cultural beliefs are constantly being tested against common experience; in most cases, they should be, as general rules of thumb, correct. However, they are also frequently mistaken in particular and systematic ways that are indicated by a scientific sociology.[3]

These systematic errors perpetuate beliefs about urban life that the research to date indicates are not true, particu-larly the belief that cities produce social isolation, amorality, and psychological disorder. Two such biases involve percep-tual distortions. One is the habit of believing in the concrete and visible, and disbelieving in the existence of the abstract and unapparent. So, for example, urbanites appear to be friendless partly because their friends tend to be geographi-cally dispersed and not concentrated near them. Ethnocentri-cism is another source of perceptual bias. We tend to inter-pret the behavior of strangers in terms of our own cultural standards, so that we often decide that strangers who have done something we find immoral or offensive must be im-moral or offensive people, when they are actually being quite proper according to the standards of their own culture. For example, young people who attend ceremonial events in ca-sual and worn clothing may be judged to be deliberately rude by their formally dressed elders, although they see them-selves as honest and free, and their elders as artificial and inhibited.

Other systematic biases involve the folk explanation de-veloped for particular observations. These explanations tend to be simple and deterministic: If city people are a certain way, it is because cities make them be that way. Such explana-tions are often blind to the subtler processes at work—the fact that many urbanites live at a faster pace because they hold high-pressure jobs, for example, or that urbanites may tend to live alone because unmarried people choose to live in cities. (This is the problem of "spurious correlation.") An-other bias in popular explanations is the practice of attribut-ing the actions of other people to their personalities while attributing similar behavior by ourselves to external circum-stances. For example, we might interpret formality by a stranger in a public place as an indication of his or her basic unsociability, while we might label identical behavior on our own part simply as appropriate to a public setting.

In these ways, the cultural themes about the urban experience turn out to be a complex and fascinating mélange of roughly correct observations and systematically erroneous interpretations. In sociological research, the actual state of affairs is usually found to be much more complex than our preconceptions had led us to believe; this clearly holds for the urban experience.

In the United States, one of those "roughly correct observations" has had serious impact on individual behavior and political decisions. American cities are seen—and correctly so —as places of great criminal violence. This observation has greatly influenced the American perspective on cities and the national dialogue on urban policies.[4] The violence has been attributed to the nature of urban life itself. This explanation is in error; great metropolises in economically advanced nations around the world are quite safe places in which to live (although their nonviolent crime rates may be relatively high). American urban violence is an aberration of the society much more than of its cities. Yet it is hard for people to think about urbanism in this country without having such a thought chased out of their minds by just plain fear. The observation makes coherent explanation difficult.

Prospects of the Urban Future

Where do we go from here? The thumbnail history of cities presented in Chapter 1 pointed out that cities are relatively new and that large metropolises are unprecedented in the development of the human species. We are now speeding toward an urban future that has outlines we can scarcely discern and human consequences we have barely guessed at. Nevertheless, let us conjecture. Drawing on our knowledge of the contemporary urban experience, what might future urbanism be like, and what sorts of urban experience might result?

Sober statistical projections have yielded startling predictions. These projections essentially extrapolate the history of the last few decades into the next few. Using such procedures, Kingsley Davis (1972) has estimated that by the year 2000 about 25 percent of the people in the world will live in cities of over one million (in 1970, 12 percent lived in such cities), and that there will be three metropolises of over 64,000,000 people each and one of over 100,000,000 (today, the New York metropolitan area contains 17,000,000). Projections made for the United States by Jerome Pickard (1972) indicate that the metropolitan population will grow from 71 percent to 85 percent of the nation by the year 2000. The Los Angeles region (which is larger than the metropolitan area) will expand from 10,000,000 to about 22,000,000, and the New York region from 18,000,000 to about 25,000,000. Many zeroes.

Valuable as they are, these projections are inevitably limited in at least two ways. They cannot incorporate into the calculations the political, technological, or cultural events that push the future out of the trajectory set for it by the past. Migration patterns in the United States are already bringing into question predictions of further metropolitan growth. As we have seen, the early 1970s witnessed more growth in nonmetropolitan counties, even remote ones, than in the metropolitan areas; the New York area even declined in population.[5] Even if the trend toward metropolitanization resumes in the late 1970s, this fluctuation testifies to the precarious fortunes of fortune-telling.

The projections are also limited in their ability to anticipate not only the size but also the shape and structure of the cities of the future. Other prognosticators have less rigorously and more speculatively estimated the form of future urban areas. A set of predictions about the future of Western cities (drawn especially from Wurster, 1963; Chinoy, 1973) is presented schematically in Figure 10, together with representations of the urban past and present. In these drawings the height of the curve indicates population concentration, and the total area under the curve stands for total population. The preindustrial, walled city was small and the populace within it highly concentrated. The modern metropolis is larger in area and population but is not as concentrated. The remaining figures illustrate possible future shapes of the metropolis, ranging from the most to the least concentrated.

It is the supercity that most captivates novelists, film

FIGURE 10

SCHEMATIC ILLUSTRATIONS OF URBAN PASTS
AND POSSIBLE FUTURES

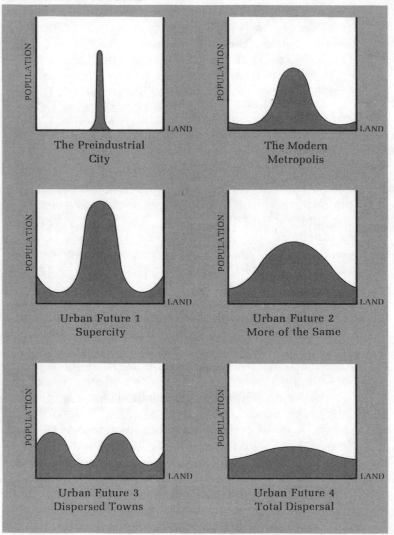

producers, and authors of "pop" sociology. In this scenario,
all the world is Manhattan, or worse; families share tiny
apartments within colossal buildings; and the negative features of congestion are multiplied manyfold. There are cir-

cumstances that might conceivably produce such a situation, but they are unlikely.[6] Trends in this century have been in the opposite direction—toward deconcentration—and popular preferences point the same way.[7]

At the other end of the spectrum is a future perhaps no more probable but far more interesting. Number 4 of Figure 10, Total Dispersal, has been called the "Post-City Age" by Melvin Webber (1968b; 1963). Advances in communications and transportation technology will eliminate the basic purpose of cities, which is the facilitation of social interaction and exchange. Physical proximity will be unnecessary to achieve these ends because proximity through videophones and 500-mile-per-hour personal vehicles will suffice. Webber (1973: 301) forecasts:

> For the first time in history, it might be possible to locate on a mountain top and to maintain intimate, real-time, and realistic contact with business or other associates. All persons tapped into the global communication net would have ties approximating those used today in a given metropolitan region.
>
> I am guessing that early in the next century, settlement patterns will be spread broadly over the continental surface, localized at those places where the climate and landscape are pleasant.[8]

This urban future, an electronic web of households and small settlements laid lightly over the land, would be a radical departure from the urban past, for, in essence, it would be a *non*urban future, indeed a "post-city age." Without any major differentiations in population density across the inhabited landscape, there would be no cities, no urban experience. Man's 6,000-year experiment of city living would be over; the urban experience would be simply a metaphor for certain ways of life thought to have been prevalent in those extinct communities called cities. (This would not be the first time in human history that cities had declined; earlier instances, such as that following the fall of the Roman Empire, have come after a collapse, however, rather than as a result of an advance in technology and communication.)

The city will probably not come to an end in the foreseeable future. It is doubtful that the necessary technology will develop—or, if it does, that it will be available to any but the very affluent few. There is a more fundamental doubt: Can electronic communication supplemented by occasional visits adequately substitute for casual, in-person interaction? Experiments are being conducted to determine whether television, conference calls, videophones, and computer link-ups can substitute for business transactions, audience participation, and social interaction. We know from our own experience with the telephone that such techniques do shrink distances. However, to the extent that there remain circumstances in which conversations in person are more efficient or more satisfying than electronic ones, and to the extent that nearer remains easier than farther, population concentration will continue. If, someday, these conditions are removed, humankind may indeed see a nonurban world.

Two more probable futures are cautious extrapolations of current trends. In More of the Same (number 2 of Figure 10), modern metropolises continue to expand in population and especially in area. At the fringes, the sprawling suburbs of different cities meld into one another; inner suburban areas are built up with apartment houses; and the relative population sizes of the center cities continue to decline. A Dispersed Towns future (number 3) is an intriguing variation on the dispersal pattern. In this case, the spreading metropolis breaks up into modest-sized towns or small cities, perhaps separated from one another by open space and parkland, and connected to one another by high-speed rail and highway. The old center city might continue as the nucleus of the region but would no longer dominate the area, for the towns would be largely self-sufficient. People would live at densities between those of contemporary suburbs and those of contemporary cities. Most important, they would live in communities of relatively modest size. (Two specific alternatives for this future are that the towns are either economically and demographically similar and are autonomous, or that they are specialized and functionally integrated—see Wurster, 1963.) We may be seeing early signs of "dispersed towns" in suburban shopping and commercial malls and industrial parks.

We should emphasize that these speculations are restricted to the economically advanced nations of the world. Any forecast at all for the developing and impoverished nations of the world other than, perhaps, catastrophe would be even more daring. Current urbanization in the developing nations is in some respects like that which took place in the West around 1880–1920. But in other ways it is critically different. For one, urbanization in the Third World is outrunning the development of an economic base for it; instead of rural workers being attracted to the city by vacant jobs, they are coming to cities with high rates of unemployment. Secondly, urban growth in developing nations is happening at a much more rapid pace than it did in the West. Third, and quite important, most of the urban growth in these nations is a result not of migration but of the general population explosion. That is, cities and rural populations are both growing rapidly through natural increase; both are threatened by economic collapse and famine (Davis, 1966, 1972; Hawley, 1971: Ch. 12; Breese, 1969). The hope is that these nations will recapitulate Western history in two respects: a drop in the birth rate and an increase in agricultural productivity. Should these occur and the present crisis be survived, then a "normal" modernization and urbanization, in which the population shifts from rural to urban areas, could occur (see Davis, 1972). In that case, the urban future of the developing nations may look like a delayed version of that facing the developed nations today.

Let us return to speculate on the social consequences of the most likely future for modern cities, a future of continued modest dispersal. In order to consider the consequences of changes in urbanism alone, we will adopt the unrealistic but useful assumption that no other social changes have been set into motion.

The greatest effects of further dispersal will be physical, in the ecological structure, as well as size, of metropolitan areas. Housing patterns will probably tend toward clustered, low-rise housing. Noise and dirt pollution will probably decrease at the points of higher concentration; whether pollution of all kinds declines or increases depends on whether dispersal leads to autonomous towns or to a more suburban-like pattern that requires a great deal of automotive transportation. These changes, in general, should satisfy popular tastes. One cost, however, will be a modest reduction in the number and, especially, the variety of available services (un-

less those futuristic communications and transportation techniques do arrive).

Based on what we have learned about the consequences
of population concentration, the social changes accompanying further dispersal will be much more modest, perhaps
barely noticeable. Differences among communities in the
ages, incomes, and other traits of their residents will diminish; similarly, economic activity and leisure pursuits will probably become more alike in various places; also, the crime
level will probably drop by a noticeable (though not great)
degree. The cohesion and importance of locally based social
groups—the community and the neighborhood—will likely
increase at the expense of those founded on other bases of
similarity, particularly occupation and life-style. (This last prediction is contingent on communications technology not making the advances predicted for it; if it does, the trend will
perhaps be reversed.)

In the personal realm, the changes are likely to be even
slighter. People will probably be neither more nor less integrated into primary social groups. There may be some minor
changes in personal relationships toward less specialization;
for example, family activities may expand and friends may be
called upon for more varied activities and assistance. At
most, there should be only marginal changes in personality,
states of mind, or behavioral styles. For the mainstream citizen, these would include greater satisfaction with the new
communities, a greater sense of belonging to the community,
and less unease about strangers—the latter a consequence of
a decline in the number of unconventional subcultures and an
increase in their spatial segregation. These small improvements in the peace of mind of "average" people may be
accompanied by a deterioration of this feeling for many "unconventional" persons, whose subcultures will have been
diminished.

Further dispersal is likely to reduce the variety and intensity of urban subcultures, but not of all subcultures equally.
Those with access to media, communications, and transport
(such as academics, other professionals, and the affluent) will
be hampered only slightly; those at the other end (such as
working-class ethnics, students, and other youths) will be

much more severely deprived of supportive social worlds. The consequences of this decline in subcultural variety for the society as a whole would be a modest diminution in innovation and change—both "good" and "bad" change.

These predictions are based on a number of "ifs"—if the urban future is one of further dispersal, if the analyses in this book are accurate, and if nothing else changes. Of course, other things will change. Although we cannot foretell what other developments will occur in modern societies, we can be almost certain that their effects on social life and personality will outweigh the consequences of changes in ecological patterns. For example, greater affluence, leisure time, and access to sophisticated technology by the general public will probably stimulate subcultural diversity and intensity, in spite of physical dispersal. Our speculations have served largely as a device for isolating the social-psychological consequences that urban developments, by themselves, would bring. We turn next to policies designed to shape that urban future.

Policies

In this section, we consider two related but distinct issues: urban policies and policies affecting urban people. The first refers to programs that would seek to alter urban factors—the size of cities, the distribution of the population within the metropolis, and so on. The second refers to social policies that would directly affect urbanites and dwellers in other areas as well—programs designed to reduce crime rates or increase housing, for example. A confusion between the two often results because of muddled use of the term "urban problems." The misconception exists that various social ills are found exclusively or primarily in cities, or that they are generated by city life. For some of these problems, as we have seen, even the simpler of these assumptions is mistaken: for example, poverty is more widespread and acute in rural than in urban areas. The problems that are disproportionately found in cities are rarely caused by urbanism, and when urbanism is a contributing factor—as in crime or group conflict—it is not a major cause. In any case, virtually all so-called urban problems are also found in nonurban areas. This confusion between urban policies and policies affecting urban people intrudes itself into the formulation of specific programs, as we shall see immediately.

One of the topics recurring among planners has been the quest for the "optimal city size": the size at which the optimal mix of urban benefits and urban costs is to be found—the highest possible level of productivity, culture, and services at the lowest commensurate level of congestion, pollution, and crime (see, for example, Dahl, 1967; Spengler, 1967). Once researchers have identified this best of all possible urban worlds, policy-makers could design strategies to encourage the growth of cities that are now too small and the diminution of those that are now too large.

Most urban scholars seem convinced, to quote a British economist, that ". . . the search for an optimal city size is almost as idle as the quest for the philosophers' stone" (Richardson, 1973: 131). The entire area of speculation is misconceived on several grounds. First, there are no substantial empirical findings pointing to a city size at which any "good"—income or innovation or governmental efficiency—is maximized, or any "bad"—crime or pollution—is minimized. In fact, some data suggest that for economic purposes an optimal city size would be larger than any we now have. We have certainly not identified an optimal size for any social-psychological variable in this book. Even if such ideals could be found, they would probably not be the same for a wide variety of social products. The size that maximizes personal incomes would differ from that which maximizes artistic creativity, or that which minimizes pollution, and so on. And it would surely be a vain task to try to sum up all these various "goods" and "bads" into a single measure.[9]

A related difficulty is the ultimately political problem of deciding what it is about a social product we wish to optimize: its best, worst, or average. Do we want a nation in which each community's citizens have access to an average art museum, or a nation in which a few (large) communities have great art museums? Do we want a nation in which everyone runs an average risk of being assaulted or one in which many run low risks and a few run great risks? (And, to repeat our previous point, how much culture is worth how

many muggings?) Another critique is similar, but more fundamental: What is optimal for one group is unlikely to be optimal for another, and what is optimal for the "average" group
is likely to be optimal for no actual groups at all. The optimal
number of library books, ethnic taverns, discothèques, or
level of traffic may suit the "average" person, but will it suit
the scholar, the blue-collar worker, the adolescent, or the
elderly person with a heart condition?

Finally, urbanists have been quick to point out that the
economic structure of a nation depends on having a hierar-
chy of cities of various sizes. Small cities serve particular
purposes—for example, functioning as service centers for
agricultural regions—and large metropolises serve others—
for example, national financial operations. It is quite improb-
able that a nation could standardize the size of its cities
without suffering acute economic disruption. For all these
reasons, the notion of an optimal city size is a myth.

While many readily concede that a single optimal city
size is a pipe dream, they are convinced of one point at least:
that contemporary metropolises are too large and that national policy should be developed to divert population from
the most populated areas to the least populated ones. This
has long been the policy in several European countries; it is
favored by many American leaders, and it is endorsed by a
majority of American citizens.[10] The underlying belief is that
great size produces social ills; reducing urban size would
alleviate those ills.[11]

Several European nations, including Britain, France, and
Sweden, have pursued major "regional growth" policies.
Through a variety of techniques ranging from tax credits to
legal injunctions, they have tried to direct industrial development—and, thus, the jobs that attract people—away from
heavily populated areas, such as the London, Paris, and Stock-
holm regions, to areas that have been losing people. Though
it is difficult to judge, these policies seem to have had some
effect in stopping or reversing the movement of people from
outlying areas to the large metropolises. It is even more
difficult to judge whether a net social benefit in lowered
urban congestion or rural employment has actually been
achieved. These policies are, nevertheless, very popular and
politically secure (Sundquist, 1975).

In addition, the British have pursued a policy of constructing "New Towns" to help stem the growth of the large "conurbations," especially London. (On the continent, the so-called New Towns are largely suburban housing developments on the outskirts of major cities.) To reach this end, the communities were planned to be self-contained small cities independent of the metropolis, to be located at a distance from the centers which the planners hoped (in vain) would be too far for commuting. Governmental pressure was exerted on industries to locate in the New Towns. And residents were brought to the New Towns by giving preference to those applicants for public housing who were willing to move there and who could fill a job in an industry located there.

Despite these strenuous and costly efforts, the New Town policy seems to have had mixed success. Many Britons have received needed quality housing; much has been learnt about urban design and planning; and the social-psychological experience of the New Towns appears to be—after a difficult transition period labeled the "New-Town Blues"—a relatively pleasant one, not unlike life in an American working-class suburb. However, the goal of self-containment has not really been met. The New Towns are only slightly more economically independent than are comparable unplanned communities, and the most successful ones seem to be those conveniently linked to London. Furthermore, New Towns have apparently not had any sizable impact on the pace of metropolitan expansion or the size of the large cities or the social problems that presumably result from "over-urbanization."[12]

Should the United States direct its population toward small communities? There are a few good reasons for supporting a policy of deurbanization: It would assist those rural places that have long lost so many of their young and productive residents, places that can no longer support vital services for the ones who remain. Deurbanization might ease congestion in the center cities, both physical congestion and strain on social services; and it would satisfy the popular preference for redistribution, a preference that has been expressed in party platforms and government declarations (see Sundquist, 1975; Elgin et al., 1974; Mazie and Rawlings, 1972). An inadequate but oft-cited reason for population dispersal is that it would improve social relations and ease psychic tensions among the American people. In view of the evidence we have reviewed here, that is quite unlikely. Redistribution might decrease crime rates and group conflict, but it would take a massive amount of migration to produce even a modest improvement in this regard (see Alonso, 1970, 1975; Whyte, 1968: Ch. 13).

There are also a few good reasons to oppose such a policy. For one, population dispersal is already happening. Within metropolitan areas, people have been dispersing outward from the center city for decades; among metropolitan areas, the largest ones have been losing ground to the others since at least 1940; and now, since about 1970, population has been shifting slightly toward nonmetropolitan areas (see Hawley, 1971; Elgin et al., 1974: 121; Sundquist, 1975: 241-253). Second, there are serious doubts about the practicality of such a policy. The cost—in tax credits, subsidies, construction, economic dislocations and inefficiencies—would be great and the effects are likely to be small. One analysis estimates that, if initiated immediately, the most strenuous (and extremely expensive) effort might reduce the populations of the New York and Los Angeles metropolitan areas in the year 2000 by only about nine percent from what they otherwise will be (Murray and Hege, 1972, especially p. 195). Third, given such expenditures, there are more efficient ways to ameliorate the various social problems. In fact, population redistribution is probably the most indirect and inefficient method possible to cure social ills. Its indirectness is reminiscent of a Rube Goldberg contraption; its inefficiency suggests the metaphor of cracking walnuts with a sledge hammer. In both cases, there is little result for much effort. Instead, direct and cheaper efforts could be made to treat the problems. For pollution, taxes or fines could be imposed; for housing, rehabilitation of dwellings is reasonable; for poverty, direct assistance in terms of jobs or money; and for congestion, the streamlining both of traffic areas and service institutions.[13]

This criticism of policies of optimal size and redistribution should not leave the impression that there can be no useful urban programs. On the contrary, there is much to be done in promoting the efficient use of urban land, in planning the growth of metropolitan areas, in providing attractive and convenient low-income housing, in facilitating the access of rural people to needed services, and generally in managing the social consequences resulting from the interaction of population and space.

One issue in particular, originally raised in Chapter 9, should be noted: the political organization of metropolitan areas. The American system of small, independent, and powerful municipalities has certainly contributed to the social problems of the inner city. In late 1975, New York City was about to go broke. Although its politicians may have done much to bring on the crisis, its fundamental problem is one almost all the major center cities face: the people and institutions that cost money are largely within the city lines; the people and institutions who can pay taxes are largely outside the city lines.[14]

Suburban municipalities can attract affluent residents through zoning and land-development regulation, while excluding low-income people. Through independent taxing and spending powers, they can provide their citizens with quality middle-class services, such as schools and recreation facilities, at relatively low tax rates. Their wealthy tax base and open land also allow suburban townships to attract modern industries providing well-paying jobs. Meanwhile, the escalating costs of maintaining a center increasingly in need of major capital improvements (for example, repaving streets), of housing low-income families who are constantly in need of special services, and of sustaining cultural institutions, such as museums (which are also used by suburbanites), are shunted to the downtown municipality. And that municipality is rapidly losing the resources necessary to fulfill those functions. This is indeed an *urban* problem: a fenced-in and decaying core, surrounded by exclusive, "beggar-thy-neighbor" suburbs. (It is ironic that many suburbanites use some of the arguments examined in this book—the contention that density has ill effects, for example—to exclude newcomers from low-density areas, thereby effectively locking their fellow citizens into the high-density core. "Preserving open space" usually means "preserving open space for the few who can afford it.")

Urban policies directed at altering this political structure would probably have a notable impact on a variety of problems. Of course, there are good arguments against metropolitan government, as well. Pursuing the democratic goal of individual participation in the community and "community control" would lead us to an opposite policy: decentralization and the dispersal of meaningful rights and responsibilities to local territorial groups. The problems mentioned previously would probably then be exacerbated. Each policy has its own benefits and its own costs.

In the final analysis, no urban policy—that is, no policy that seeks to manipulate a population's physical environment and spatial distribution—will have as sizable an impact on our critical social problems as would policies directed specifically at those problems. Arguments that stress "urban" solutions to such problems as pollution, poverty, and crime are usually misinformed, visionary, and, ultimately, temporizing.

Straightforward solutions to most of those problems exist, and we do not need to be sociologists to recognize the answers. Whether the need is to reduce pollution, poverty, crime, political disaffection, or whatever, relief is most likely to come from redistributing income, power, and social responsibility. Yet these solutions have their own costs. The difficulty in social problems is less often a technological one of finding solutions than a political one of deciding among alternative costs and who shall pay them. (This usually seems to be the case when sociologists are called upon for answers; what people really want is a magic solution which will cost no one.) The "urban crisis" is thus less a crisis in need of answers than a crisis in need of choices. While we await these choices, we must often listen to a lot of distracting and temporizing speculations about urbanism and the "decline of community."

Having said my piece about social policy and the urban experience, I will end with a few comments about the policies of individuals in their personal lives. The truths sociology uncovers are truths about people in general, and, as such, they are not all true for any specific person. So it is with the findings and conclusions of this book. Even when we considered specific categories of people—such as the young, or housewives, or blacks—none of the generalizations we made are valid for each member of these social categories. The individual is just that: individual in history, interests, and preferences. So, ultimately, each person must make choices founded on unique needs and desires. Some will seek and enjoy less of the urban experience; others will prefer and thrive on more of the urban experience. It is my hope that this book will help make these choices better informed, and that we will share a society in which each individual has the freedom to make such a choice.

NOTES

CHAPTER 1

1. General histories of urbanization include: Hawley (1971), Sjoberg (1960), Mumford (1961), and Childe (1951).

2. Popular examples include Ardrey (1966), and Morris (1969). Even as serious a scholar as Kingsley Davis (1973) has worried that man's genetic heritage may be unable to adjust to cities.

3. This interpretation of "urban" is neither self-evident nor universally accepted, and a portion of the next chapter will be devoted to arguing the question. I note here only that there are other ways of defining the term, with different implications for the proper study of the issue. For instance, some scholars (such as Castells, 1968) are convinced that urbanism is so fundamentally intertwined with modernization or industrialization that the only truly "rural" communities are those totally isolated from modern influences. Since according to this view "urban" refers to general economic and cultural attributes, a modern nation such as the United States is, for all essential purposes, urban throughout. (That is, virtually all Americans watch television, buy mass-produced goods, and so on.) The resulting implication is that comparing urban and rural places and people is a vacuous exercise, for there is no rural left (e.g., Firey et al., 1957). According to another and related view (e.g., Reissman, 1964, and Greer, 1962), urbanism is not a property that communities have in greater or lesser degrees, for all communities are inevitably and fundamentally linked to each other. Instead, urbanism is a property of *societies;* they vary in their degree of urbanization (the scale of their institutions), and that has consequences for their communities. Had I adopted either of these positions, or other variations, the investigation in this book would have proceeded far differently. But it is my firm conviction that communities do form distinct entities, and, as set forth in Chapter 2, that the best definition of "urbanism" is in terms of population size. (Further discussion appears in Fischer, 1975a. See also Reiss, 1959a; Arensberg, 1965).

4. This question, whether differences between urban and rural people are due to urbanism—population concentration—itself, becomes a refrain throughout the book for several reasons: First, popular beliefs about urban life are basically concerned with this issue. Even casual comments on urban ways usually imply that the phenomena are inherent and inescapable concomitants of just living in the city. Second, social scientists' interest in urbanism derives mainly from the city's intrinsic quality of scale, a quality which means that studies of urbanism might yield lessons applicable to modern society as a whole. Third, many features common to cities of our time (such as bureaucracies and subordination to a national state) are not common to cities in other cultures and historical periods. Any effort to make generalizations about city life from these heterogeneous cases must examine the concomitants of the elementary constant in all these specific instances: population concentration. Fourth, for the purpose of constructing urban policy, it is necessary to determine which specific causes produce which specific effects. Is crime, for example, inevitably associated with population concentration, or does it appear disproportionately in modern American cities because of other special conditions in those cities?

5. The reference is to multivariate techniques, including cross-tabular and regression methods. No orthodoxy is imposed as to the best technique or the most appropriate controls. In general, I have settled for what the literature provides.

6. A few authorities in the field have argued that any effort to formulate generalizations about urban life that are valid cross-culturally and historically is misguided. In particular, they contend that the ways of life in preindustrial and industrial cities are qualitatively distinct (Sjoberg, 1960; Reissman, 1964). I will nevertheless move ahead with my analyses and, by the end of the book, I will have proposed a few universal generalizations.

7. A sample of general historical and cross-cultural discussions of urbanism is: Sjoberg (1960), Mumford (1961), Hawley (1971), Southall (1973a), Davis (1973), Callow (1973), and Handlin and Buchard (1963). Several authors have presented historical typologies of cities, among them Sjoberg (1960, 1965a), Arensberg (1968b), and Redfield and Singer (1954).

257

CHAPTER 2

1. A general source of ancient, classical, and renaissance views of urban-rural differences is Sorokin et al. (1930).

2. Regular reading of *The New York Times* yields a steady supply of introspective reflections on the city. One might also consider the New York movie. In an earlier cinematographic era, it portrayed dancing in the streets *(Singing in the Rain)*, frolicking in the grass *(Barefoot in the Park)*, and using the metropolis as one huge, joyful playground *(A Thousand Clowns)*. Recent films have employed a sad, violent and brutalizing New York as a vehicle for exhibiting the ills of modern life *(Midnight Cowboy, Little Murders, Death Wish,* etc.). The changing trend has been noted by the *Times*'s film critic, Vincent Canby (1974).

3. Similar discussions appear in White and White (1962), Schorske (1963), and Strauss (1961).

4. The *Gallup Opinion Index* is published monthly by the American Institute of Public Opinion, Princeton, N.J. Their reports of survey findings will be abbreviated as G.O.I. henceforth, and will be referred to by year and report number.

5. See also Fuguitt and Zuiches (1973), Mazie and Rawlings (1972) and Fischer (1973b).

6. Various studies highlight different characteristics of those less hostile to cities. The reports include: G.O.I. (1973, #94:31), Zuiches and Fuguitt (1972), Mazie and Rawlings (1972), Cantor (1975), Zelan (1968), and Bell (1958).

7. Recent reports from the U.S. Census indicate that, from 1970 to 1975, there has been some migration from Standard Metropolitan Statistical Areas to nonmetropolitan areas (Bureau of the Census, 1975; Reed, 1975a). Much of this movement, however, is not urban-to-rural; it only reflects the spillover of suburbs across arbitrary metropolitan boundaries. Another qualification is that the move may be temporary, a result of recessions in the early 1970s. (Rural-to-urban migration dropped sharply during the Depression decade of 1930–1940). But some of this reversal is no doubt real—if for no other reason than the simple fact that, as the United States becomes over 75 per cent metropolitan, fewer rural people are available to move to cities, and more are available to do the reverse. (A similar trend is reported for Britain: Royal Commission, 1969: 35.)

8. In this regard, a recent survey of New Yorkers revealed that well-to-do residents of the city were much more likely to be living there out of "free choice" than were the less economically fortunate. Forty-five percent of blue-collar workers said they had no alternative but to live in the city (Lynn, 1974: 18). See also Mazie and Rawlings (1972).

9. A prior issue is the epistemological utility of the concept of urban, however it is defined. The challenge is presented, for example, by Castells (1968, 1969). See the discussion in Fischer (1975a).

10. A technical concept that comes close to capturing this definition is "population potential" (Carrothers, 1956). The relativistic definition of "city" is actually not unusual. Webster's Collegiate Dictionary defines a city as "an inhabited place of greater size, population, or importance than a town or village." A town is defined as intermediate between city and village; a village intermediate between town and hamlet; and a hamlet as smaller than a village.

11. Demographic definitions also have disadvantages, one of which is determining the boundary of the city or urban area: Where does suburb become countryside? Another is the opening it provides for unusual cases. Is a downtown where no one resides not part of a city? Finally, such a reductionist definition seems to lose some of the flavor associated with the term "city." In contrast, the other types of definitions seem to capture some of the meanings of city life as they have been expressed in Western culture. The cost of making this connection, however, is the sacrifice of scientific utility. For one, these definitions leave anomalous cases in limbo; for example, one author excludes from urban consideration the large settlements of the Incas, because they did not have writing (Sjoberg, 1960). Others exclude the large communities of pre-colonial West Africa because their economies were predominantly agricultural. More important, such definitions close off from investigation the relationship among critical urban-linked factors. To define a city as a large settlement in which certain activities occur is to preclude an inquiry into whether or not population size is related to those activities by asserting

arbitrarily that it is. A preferable scientific procedure is to make a minimum number of restrictive assumptions and to permit a maximum number of empirical inquiries.

12. I am aware that this synopsis, based largely on Durkheim, does not do full justice to the classic sociological tradition. However, it does highlight the basic features of "Great Transformation" theories, particularly as they have influenced sociology.

13. The parallels are explicit. Simmel (1905: 47) wrote: "An inquiry into the inner meaning of specifically modern life ... must seek to solve the equation which structures *like the metropolis* set up between the individual and super-individual contexts of life" (italics added). Durkheim (1893: 299): ". . . Insofar as the moral density of society is increased, it becomes similar to a great city which contains an entire people within its walls."

14. Some have claimed that Park disagreed with Wirth's argument that urbanism leads to isolation and disorganization (e.g., Kasarda and Janowitz, 1974: 328). Park said many things, but few statements more succinctly state the thesis that Wirth championed than a passage in Park's 1916 paper: "It is probably the breaking down of local attachments and the weakening of the restraints and inhibitions of the primary group, under the influence of the urban environment, which are largely responsible for the increase of vice and crime in great cities" (Park, 1916: 112).

15. The following exposition summarizes a longer exegesis in Fischer (1972); another extended treatment is in R. Morris (1968).

16. Among the systematic adaptations that Milgram lists as ways by which urbanites protect themselves from overload are: attending less to any particular stimulus—for example, cutting short discussions with sales clerks when purchasing an item; ignoring low-priority demands (brushing aside mendicants); blocking off intrusive stimulations (avoiding eye contact when walking through a crowd); filtering the intensity of stimulations (using small talk to dilute any serious involvement with another individual; and establishing mechanisms to divert unwanted inputs (employing a telephone answering service). These various techniques are all means which separate a person from others around him. Individuals who adopt them become increasingly isolated and uninvolved, not only with respect to strangers, but ultimately from people they know, as well.

17. They are said to "arise" only in the sense that communities which fail to employ them disintegrate.

18. Merton (1938a: 222–25) has suggested an alternative branch in the argument that urban differentiation leads to anomie. According to his analysis, the visibility in the city of affluent life-styles raises aspirations among the general population—aspirations that will not be met in most cases. Individuals suffering from this condition form a pool of potentially withdrawn, deviant, or rebellious urbanites.

19. Consequently, I have called this position "nonecological" (Fischer, 1975a, b), a term modified from "non-materialist," used by Sjoberg (1965b). I should add that there are a great number of ecological theories and approaches in urban sociology that compositionalists do not dispute—for example, those dealing with neighborhood succession. The ecological debate here speaks only to the issue of the social-psychological consequences of urbanism.

20. The concept of "subculture" is sufficiently controversial (Clarke, 1974; Valentine, 1968: 103–14) to warrant further comment. Subcultures are composed of two parts: a "subsystem"—a set of interconnected social networks (in a sense, overlapping and superimposed social circles)—and the associated subculture proper—a set of norms and behaviors common to the subsystem. The term "subculture" will be used for both the network set and its culture; it is loosely synonymous with "social world." It must be understood that the defining traits of a subculture are not absolute criteria but variable dimensions—the degree of relational separateness (boundary) and internal coherence of those cultural elements. This does not invalidate the concept, but instead reveals that the specificity with which subcultures are defined is a matter of analytical purpose and empirical convenience. (The limiting case is when all interacting pairs of individuals are called subcultures.) Furthermore, an individual can be a member of more than one subculture (depending partly on the minuteness of the analytical distinctions), but the number of substantial subcultures to which an individual can belong is probably severely limited by time, energy, and conflicting demands.

21. Of course, what is unconventional in one period can become quite conventional in the next. What then occurs is that a new deviance develops in reaction to that norm.

CHAPTER 3

1. The topics of urban ecology and social geography that are touched upon in this section are introduced more fully in Hawley (1971), Johnston (1971), Herbert (1972), Yeates and Garner (1971), Schwirian (1974), and Bourne (1971).

2. Some specific cases are: Teotihuacan (Millon, 1967), Cairo (Abu-Lughod, 1971), Damascus (Lapidus, 1966), Moscow (Abbott, 1974), and Osaka (Yazaki, 1973). General descriptions appear in Sjoberg (1960), Hawley (1971), and Pirenne (1956).

3. This interpretation of the changes in urban ecology leans heavily on a technological determinism (Hawley, 1971), supported by a number of historical studies that seem to demonstrate the relationship (e.g., Warner, 1962; Conzen, 1975; Jackson, 1975). However, many other forces no doubt also contributed to the modern pattern of residential segregation, some occurring before these technological changes (e.g., in seventeenth-century London—Carr, 1975).

4. These comments are based on the literature in factorial ecology. For summaries, see Rees (1972) and Herbert (1972: Ch. 6). See also Schwirian (1974) and Yeates and Garner (1971: Ch. 11).

5. The same is true elsewhere, in Japan, for example (Carpenter, 1960).

6. For example, cities were particularly vulnerable to the Black Plague in the mid-1300s, sometimes losing half or two-thirds of their populations (Langer, 1964).

7. However, the difference between cities in developed and developing nations remains critical. Calcutta, for example, painfully resembles the stark description of a preindustrial environment at its worst.

8. These two arguments were raised, for instance, against the National Academy report that urbanites suffered lung cancer death rates twice those of rural persons (*San Francisco Examiner,* September 14, 1972).

9. Most descriptions of housing in industrializing cities are much like this one. See, for instance, Handlin (1969) and Banks (1968).

10. For example, a survey conducted in the Detroit area revealed that over 90 percent of persons with children preferred single-family homes. The only groups who did not by a majority prefer single dwellings were unmarried and childless individuals currently living in multiple-unit dwellings (Lansing and Hendricks, 1967). See also Michelson (1970, 1973a) and Wright (1970).

11. So, for example, one study indicated that high housing density reduced people's feelings of satisfaction with their neighborhoods. However this effect was mediated entirely by perception of density. That is, only as it affects the extent to which people *think* that their neighborhood is dense does the actual density of the neighborhood operate to reduce their satisfaction (Marans and Rodgers, 1975).

12. This conclusion violates many preconceptions we have about high-rise living. In some cases, researchers prefer to keep their preconceptions. At a conference on housing, the chairman of the panel on space and privacy reluctantly summed up:

> We came to some conclusions that we really didn't want to, but to get on with it, I will read what we wrote down last night.
>
> We said that according to present evidence, space and privacy have only dubious and perhaps undiscovered causal relationships to health or illness. Some concern was expressed that our measuring techniques may be too crude to find the relationship between space, privacy and health which many of us believe exists. But I think what we were saying to ourselves is that we know what we are finding is not true but we don't know how to prove that it isn't (A.P.H.A., 1970: 10).

13. Michelson (1973b), Wellman et al. (1973), Baldassare (1975), Lopata (1972: 269ff.), and Fischer et al. (1976).

14. Other sources on size and the availability of general services include Yeates and Garner (1971: Ch. 7), Swedner (1960: 107-121), Keyes (1958), and W. R. Thompson (1965). Sources dealing with specialized services include Ogburn and Duncan (1964), Abrahamson (1974), Marden (1966), and Reskin and Campbell (1974).

15. A more recent survey has confirmed the general findings on urban-rural differences—*The New York Times,* August 10, 1975: E-6.

16. Geographers have studied this phenomenon intensively, generally under the rubric of "central-place theory." For introductions, see Berry (1967) and Yeates and Garner (1971).

17. On complaints, see, for instance, Hawley and Zimmer (1971). Most people usually place access to services relatively low on their list of considerations when choosing a place to live (e.g., Butler et al., 1968), sometimes to their later chagrin (Michelson, 1973a). See also Fischer (1973b).

CHAPTER 4

1. In general, attributes of individuals, such as age or income, are "held constant" in the determinist and subcultural models. That is, the theories assume that urbanism has effects on individual behavior irrespective of these traits. However, individual attributes are in fact related both to urbanism and to many dependent variables, such as unconventional behavior, thus raising the possibility that the associations of urbanism to these dependent variables are spurious. Indeed, the proposition that those associations are spurious is cen●al to compositional theory (see Fischer, 1972).

2. General discussions of this difference can be found in Jones (1966), W. Petersen (1961); of England, in Mann (1964); of the United States, in Taeuber (1972), and Fuguitt and Field (1972).

3. Patterns of urban homogeneity have been described in various studies of preindustrial cities, for instance, of native Yoruba towns (Krapf-Askari, 1969). But even in these types of towns, the general case was of even greater homogeneity in the countryside (Sjoberg, 1960).

4. This point was suggested by Ann Swidler.

5. A study of a Guatemalan village, small town, and small city showed that while villagers could distinguish people only by race and wealth, the townsmen had seven categories of rank, and the city people ten (Roberts, 1973: 54). Similar findings have resulted from the study of American college students (Lasswell, 1959). Outside observers also note greater class differentiation in larger communities (Fuguitt and Field, 1972; Ogburn and Duncan, 1964). Data on the economic diversification associated with city size is available in many sources, including Crowley (1973).

6. The pattern of migration does not imply that urbanites change residences more frequently than do rural people. Modern data indicate that rural populations are, on the average, as restless as urban ones. Evidence on mobility is available, for twentieth-century America, in Bureau of the Census (1968), G.O.I. (1974, #110: 15), and for the nineteenth century, in Thernstrom (1973); for modern France, Bastide and Girard (1974a); and for pre-Western Japan, R. J. Smith (1973).

7. On the United States, see Tilly (1970a); France: Bastide and Girard (1974b); Africa: Hanna and Hanna (1971) and Little (1973); Latin America: Bradfield (1973) and Perlman (1975).

8. J. M. Nelson (1969) provides a cross-national review on the topic of urban migrants and social disorganization; Cornelius (1971) reviews Latin America; Hanna and Hanna (1971: Ch. 4), Africa; Tilly (1969; Tilly et al., 1975), Europe. On racial disorders in the United States, see Kerner Commission (1968).

9. A sample of studies—the United States: Tilly (1965), Snyder (1971), McDonald and McDonald (1974); Latin America: Lewis (1952), Roberts (1973), Perlman (1975); France: Girard et al. (1966); for Africa, see Hanna and Hanna (1971: Ch. 3).

10. A large-scale survey conducted in 1973 demonstrated that, compared with the nation's other large cities, New York City had relatively low rates of serious crimes.

11. It might be argued that biases in official crime-recording inflate the urban-rural contrast (e.g., Stinchcombe, 1963). However, distortions in the opposite direction are probably as great or greater still (e.g., lower police-to-number-of-crimes ratios; greater distrust of the police). In their study on the accuracy of crime statistics, Reynolds and Blythe (1974) present evidence that suggests as much. In any case, the proposition that crime rates are positively correlated with urbanism seems quite secure, supported by the extreme differences in official rates shown in Figure 5, independent surveys (e.g., Ennis, 1967), and confirmation in other nations (Wolfgang, 1970).

12. On Tokyo: "Crime in Tokyo a Minor Problem," *New York Times* (January 3, 1971: 6); Hong Kong: Michelson (1970:154-155); Rome: "Non-violent cities," *Newsweek* (January 5, 1970: 33).

13. For a general review of urbanism and crime, see Wolfgang (1970), and Mulvihille and Tumin (1969). On rural homicide, see Wolfgang and Ferracuti (1967: 276ff). Specific discussions include, on pre-modern England, Tobias (1966); on modern England, Mann (1964: Ch. 2) and H. L. Richardson (1973: 97); nineteenth-century France, Lodhi and Tilly 1973); modern France and Belgium, Szabo (1960); Scandinavia, Westergaard (1966); Africa, Hanna and Hanna (1971); Asia, Hauser (1957: 221–33); and developing nations in general, Clinard and Abbott (1973: 81–91).

14. In his study of a Washington slum, Hannerz (1969) observed that many of the local criminals were well known—and feared—by the neighborhood residents.

15. One could suggest, however, that urban aspirations are raised still higher than urban income, and thus argue that urbanism produces relative deprivation. On the other hand, there is little empirical evidence that urbanites are more relatively deprived than ruralites, or that the difference in such feelings could account for the great variation in crime rates (See Fischer, 1973b).

16. On the group nature of delinquency, see Erickson (1971), Einstadter (1969), and Cloward and Ohlin (1961), among others. See general discussion in Wilks (1967:140–42).

17. This analysis of urban violence is pursued at greater length in Scherer et al. (1975: Ch. 8). The major source on the topic of violent subcultures is Wolfgang and Ferracuti (1967). The kind of evidence that has been offered *for* the proposition that certain subcultures teach their members to use violence readily includes, first, statistics showing huge variations between particular groups (the poor, the black, etc.) and others in rates of criminal violence; and, second, ethnographic descriptions of violent groups (e.g., Horowitz and Schwartz, 1974; but also Rossi et al., 1974). The kind of evidence presented *against* the proposition is the absence of major differences between such groups and the rest of the population in their answers to survey questions about their attitudes concerning violence and their personal experiences with noncriminal violence (Erlanger, 1974; Ball-Rokeach, 1973). Although the documentation in support of the negative position is quite persuasive, I am not fully convinced that the probes used in these surveys capture the essence of the "subculture of violence" thesis: that certain groups have, and perpetuate through socialization, a higher tendency to resort to violence and, consequently, greater proportions of their members who commit serious violence.

CHAPTER 5

1. A discussion of the Chicago School's concept of "social world" appears in Short (1971). On "social networks," see Boissevain (1973), J. C. Mitchell (1969), and Fischer et al. (1977).

2. Boissevain (1973) actually provides a quantitative comparison between a resident of a village and one of a city.

3. Wirth, for example, wrote:

The bonds of kinship, of neighborliness, and the sentiments arising out of living together for generations under a common folk tradition are likely to be absent, or, at best, relatively weak in an aggregate the members of which have such diverse origins and backgrounds. Under such circumstances, competition and formal control mechanisms furnish the substitutes for the bonds of solidarity that are relied upon to hold a folk society together (Wirth, 1938: 152).

And Park:

The form of government which had its origins in the town meeting and was well suited to the needs of a small community based on primary relations is not suitable to the government of the changing and heterogeneous population of cities of three or four million. . . . Besides all the rest, [the voter] is too busy elsewhere to inform himself about the conditions and needs of the city as a whole. (Park, 1916: 120).

4. For example, one student of nineteenth-century America concludes:

The probability that only between 40 and 60 percent of the adult males to be found in an American community at one point in time could still be located there a decade later held not only for most cities throughout the nineteenth and twentieth centuries; it applied in farming communities untouched by urbanization as well. . . . Approximately half of their residents at any date were destined to disappear before ten years had elapsed. . . . This was not a frontier phenomenon, or a big-city phenomenon, but a national phenomenon (Thernstrom, 1973: 225, 227).

Another possible index of community concern might be contributions to local charities. One study indicates that large-city residents were slightly *more* likely to make an effort to contribute to the community chest than small-city residents (Alford, 1972).

5. For example, the boundaries of the political community are not always identical to those of the social community, as in the case of small suburbs. This boundary problem is a particularly American phenomenon.

6. See Dahl and Tufte (1973), Tilly (1973, 1974), Prewitt and Eulau (1969), Black (1974), Coleman (1957), Spilerman (1971), and Kesselman (1966).

7. This analysis is drawn in part from studies of differences in school sizes and the consequences for student participation in school activities (Barker and Gump, 1964; cf. J. Nelson, 1973). See also studies on "over-manning" (Wicker, 1968, 1969); on city councils, Prewitt and Eulau (1969).

8. See discussions in Dahl and Tufte (1973) and Tilly (1973). Studies include, on international data: Nie et al. (1969), Burstein (1972), Dahl and Tufte (1973), Tilly (1973); U.S. data: Verba and Nie (1972: Ch. 13), Alford and Lee (1968), Fischer (1975d), van Es and Brown (1974); England: Royal Commission (1969); France: Tarrow (1971) and Kesselman (1966); and Japan: B. M. Richardson (1973).

9. See studies cited in previous note.

10. The substitution of instrumental and single-purpose associations for primary and diffuse groups during the process of urbanization is the essential dynamic of *Gemeinschaft* (community)-*Gesellschaft* (association) theory. "All praise of rural life has pointed out that Gemeinschaft among people is stronger there and more alive; it is the lasting and genuine form of living together. In contrast to Gemeinschaft, Gesellschaft is transitory and superficial . . . a mechanical aggregate and artifact"—Tönnies 1887: 35). Wirth (1938: 162):

Reduced to the stage of virtual impotence as an individual, the urbanite is bound to exert himself by joining others of similar interests into groups organized to obtain his ends. This results in the enormous multiplication of voluntary organizations directed toward as great a variety of objectives as there are human interests and needs. . . .

It is largely through the activities of voluntary groups, be their objectives economic, political, educational, religious, recreational, or cultural, that the urbanite expresses and develops his personality, acquires status, and is able to carry out the round of activities that constitute his life career.

11. On associations among American immigrants, see Handlin (1969); on Africa: Hanna and Hanna (1971), Epstein (1967), and Little (1965); on Latin America, the collection edited by Mangin (1970).

12. Single cities studied include Detroit (Axelrod, 1956), San Francisco (Bell and Boat, 1957), New York City (Komarovsky, 1946), and New Haven (Dotson, 1951). Comparative studies include Curtis (1971), Babchuck and Booth (1969), van Es and Brown (1974), and Fischer (1973a). The latter study showed, for example, that among middle-income whites, 65 percent of those living in nonmetropolitan areas and 60 percent of those in metropolitan areas never attended club meetings.

13. For studies, see Bell and Boat (1957), Axelrod (1956), Kasarda and Jonowitz (1974), Litwak and Szelenyi (1969), and Wellman et al. (1973).

14. Park, for example, states:

The outcome of [urban specialization] is to break down or modify the older social and economic organization of society, which was based on family ties, local associations, on culture, caste and status, and to substitute for it an organization based on occupation and vocational interests. . . . The different trades and professions seem disposed to group themselves in classes, that is to say, the artisan, business, and professional classes (Park, 1916: 102).

Durkheim (1893), Simmel (1905) and Wirth (1938) also refer to the rise of economic structuring in the city.

15. A random sample of 36 metropolitan areas was drawn from those listed in the Bureau of Labor Statistic's (1969) report on work stoppages in 1968. The number of lost worker-days increased exponentially with increases in population size.

16. This argument can be taken to a reductio ad absurdum. I have been asked, for example, whether pipe-fitters form a separate subculture. The answer is yes, if the number of pipe-fitters in a superlarge city were great enough. Obviously, this does not occur in most, if any, contemporary cities. Also, additional factors help determine at what threshold of size occupations will develop distinctive cultures, factors including degree of separation from other walks of life (because of schedule or physical location), exclusivity of recruitment, degree of specialized training, and degree of task-related communication, among others. (See Wilensky [1964] on the cultural differentiation of occupations.)

17. The informal associations discussed here are unofficial and smaller versions of the formal associations discussed earlier. "A special-interest group is a phenomenon of Gesellschaft," wrote Tönnies (1887: 213). It is basic to the concept of Gesellschaft that its social relations are essentially impersonal and instrumental. "A special-interest group is a fictitious being which serves its authors, expressing their common rational will in certain relationships" (Tönnies, 1887: 214). "Rational will" in this context is impersonal: "In rational relations man is reckoned with like a number, like an element which is in itself indifferent" (Simmel, 1905: 49). Consequently, "in Gesellschaft every person strives for that which is to his own advantage and he affirms the actions of others only in so far and as long as they can further his own interest" (Tönnies, 1887: 77). "Our acquaintances tend to stand in a relationship of utility to us in the sense that the role which each one plays in our life is overwhelmingly regarded as a means for the achievement of our own ends" (Wirth, 1938: 153).

18. An exponent of the popular view is Packard (1972), and of the scholarly positions, Tönnies (1887), Durkheim (1893), Park (1916), Nisbet (1967), and Alexander (1967). Tönnies (1887: 42) called the neighborhood the "Gemeinschaft of locality . . . a community of physical life." Park (1916: 111) described the characteristics of such natural or "primordial" relationships as including interactions that are "immediate and unreflecting . . . carried on largely within the region of instinct and feeling . . . in direct response to personal influences and public sentiment . . . and [not the result] of a rational and abstract principle."

19. The survey statistics came from an unpublished table prepared for Fischer (1973a). See also Swedner (1960), Key (1968), Bradburn et al. (1970), and B. M. Richardson (1973). Migrants to cities often report that their home villages were more neighborly than their current places of residence (e.g., K. K. Petersen, 1971). A major exception to this pattern of findings are those of Kasarda and Janowitz (1974), who discovered only negligible associations between community size and local involvement in their secondary analysis of an English survey.

20. General discussions of neighboring appear in Keller (1968), Mann (1965), and Michelson (1970). Specific studies include Fischer et al. (1976: Ch. 7), Gates et al. (1973), McGahan (1972), Kasarda and Janowitz (1974), Fava (1959), and Fellin and Litwak (1963).

21. For example, in one study (Fischer, 1973a), statistically controlling for individual traits still left a large association between community size and knowing one's neighbors. In another (Bradburn et al., 1970), a variable measuring "urbanization" was more highly associated with the extent to which individuals neighbored than any other factor.

22. This analysis draws heavily from Heberle (1960) and Suttles (1972). See also Keller (1968).

23. This generalization assumes that social class is held constant. Neighboring tends to increase with an individual's social class as part of a general increase in social activity of all kinds. Thus, well-to-do people are more neighborly (in terms of casual interaction) than less affluent people; among their total social relationships, however, people in higher classes emphasize the neighborhood ties less than do people of lower rank (see Keller, 1968; Fischer et al., 1977: Ch. 7).

24. Keller (1968: 44) suggests that neighbors exchange four kinds of services—help of a casual nature, help in an emergency, joining in the celebration of special events (e.g., a birth), and assisting at cyclical events (e.g., harvests). But the latter two are not inherent in the role. See also Useem et al. (1960).

25. J. Smith et al. (1954), Bell and Boat (1957), Riemer and McNamara (1957), Tomeh (1967), K. K. Petersen (1971), Key (1968), Koyama (1970), Fischer (1973a), Hawley and Zimmer (1971: 54), and Keller (1968).

26. "For social control to be rigorous and for the common conscience to be maintained, society must be divided into rather small compartments completely enclosing the individual"—Durkheim (1893:300).

CHAPTER 6

1. Several "conflict theorists" (such as A. Cohen, 1969; Schildkrout, 1974; and Hechter, 1974) have advanced the thesis that ethnicity, at least in the urban setting, is often a culturally empty institution. In this view, ethnic groups are primarily economic and political conflict groups that employ ethnicity only as a political tool. This argument over the "real" content of ethnicity is partly a matter of judgment—how distinctive must a culture be to be distinctive?—and partly one of research. Without pressing the argument, I would suggest that the identifiability of ethnic boundaries, even for political purposes, is strongly associated with cultural differences, so that without these differences political cohesion becomes unlikely.

2. At first glance, it may not be clear how both cultural intensification and diffusion can occur simultaneously. Yet such cases are common. They involve selective acceptance of cultural items from other groups. These "peripheral" items are borrowed either because they are convenient (say, clothing styles) or useful (for example, political organization). But this borrowing occurs together with an emphasis on "central" identity and core values. Examples will be given in the text. The same pattern holds true for personal contacts across ethnic lines. As an anthropologist of ethnicity writes:

> It is clear that [ethnic] boundaries persist despite a flow of personnel across them. In other words, categorical ethnic distinctions do not depend on the absence of mobility, contact and information, but do entail social processes of exclusion and incorporation whereby discrete categories are maintained despite changing participation and membership. . . . Ethnic distinctions do not depend on the absence of social interaction and acceptance but are quite to the contrary often the very foundations on which embracing social systems are built [Barth, 1969: 9-10].

3. The following is only a partial bibliography. North America: Gans (1962b), Glazer and Moynihan (1970), Handlin (1969, 1951), Snyder (1971); Latin America: Butterworth (1962), Doughty (1970), S. I. Thompson (1974); Europe: Halpern (1965), Willems (1970); Africa: Shack (1973), Hanna and Hanna (1971); Asia: Rowe (1973), Husain (1956).

4. Gans (1962b) makes such an observation in The Urban Villagers (p. 208): "American cities, however, could not penetrate the family circle. Thus, whereas the children became adults of the second generation retained little of the Italian culture [meaning peripheral items], they did retain most of its social structure [a central item]." Sengstock (1969) presents a study that illustrates this distinction.

5. There are other, similar problems common to such ethnographic studies. Researchers who have assigned themselves the task of studying ethnicity (or kinship, for that matter) tend to "see" it even where others might not. And there is a tendency to select distinctive groups for case study, often groups more ethnically defined than the average.

6. Epstein (1967); J. C. Mitchell (1970); see, also, Hanna and Hanna (1971). On tribal associations, see Little (1965b); Bascom (1968).

7. Another example, this one highlighting the difficulty of maintaining ethnicity in a small community, was provided by a conference held on Jewish life in American small towns:

> ". . . With less than 29 youngsters, 3-year-olds to high school age," said a participant from a midwestern town with 35 Jewish families, "how can we manage an effective Hebrew school to educate them?"
> Community centers, nurseries, homes for the aged, all-day Jewish schools, adult study programs, and other communal and social service programs are a rarity in small towns [Spiegel, 1973].

Other illustrations are provided by Suttles (1968: 150), and Doughty (1972).

8. This, of course, simplifies a complex pattern in at least two respects: 1) To the degree that community size is not correlated with the size of a given ethnic group, the urbanism-ethnicity association is weakened. Clear instances of minority concentrations in rural areas can be noted; for example, California's Japanese-Americans. But, in general, the correlation is there. 2) It is very difficult to say whether members of an ethnic minority in a city, no matter how numerous, can be as culturally distinctive as their relatives in an isolated and homogenous village, no matter how few. For many peripheral cultural items, they cannot. The rural group is more ethnically "pure." For other items, certainly for self-conscious identity, perhaps they can. What does seem clear is that, for a minority, being sizable and in a large city is conducive to ethnic persistence.

9. Compared to most nations, the United States imposes a uniform and pervasive language and culture on its minorities. In the majority of cases, these minorities are separated by great distance and cost from their homelands, thereby reducing the sort of continuing support and immigration available to minorities in the cities of most other nations (see Lieberson et al, 1975).

10. If we consider groups of friends, the contrast is sharper still. The town of 10,000 provides about 1000 times as many possible, unique, three-person groups as does the town of 1,000. The general formula for the number of possible unique combinations, C, of size S, which can be extracted from a total population of elements, N, is:

$$C = \left[\prod_{S=1}^{S} (N-S+1) \right] / S!$$

The difference between two populations of size, N_a and N_b, in the number of combinations, C_a and C_b, possible at a given size is an exponential function:

$$C_a / C_b > (N_a / N_b)^S$$

11. A sample of such studies: W. F. Whyte (1955), Young and Wilmott (1957), Gutkind (1969), Pons (1969), and Roberts (1973). Other studies, many of which will be cited in the discussion of kinship, present the same conclusion.

12. See Wylie (1964), P. Smith (1968), G. M. Foster (1967), and Banfield (1958).

13. Other such studies include, in Detroit: Axelrod (1956); in Los Angeles: Greer (1956); in Toronto: Wellman et al. (1973); in Rio de Janeiro: Perlman (1975).

14. For similar findings, see Sutcliffe and Crabbe (1963), Key (1968), Kasarda and Jarowitz (1974), and Swedner (1960). Two surveys of leisure-time habits show essentially no size-of-community differences in the proportions of residents who prefer to visit or entertain friends (de Grazia, 1962: 461; A.I.P.O., 1974, #105: 12). There is one study that claims to find such differences, but the research suffers from serious difficulties (an odd sample, no third-factor controls, marginal differences), and, at best, demonstrates only that New Yorkers differ from residents of other cities (Guterman, 1969).

15. Apart from Koyama (1970), there are few comparative studies on the specialization of networks. Verbrugge (1973) presents data on personal networks for Detroit and for a small city in Germany. Specialization seemed to be greater in Detroit, but the comparison is a crude one. See also Frankenburg (1965) and Boissevain (1974: 71ff.). Most network surveys have been solely urban, e.g., Litwak and Szelenyi (1969), Laumann (1973), and Wellman et al. (1973).

16. Wirth's statement (1938: 160-161), in more detail:

> ... The city is not conducive to the traditional type of family life, including the rearing of children and the maintenance of the home as the locus of a whole round of activities. The transfer of industrial, educational, and recreational activities to specialized institutions outside the home has deprived the family of some of its most characteristic historical functions. ... The family as a unit of social life is emancipated from the larger kinship group characteristic of the country, and the individual members pursue their own diverging interests in their vocational, educational, religious, recreational, and political life.

See also Burgess and Locke (1953: Ch. 4), Obgurn (1954), Tönnies (1887: 229), Park (1916).

17. In 1965, metropolitan counties had a divorce rate of 2.6 per thousand people, and nonmetropolitan counties 2.2 per thousand (NCHS, 1969c: 24). See also Goode (1963), Carpenter (1960), Mann (1965: 59), Clinard (1964).

18. Results from unpublished table prepared for Fischer (1973a).

19. Other studies include, in North America: Gans (1962b), Suttles (1968), Lewis (1952), Garigue (1956); in Europe: Halpern (1965), Willems (1970); in Africa: Aldous (1962), Schwab (1968); in Asia: Vatuk (1972), Nayacakalov and Southall (1973). See also citations in note 11, on studies of friendship.

20. For reviews of the survey literature on urbanism and kinship, see Greer (1962), R. N. Morris (1968), and Goode (1963: 70-76). Studies include Axelrod (1956), Wellman et al. (1973), Simic (1973), Cantor (1975), and Lees (1969).

21. A related finding, but one somewhat difficult to interpret , was reported by Hadley Cantril (1965: Appendix E). Data from surveys conducted in several developing nations (Brazil, pre-Castro Cuba, Egypt, Nigeria, and Panama) indicate that people in urban places tended to have more personal fears (and hopes) about their families than did people in rural places. In more economically advanced nations (Israel, West Germany, the United States, and Yugoslavia), there were no substantive urban-rural differences in family worries.

22. See Litwak (1960), Adams (1966), Wellman et al. (1973), Koyama (1970), Vatuk (1972), Fischer et al. (1977).

23. Winch and Greer (1968) found no size-of-community differences in "extended familism" for nonmigrants, but found such differences among migrants, the rural ones being more familistic (p. 42). This difference is probably a result of migrants having moved to small communities precisely *because* of their kin, while people tend to move to large cities for different reasons (see Bastide and Girard, 1974).

CHAPTER 7

1. The book that sparked studies of urban cognitive maps was Lynch (1960). Other studies include Horton and Reynolds (1971), and de Jonge (1962).

2. Much of the following discussion is expanded upon in the review of the crowding literature by Fischer et al. (1975).

3. Other extrapolators in this vein include Calhoun (1962), Hall (1966), and van den Berghe (1974).

4. Among the popularizers of this thesis are Ardrey (1961) and D. Morris (1968). Scholars who make this argument include Lorenz (1966), Leyhausen (1965), Carstairs (1969), and van den Berghe (1974).

5. Critiques of the ethology-territoriality model include: Montagu (1973), Alland (1972), Martin (1972), S. Nelson (1974), Freedman (1975), and Fischer (1975e). See also discussions by Wynne-Edwards (1964) and Dubos (1970).

6. See Calhoun (1962), Hall (1966), Meier (1962), Milgram (1970), Desor (1971), Aiello et al. (1975), and Freedman (1975: 93-95).

7. See Somer (1969), Hall (1966), and Goffman (1971). Reviews and theoretical critiques appear in Watson (1972), Evans and Howard (1973), Baldassare and Feller (1976), and Pedersen and Shears (1973).

8. This cultural model meshes with the nonverbal-communications version of the "personal space" model. If one person moves closer to another, that person is saying, "This situation is not one of strangers, but of friends." The illustration of the New York subway suggests that riders come to expect and accept crowding. This deduction finds empirical support in a survey of New Yorkers (Morton, 1972), which showed that riding the subways was not related to disliking the city (though other things, especially neighborhood quality, were).

9. We cannot hope to review in detail the massive amount of research in the crowded field of crowding. See the several recent reviews of the literature: Fischer et al. (1975), Stokols (1977), Lawrence (1974), and Freedman (1975; 1973).

10. One curious finding has emerged from a few studies in this line: Groups of males seem to be more upset and aggressive in small (dense) rooms than in large ones, but with groups of females, it is the reverse. In groups including both sexes, no difference was observed between the rooms. A small sample of studies of this type of research: Freedman et al. (1971, 1972), Stokols et al. (1973), and Ross et al. (1973). See reviews cited in previous note.

11. One oft-cited study (Galle et al. 1972) presents evidence suggesting that crowding within households is related to pathologies. However, there are serious questions about the results of this study (S. Ward, 1974; Fischer et al., 1975; McPherson, 1975).

12. There is an unfortunate scarcity of studies on this key issue that are comprehensive, relevant to general populations, and analytically sophisticated (e.g., systematically controlling for confounding variables). Most studies, though helpful, are limited. For instance, one study compared a small sample of Algiers residents with their kin and friends in a rural oasis, and found more tension among the former (Miner and DeVos, 1960). But a comparison of stress symptoms among residents of a slum in Lima, Peru with those of residents in a peasant village showed little difference (Rotondo, 1962).

13. No contemporary urban-rural difference in suicide rate has been reported for the United States (N.C.H.S., 1967b), Japan (Carpenter, 1960), or France (Szabo, 1960). A higher urban than rural rate has been reported for England (Mann, 1964: 48) and Scandinavia (Westergaard, 1966).

14. The seventeen were totaled from those reported by Swedner (1960: 30-45), and Nelson and Storey (1969), plus others, e.g. Schooler (1972), Sewell and Amend (1943), and Haller and Wolff (1962). The last found signs that seventeen-year-old boys in two towns were more nervous than those in nearby villages, but with no more tendency to suffer from pathological symptoms.

15. Dohrenwend and Dohrenwend (1972) review a mixed bag of nine epidemiological studies that compared populations in larger and smaller communities. They conclude that mild neuroses are more common in urban areas, while serious psychoses are more common in rural ones. However, the studies are quite limited with regard to samples, procedures, and controls for spurious relationships and for "drift." Furthermore, the differences are essentially small ones (see critique by Srole, 1972; Schwab et al., 1972). An earlier review concludes that there is as yet no clear evidence of urban-rural differences in mental health (Freeman and Giovannini, 1969).

16. The present usages of alienation are derived from the work of Melvin Seeman (1959, 1972, 1975); a good history of the concept appears in Schacht (1971).

17. An interesting exception to this generalization comes from Uganda, where a small survey found that residents in the city felt more powerless than residents in a village. The researcher attributed the finding in part to political repression and terror, which were more widespread in urban areas (R. W. Thompson, 1974).

18. Various scales have been constructed to measure "normlessness," the most well-known of which is the Srole Anomia Scale. However, it is not clear that these scales do measure normlessness (see Seeman, 1972; Fischer, 1976); in any case, studies using them fail to show any major relationship with urbanism (see Fischer, 1973a: fn. 2).

19. This pattern of mistrust prevailed when the village was revisited in 1973 (Wylie, 1973). See also Foster (1967), and Lantz (1971).

20. Tabulation from the National Opinion Research Center Social Survey, 1972, was kindly provided by Susan Issel.

21. We have not discussed three other varieties of alienation listed by Seeman (1972): *Self-estrangement,* which refers to alienated labor, is not directly germane. *Meaninglessness* refers to the feeling that events in the world around an individual are incomprehensible. This has been researched very little, but indications (from survey items such as: "The way things are going, it is not fair to bring children into the world—agree or disagree?") are that it is not associated with urbanism. *Value isolation* refers to a lack of esteem for those goals that are generally considered important in an individual's society. In the next chapter, we shall see that this form of alienation probably *is* related to urbanism. Finally, *political alienation* was discussed in Chapter 5, where evidence was reviewed indicating that, although alienation from political activities as such is not associated with urbanism, detachment from local politics is.

22. One might wonder whether urban and rural people differ (as Charles Tilly suggests) in *what* they are anxious or concerned about. In Hadley Cantril's (1965) international survey, people in fourteen countries were asked to name their greatest hopes and fears for themselves and their nations. From a visual inspection of the published tables, little in the way of systematic urban-rural differences emerge in these responses. However, in the developing nations, urban people seem more likely than rural people to express hopes *and* fears about both their families and their countries' political and economic situations.

CHAPTER 8

1. The terms Wirth (1938) used that imply impersonality include "rationality," "sophistication," "tolerance," etc. The same general meaning also seems to be captured in Parsons' (1951) "pattern-variables" at the poles of universalism—specifically, affective neutrality and self-orientation (noted also by Kolb, 1954).

2. Unfortunately, studies of "modernity" such as Aksoy's combine modernity as a cognitive state—a way of viewing the world, such as impersonality—with modernity as a set of values; the latter usage we will employ later in this chapter.

One particular form of impersonality is ethnic tolerance or absence of prejudice. Research in North America generally finds that urban people are substantially less prejudiced—thus, more impersonal—than are rural people. However, controls for social class, religion, and other covariates tend to render the differences marginal (Selznik and Steinberg, 1969; Curtis and Hawkins, 1975; Fischer, 1971; Whitt and Nelsen, 1975). Moreover, such residual differences may reflect not cognitive styles, but liberal ideologies that are currently more prevalent in cities than in small towns.

3. Blumenthal et al. (1972) found in a national sample of men that rural residents scored slightly *higher* than urban residents on a "materialism" scale (p. 114), but also scored higher on a "kindness" scale (p. 122).

4. Milgram (1970) reports two pilot studies that found somewhat greater willingness to help strangers on the telephone or at the door in small towns or suburbs than in large cities. Though these studies are modestly suggestive about the chances of any given "victim" being assisted by any given "bystander," they do not speak to our theoretical concern about personality dispositions to help, because they did not standardize for extenuating circumstances: press of business in the stores or homes that were telephoned, crime rates in areas visited, the plausibility of the "victim's" requests in each place, background characteristics, etc. As Milgram says, these are illustrative pilot studies, and "at this point we have very limited objective evidence." Also, different results were obtained by Forbes and Gromoll (1971). They found no differences among communities in the likelihood of "lost letters" being mailed by strangers. Two very recent studies have added yet more conflicting data. One found that people in small towns in Massachusetts were slightly more willing to help a stranger in need than were people in Boston (Korte and Kerr, 1975). But the same research conducted in the Netherlands found no such differences between people in large cities and those in small cities (Korte et al., 1975). These studies, though more exact than the ones reported by Milgram, still share similar limitations. Finally, Alford (1972: 349) reports that there is a positive correlation (.18) between city size and contributions to the Community Chest as a proportion of local wealth.

5. Studies which show that the probability of any one observer intervening *declines* with increases in group size also show that the probability of someone helping at all *increases* with group size (e.g., Latané and Dabbs, 1975).

6. And stories such as the following appear often enough in the press to instill caution in most people: "'I was trying to be a good neighbor and now my wife is dead,' said Earl Harshman, the victim of a brutal beating at his home by two men he permitted to use his telephone." (*San Francisco Chronicle*, Dec. 19, 1974: 5).

7. Jones and Nisbett (1972) discuss the perceptual bias people tend to show when they attribute their own actions to *situational* constraints ("I had to do it") but attribute the same behavior by another to that individual's *personality* ("He wanted to do it").

8. Another contributor to the impression of impersonality is simple numbers. Given the larger size of the urban population, the chances are greater that someone will misbehave and annoy others there than in small towns. An illustration is provided by a widely publicized "experiment" conducted by Stanford University psychologist Philip Zimbardo (1969). He abandoned a car on a Bronx, New York expressway, and within hours it was completely vandalized. A car similarly abandoned on a Palo Alto, California street went undamaged for days. It was illegitimate to conclude, as he did, anything about people in large cities versus those in smaller ones. One crucial fact is that far more people passed the Bronx car than passed the Palo Alto car, exposing the former to much greater risk. The New York people were not necessarily any different from the Californians. (Moreover, the cars were left in neighborhoods of very different social class; the Bronx expressway is a notorious dumping ground for ailing automobiles; and the places chosen were hardly representative of each community.)

9. Waves of social innovation build up in cities and wash over the surrounding hinterlands in the same way that material innovation diffuses. An illustration of this wave phenomenon is provided by two polls, taken seventeen years apart, which asked national samples of Americans whether they drank alcohol (G.O.I., 1956; 1974, #108). The percentages who said yes were, by size of community:

	1957	1974	Difference
Communities over 500,000	73%	80%	7%
50,000 to 500,000	51	71	20
2,500 to 50,000	48	65	17
Under 2,500	46	55	9

The proportions who admit to drinking have increased least in the largest and smallest communities and most in the medium-sized communities. These differences can be interpreted to indicate that the crest of the wave is now hitting small cities but has yet to reach rural places in full force.

10. Peasant revolts are, of course, common and were actually the rule in Communist successes. However, peasant uprisings are usually, at least initially, restorative and not radical (Hobsbawm, 1970; Tilly et al., 1975). The advantage of peasants over urban workers in modern times has probably less to do with motivation than with the tactical advantages of remote bases (see Gurr, 1971).

11. Rhoads Murphey (1954) has argued, in a vein similar to others (e.g., Redfield and Singer, 1954), that cities were conservative forces in certain societies, specifically precolonial China. It was in the cities that the orthodox centers of Chinese government and religion were located. However, he presents no evidence to challenge the generalization that, although the cities were the seat of the establishment (as they are today), they were simultaneously the site of progressive dissent. The Chinese-European comparison suggests, instead, two noteworthy features of urban radicalism. One, during periods of nation-building, forces for the creation of a state build up in and flow from the urban centers. Rural regions resist this innovation, as they resist other innovations, not because the peasants are revolutionary but, to the contrary, because they are conservative (see Tilly et al., 1975). Two, in nation-states, cities will be simultaneously the seedbeds of dissent and, for reasons of communications and economics, the headquarters of the establishment. The popular support for the establishment comes, however, from the hinterland. In France, the government has almost always been located in Paris, but so have the threats to its power, so that it has depended on the provinces for the necessary support to maintain itself in Paris.

12. See Fischer (1975c), Nelson et al. (1971), Schnaiberg (1971), Seligson (1972), G.O.I. (1975, #114), and Argyle (1968). Negative evidence on the association of urbanism and irreligiosity appears occasionally, e.g., van Es and Brown (1974). The examination of this topic cross-culturally is somewhat confounded by the differences between what anthropologists call the "great" and "little" traditions. The urban elite version of a society's religion is frequently far more sophisticated than that of the peasantry, or of the urban proletariat. Yet, interestingly, the cities are where these intellectualized doctrines are promulgated, and thus they are another form of urban innovation.

13. On urban innovation and diffusion in general, see Turner (1940) and Rogers (1962). On inventions, see Ogburn and Duncan (1964), Feller (1973), Merton (1938b: 211-224), Higgs (1975), and H. L. Richardson (1973: 40-43).

14. Fischer (1975c), Hoch (1972), Nelsen et al. (1971), Willitis et al. (1974), and Lowe and Peek (1974); see review in Swedner (1960: 30-45). Two studies that found no residual urban-rural differences after controls are Grasmick (1974) and White (1973: 27-8).

CHAPTER 9

1. The statistics used in Figure 9 actually underestimate suburban growth because they include annexed areas within center cities. See Kasarda and Redfearn (1975). Shortages of and increased prices for gasoline have suggested the possibility of a check on suburban growth. However, an analysis of gas prices in relation to incomes suggests that this will not be a major factor (Bruce-Briggs, 1974).

2. Defining "suburb" requires more comment. Any satisfactory definition should neither severely violate nor bow to the common usage of the term. Therefore, any definition that categorizes a locality near the central business district as a suburb, or an area on the urban fringe as city, is unsatisfactory. A number of suggested criteria fail this test. These criteria include residential land use (what does one do with center-city residential areas?); density (outlying apartment areas exist; in-lying low-density areas, while uncommon, do exist); housing type (most metropolitan areas have single-family housing throughout); commuting (virtually everyone who works commutes); recency of development (what does one do with engulfed villages or redeveloped downtowns?). To define suburbs in terms of "familism" begs the sociological question about the relationship between suburbanism and ways of life. The political definition has its virtues, but also its anomalies. (Los Angeles is a classic example, where the "suburb" of Compton is a stone's throw from City Hall, but where it takes about an hour on the freeway to reach the city limits at the north end of the San Fernando Valley.) Virtually all of these definitions have something to recommend them; and virtually all are strongly related to distance. But none do quite as well as distance in providing a definition.

Five arguments support a definition based on distance: 1) distance appears in many common usages of suburb—e.g., that a suburb is an outlying *and* residential area, or an outlying *and* low-density area; 2) distance is related to the historical meaning of the term—a residential area outside city walls; 3) distance is cross-culturally useful; in foreign nations, many of the other variables are inappropriate (e.g., political lines) or inconsistent there (e.g., residentiality), while distance is a simple universal; 4) distance determines the other definitions—e.g., the farther out, the easier it is to maintain low density; and 5) distance is parsimonious and a simple ecological variable.

3. The basic sources on popular and scholarly views of suburbia are *The Suburban Myth* by Scott Donaldson (1969), and a chapter with a similar title in Bennett Berger's *Working-Class Suburb* (1960).

4. Two research items support this conclusion. Guest (1972) found that the concentration of child-rearing families in outer areas can be explained statistically by the spaciousness and newness of the dwellings. And a recent study of movers in metropolitan areas found that those moving from the cities to the suburbs were *not* much more likely to endorse pro-suburban views than were those moving within the city (Butler et al., 1968). For a thorough discussion of the effects of housing economics on suburban expansion, see Evans (1973).

5. Most of the studies cited in the discussion of pollution in Chapter 3 point out that irritant levels are lower in suburban than in city districts.

6. In 1970, almost half the suburban households in the United States had two or more cars; only about one-fourth of city households did (Bureau of the Census, 1973).

7. Press accounts suggest that the construction of single-family houses in the suburbs has been severely curtailed recently *(The New York Times,* Jan. 20, 1974, p. E-6; April 27, 1975, p. E-6; *San Francisco Chronicle,* Jan. 13, 1975). Whether this is a temporary or a long-term change remains to be seen.

8. Von Rosenbladt (1972) provides a tally of services by distance from the city center in a German community. On complaints by suburbanites about lack of services, see Warner (1962: 158), Hawley and Zimmer (1971), Michelson (1973a), and Fischer and Jackson (1976: fn. 19). Gans (1967) points out that groups with specialized needs, e.g., adolescents, suffered most from this problem. On the elderly, see Bourg (1975). Suburbanites tend to travel farther to schools, churches, stores, and jobs than do city residents. However, they seem not, on the average, to spend more *time* on these trips, because a higher proportion of suburbanites than city dwellers drive cars. See Hawley and Zimmer (1971), von Rosenbladt (1972), Oi and Shuldiner (1962), and Stegman (1969).

9. White city residents are about 50 percent more likely to be of foreign stock than suburbanites (Bureau of the Census, 1972: Table 108).

10. Unfortunately, the statistics and studies we are citing often vary on their operational definition of "suburban." Some use the entire Standard Metropolitan Statistical Area (SMSA) outside the center city; others use only the urban parts, excluding rural portions of counties within the SMSA. Generally, although the numbers will differ as a consequence, the conclusions will not. The median income data cited initially in the

text are based on the first definition; the 29 metropolises data are based on the second.

11. Some have failed to find social-class differences between cities and suburbs. Anderson and Egeland (1961) and Guest (1971) report that occupational prestige did not increase much with distance from city center in their ecological studies. The problem seems to have been the use of prestige instead of income. The census reports that, within occupational types, suburbanites earn more than city dwellers (Bureau of the Census, 1972: Table 116). And, in preparing Fischer and Jackson (1976), we found, in a sample of white males in Detroit, that distance from the city center was correlated about .3 with respondents' family income, though only about .2 with their education and occupational prestige. Another problem that has bedeviled the literature on this issue is the technical difficulties which arise as a result of arbitrary city boundaries (see Schnore, 1972).

12. The historical reversal in the association between suburbanism and social class is briefly explained in Chapter 3 (pp. 42–44). See Evans (1973: Ch. 10) for a more sophisticated economic model. In the United States, small metropolitan areas less often exhibit the pattern of suburban affluence than large metropolises do. This appears to be a result partly of statistical artifacts produced by political boundaries, partly of less developed transit systems in smaller communities (which reduce the attraction of suburban residence), and partly of less congestion and deterioration in their centers (making city residence less offensive). See Schnore and Winsborough (1972).

13. Methodological difficulties confound analyses of homogeneity. One problem is the measurement of variability: Inevitably, it seems, the measure is affected by the direction of skewness in the distribution of the given attribute, thus producing a correlation between measures of central tendency and measures of dispersion. Another problem is the unit of analysis. At the largest level, city municipalities versus suburban townships, it is clear that the latter are more homogeneous than the former. At the smallest level reported in the literature, census tracts, the results are ambiguous (Fine et al., 1971). This probably results from the different areal sizes of city and suburban tracts. At intermediate levels—zones and neighborhoods—it appears that suburban localities are slightly more homogeneous than city localities (Kish, 1954; Bradburn et al., 1970). For a discussion of the methodological problems, see Roof and Van Valey (1972).

14. For the purpose of completeness, brief comments about the two omitted secondary groups are in order. 1) *Formal associations.* Two contrary speculations have been offered in this regard: one that suburbanism produces a veritable mania of joining and organizational activity (e.g., Whyte, 1956); the other that the drain of commuting reduces organizational participation, at least for males (e.g., W. T. Martin, 1959). There seem to be no major differences in membership not explainable by personal characteristics. (see, for example, Hawley and Zimmer, 1971: 56; Berger, 1960: 59-64; cf. Gruenberg, 1974). Gans' (1967) study does indicate much joining during the early period of suburban settlement, but this is probably a passing phase (see Dobriner, 1963). 2) *Occupational and class groups.* I would speculate here that suburbanism (slightly) encourages the strengthening of class groups at the expense of occupational groups. The argument is twofold: Residential location is based on income, not job, so that the locality group overlaps more with the *class* group in the suburbs than in the city; at the same time, residential dispersal makes contact among occupational associates more difficult.

15. On suburban resistance to metropolitan government, see Greer (1963), Campbell and Dollenmeyer (1975), and Hawley and Zimmer (1971).

16. At least two studies have found that white suburbanites, though not particularly prejudiced in general, are more resistant to housing integration than are white city dwellers (Campbell, 1971; Wirt et al., 1972). For general discussions of suburban politics, see Wirt et al., (1972), Wood (1958), Gans (1967), Greer and Orleans (1962), and Greer and Greer (1976).

17. A list of studies on neighboring, as well as further data, appears in Fischer and Jackson (1976). Most notable in that list are Michelson (1973a), Tomeh (1964), Fava (1959), Tallman and Morgner (1970), Berger (1960), and Gans (1967).

18. Hawley and Zimmer (1971: 58-64) examine the "scope" of daily activity engaged in by respondents to their survey, including distance to work, stores, friends, and the like. Not surprisingly, suburbanites travel farther, on the average, than city dwellers do (see note 8). After all, suburbs are more dispersed. However, the differences are not

great. And among residents in the larger metropolitan areas who had not moved from the adjacent city (i.e., had not left behind social ties), the differences were reversed; their lives were more spatially circumscribed than those of comparable city dwellers.

19. Tomeh (1964) found in a Detroit study that suburbanites reported seeing friends (and neighbors) slightly more often than did city dwellers, and had just as frequent contact with kin and co-workers. However, in analyses performed by the author and his associates on a survey of Detroit men conducted in 1965, no association was found between suburbanism and either reported number of friends or friendship intimacy (Fischer and Jackson, 1976; Baldassare and Fischer, 1975). See also Sutcliffe and Crabbe (1963).

20. Michelson (1973a), Gans (1967), Clark (1966), Berger (1960), Young and Willmott (1956), Smith et al. (1954), and Fischer and Jackson (1976).

21. See Tallman (1969), Gans (1967), Young and Willmott (1957), Clark (1966), Michelson (1973a), Foote et al. (1960: 186), Gillespie (1971), and Fava (1975). Berger (1960) footnotes this problem in passing. He also remarks that the rate of employment among the wives of the newly suburbanized auto-workers whom he studied dropped precipitously after the move. In fact, two of Berger's fifty male respondents had been deserted by their wives because of the women's inability to adjust to suburbia (p. 70, fn. 31)! L. M. Jones (1974) has documented suburban women's low access to jobs and supportive services, which probably reduces their chances for employment. In preparing Fischer and Jackson (1976), we found, while analyzing a national survey, that the suburban-city distinction was significantly related to men's responses to the question of whether they would be unhappy if they had to move ($\gamma = .19$—suburban men more unhappy), but only marginally related to women's responses ($\gamma = .07$).

22. For example, Gallup Polls report attitude differences by metropolitan size, but rarely distinguish center cities from suburbs; and studies in foreign nations are, because of population distributions there, largely focused on urban-rural rather than city-suburban contrasts.

23. Carlos (1970), Tallman and Margner (1970), Fischer (1975c), and Berger (1960). Contrary data are reported by Zimmer and Hawley (1959). See also Newman (1976).

24. The application of Wirthian theory to differences within an urbanized area is hindered by one major difficulty: Its primary process is the structural differentiation that results from urbanism. Suburbs are a part of that structural differentiation. That is, suburban communities are specialized territorial units within the greater metropolitan area, emphasizing residence, or in some cases, industry, and housing a selected subsection of the population (Obgurn, 1937). In this sense, the Chicago School theory is about a whole metropolis and thus cannot be applied to differences within it. However, the secondary process in the Wirthian theory might be applicable. This is the argument concerning direct psychological experiences—the "psychic overload" analysis (see Chapter 2).

CHAPTER 10

1. One of the more important of these questions concerns the term "community" as used in reference to human settlements. Are towns and cities, particularly in modern societies, socially significant social forms or are they just differentiated pieces of a national social structure, their cultures simply local manifestations of a national one? More broadly, to what degree is "community"—rural, urban, or suburban—a useful concept in sociology? (See Greer, 1962; Castells, 1968, 1969; Pickvance, 1974). Similarly, what is the significance of a particular geographical location for an individual, particularly in an age of telephones, television, and supersonic airliners? Phrased another way, what is the essential role of space in human relationships? (See Webber, 1963, 1970; Bernard, 1973). Another issue concerns the urban-rural distinction. Urban sociology has long used the rural-urban continuum as a basic conceptual scheme for sorting communities. And this book has followed that tradition. But perhaps there is a quite different and more revealing conceptual scheme that could be used. Several have been casually suggested—for example, schemes based on economics or political structure—but no alternative to the variable of urbanism has been fully developed yet (see Fischer, 1975a).

2. In the first chapter, we pointed out that one motive for sociologists to study the city is their impression that the processes set into motion by urbanization at the local level parallel and forecast processes accompanying modernization at the societal level.

In particular, the joining together of a nation by modern communication and transport has been regarded as similar to the coming together of people in cities. Assuming that the notion of parallelism is valid, our conclusions have direct implications for certain theories about the direction of modern society, in particular, for those about "mass society"—the thesis that modernization erases cultural differences among social units, such as ethnicity, regions, and classes, and results in an atomized mass of individuals who are spoon-fed a homogeneous cultural pabulum by the media. The conclusion that follows from our analysis holds quite the opposite: that the development of communications and transportation leads to the differentiation of cultural groups, including the appearance of groups founded on new bases of association (hobbies, politics, life-styles, and the like) and to an increased freedom of choice for individuals in the society; in short, to a pluralist society rather than a mass society (see also Shils, 1962; Wilensky, 1964; Webber, 1968a: 189).

3. Let me expand to avoid the impression that, in this passage, I have endorsed the canard that sociology merely ratifies common sense. An analogy can be made to folk astronomy. Primitive beliefs about celestial processes were fairly accurate descriptors and predictors of, for example, sunrises and seasonal changes, in spite of the fact that they were greatly mistaken in their explanations of those events. Scientific astronomy is, in practical terms, not so much better in predicting our common folk experience, though it provides a much improved explanation of those experiences. In that sense, sociology should not be expected, in most cases, to find popular *descriptions* of events to be altogether mistaken but only to provide better *explanations* of those phenomena.

4. Urban violence provides a major impetus for national programs that would redistribute population away from the large metropolises (see Sundquist, 1975: Ch. 1).

5. Between 1970 and 1973, metropolitan areas of over three million grew one percent in size (losing I.2 percent in net migration); areas between one and three million grew 3.6 percent, other metropolitan areas, 4.1 percent. Nonmetropolitan counties close to metropolitan areas grew 6.5 percent; others somewhat farther away grew 4.5 percent; and peripheral counties grew 4.0 percent (Forstall, 1975).

6. One concern is the possibility of a catastrophic energy shortage. Even were this to become a drastic reality, it is still unlikely that "supercity" would result. Large cities are highly dependent on cheap energy to bring resources to their residents from the hinterland. The more likely consequence of an "eco-catastrophe" would be dense but small and scattered communities.

7. One statistical projection forecasts that center-city population in the United States will grow only about 15–33 percent from 1970 to 2000, while suburban population will approximately double (Bureau of the Census, 1973).

8. For similar speculations, see Willbern (1964), Friedman and Miller (1965), Greer (1962), Abu-Lughod (1966), and J. Ward (1972).

9. This does not stop people from trying to come up with summary "quality of life" measures and then ranking communities accordingly, a procedure which ignores the fact that one man's quality of life is another man's poison (see Park, 1952). (Unlike combining different indicators of similar phenomena—say, measures of health, or wealth—this procedure sums indicators of quite disparate phenomena, largely on the basis of the researcher's values concerning what is "good" or "bad.") On the question of optimal city size, see Richardson (1973), Duncan (1957), Alonso (1971, 1975), Edel et al. (1974), Hoover (1972), and Dahl and Tufte (1973).

10. In one survey, a majority of Americans agreed that the "Federal government should discourage further growth of large metropolitan areas" (52 percent) and that it should "encourage people and industry to move to smaller cities and towns" (58 percent). Interestingly, agreement was strongly and positively related to the educational level of the respondent—Mazie and Rawlings (1972: 614). See also Sundquist (1975: Ch. 1).

11. The theory economists have developed to explain how a city could get larger than it "should" is based on the notion of "externalities." Each extra resident of a city does not have to pay the full cost his or her presence brings in pollution, congestion, and so on. Instead, that cost is shared by all the residents of the city. Consequently, each individual is encouraged to come and stay, even though for the city as a whole the resulting costs outweigh the benefits. (This is one variation on the general problem of "collective irrationality.") For a discussion of this thesis, see Alonso (1975).

12. There are apparently few, if any, objective summary assessments of British New

Towns. The comments in the text are based largely upon R. Thomas (1969), Eldridge (1967), Gutheim (1967), and Willmott (1967). There are several studies of specific New Towns, e.g., Willmott (1963), and Mogey (1956).

13. A number of these direct solutions involve changing "externalities" to "internalities." For general discussions, see Alonso (1971, 1972, 1975).

14. The writer Jimmy Breslin put it forcefully, but not inaccurately:

The official policy of New York was to deny food or housing to no one. . . .

From this our troubles came. New York lost jobs and gained people who needed jobs. Crime rose and the schools fell and more whites fled. And now suddenly everybody screams in horror: The city cannot pay its bills. Of course the city cannot pay its bills. Is not a house of the poor always poor? (New York Times, August 20, 1975)

REFERENCES

The page of the text on which a particular study is discussed is indicated by the bold-face page number at the end of the entry.

A.P.H.A. (American Public Health Association). 1970. *Proceedings of the First Invitational Conference on Health Research in Housing and Its Environment.*

Abbott, W. F. 1974. "Moscow in 1897 as a pre-industrial city." *American Sociological Review* 39 (August): 542–550. **214, 216**

Abrahamson, M. 1974. "The social dimensions of urbanism." *Social Forces* 52 (March): 376–383.

Abu-Lughod, J. A. 1966. "The city is dead—long live the city: Some thoughts on urbanity." Monograph 12, Berkeley: Center for Planning and Research.

Abu-Lughod, J. A. 1971. *Cairo.* Princeton: Princeton Univesity Press. **11, 44, 49, 116**

Adams, B. 1966. *Kinship in an Urban Setting.* Chicago: Markham.

Aiello, J. R., Y. M. Epstein, and R. A. Karlin. 1975. "Effects of crowding on electrodermal activity." *Sociological Symposium* 14 (Fall): 43–58.

Aiken, M., and R. R. Alford. 1974. "Community structure and innovation: The case of urban renewal." *American Sociological Review* 39 (February): 19–28. **103**

Aksoy, S. 1969. "The impact of urbanization on change." Mimeo. Harvard University Center for International Affairs (January); findings reported in Inkeles (1969). **185**

Alden, A. 1887. *Poems.* Wilton, Me. **19**

Aldous, J. 1962. "Urbanization, the extended family, and kinship ties in West Africa." *Social Forces* 61 (October): 6–12.

Alexander, C. 1967. "The city as a mechanism for sustaining human contact." In J. Helmer and N. A. Eddington (eds.), *Urbanman.* New York: Free Press (1973): 239–274. **8, 128, 138, 172, 180**

Alford, R. R. 1972. "Critical evaluation of the principles of city classification." In B. J. L. Berry (ed.), *City Classification Handbook.* New York: Wiley: 331–359.

Alford, R. R. and E. C. Lee. 1968. "Voting turnout in American cities." *American Political Science Review* 62 (September): 796–813.

Alford, R. R. and H. M. Scoble. 1968. "Sources of local political involvement." *American Political Science Review* 62 (December): 1192–1206. **218**

Alland, A., Jr. 1972. *The Human Imperative.* New York: Columbia University Press.

Alonso, W. 1970. "What are new towns for?" *Urban Studies* 7 (February): 30–55. **253**

Alonso, W. 1971. "The economics of urban size." *Papers of the Regional Science Association* 26: 67–83. **64, 77**

Alonso, W. 1972. "Problems, purposes, and implicit policies for a national strategy of urbanization." In S. M. Mazie (ed.), *Population, Distribution, and Policy,* Volume V, Research Reports, U. S. Commission of Population and the Future. Washington: U.S. Government Printing Office: 631–648.

Alonso, W. 1975. "City sizes and quality of life: Some observations." Paper presented to the American Association for the Advancement of Science, New York City (January). **77, 253**

Alonso, W., and M. Fajans. 1970. "Cost of living and income by urban size." Working Paper No. 128. Berkeley: Institute of Urban and Regional Development. **24, 76**

American Institute of Public Opinion. *Gallup Opinion Index.* Princeton, New Jersey.

Anderson, E. N., Jr. 1972. "Some Chinese methods of dealing with crowding." *Urban Anthropology* 1 (Fall): 141–150. **162**

Anderson, T. R., and J. A. Egeland. 1961. "Spatial aspects of social area analysis." *American Sociological Review* 26 (June): 392–399. **213**

Ardrey, R. 1961. *African Genesis.* New York: Atheneum.

Ardrey, R. 1966. *The Territorial Imperative.* New York: Atheneum.

Arensberg, C.M. 1965. "The community as object and as sample." In C. M. Arensberg and S. T. Kimball (eds.), *Culture and Community.* New York: Harcourt Brace Jovanovich: 7–27. **6**

276

Arensberg, C. M. 1968a. *The Irish Countryman*. Revised Edition. Garden City, New York: Natural History Press. **117, 183**

Arensberg, C. M. 1968b. "The urban in crosscultural perspective." In E. M. Eddy (ed.), *Urban Anthropology and Urban Studies*. Athens: University of Georgia Press. 31–47.

Argyle, M. 1968. "Religious observance." In D. L. Sills (ed.), *International Encyclopedia of the Social Sciences*. New York: Macmillan and Free Press.

Axelrod, M. 1956. "Urban structure and social participation." *American Sociological Review* 21 (February): 14–18.

Babchuck, N. and A. Booth. 1969. "Voluntary association membership: A longitudinal analysis," *American Sociological Review* (February): 31–45.

Bach, W. 1972. "Urban climate, air pollution and planning." In T. R. Detwyler and M. G. Marcus (eds.), *Urbanization and the Environment*. Belmont, Cal.: Duxbury: 69–96. **50**

Bagley, C. 1968. "Migration, race and mental health: A review of some recent research," *Race* 3. **80**

Bahr, H. M. 1973. *Skid Row: An Introduction to Disaffiliation*. New York: Oxford. **110, 138**

Baldassare, M. 1975. "The effects of density on social behavior and attitudes." *American Behavioral Scientist* 18 (July/August): 815–825.

Baldassare, M. and S. Feller. 1976. "Cultural variation in personal space: Theory, methods and evidence." *Ethos* 3 (Winter): 481–503. **158, 160**

Baldassare, M., and C. S. Fischer. 1975. "Suburban life: Powerlessness and need for affiliation." *Urban Affairs Quarterly* (March): 314–326. **220, 226**

Baldassare, M., and C. S. Fischer. 1976. "The relevance of crowding experiments to urban studies." In D. Stokols (ed.), *Psychological Perspectives on Environment and Behavior*. New York: Plenum Press: forthcoming. **163**

Ball-Rokeach, S. J. 1973. "Values and violence: A test of the subculture of violence thesis." *American Sociological Review* 38 (December): 736–749.

Balzac, H. de. 1962. *Pere Goriot* (trans. H. Reed). New York: New American Library. **95**

Banfield, E. C. 1958. *The Moral Basis of a Backward Society*. New York: Free Press. **17**

Banks, J. A. 1968. "Population change and the Victorian city." In C. Tilly (ed.), *An Urban World*. Boston: Little, Brown (1974): 358–368.

Barker, R. G. and P. V. Gump. 1964. *Big School, Small School*. Stanford, Cal.: Stanford University Press. **138, 182**

Barnett, S. 1973. "Urban is as urban does." *Urban Anthropology* 2 (Fall): 129–160. **135**

Baroja, J. C. 1963. "The city and the country: Reflexions on some ancient commonplaces." In C. Tilly (ed.), *An Urban World*. Boston: Little, Brown (1974): 473–485. **16**

Barth, F. 1969. "Introduction." In Barth (ed.), *Ethnic Groups and Boundaries*. Boston: Little, Brown.

Bascom, W. 1963. "The urban African and his world." In S. F. Fava (ed.), *Urbanism in World Perspective* (1968). New York: Crowell: 81–92. **78**

Bastide, H. and A. Girard. 1974a. "Mobilité de la population et motivations des personnes." *Population* 29 (May-June): 579–607.

Bastide, H. and A. Girard. 1974b. "Mobilité de la population et motivations des personnes, II: Les motifs de la mobilité." *Population* 29 (July): 743–769.

Bell, W. and M. Boat. 1957. "Urban neighborhoods and informal social relations." *American Journal of Sociology* 62 (January): 391–398. **139, 145**

Bell, W. 1959. "Social choice, life styles, and suburban residence." In W. M. Dobriner (ed.), *The Suburban Community*. New York: Putnam: 225–247. **220, 229**

Beranek, L. L. 1966. "Noise." *Scientific American* (December); Reprinted in K. Davis (ed.), *Cities*. San Francisco: Freeman (1973): 158–168. **50**

Berger, B. 1960. *Working-Class Suburb*. Berkeley: University of California Press. **210, 212, 220, 223, 226, 227, 230**

Berger, P., B. Berger, and H. Kellner. 1973. *The Homeless Mind*. New York: Vintage. **183**

Berkowitz, L. and B. McCaully. 1972. *Altruism and Helping Behavior*. New York: Academic Press. **187**

Bernard, J. 1973 *The Sociology of Community*. San Francisco: Scott Foresman.

Berry, B. J. L. 1967. *Geography of Market Centers and Retail Distribution*. Englewood Cliffs, N.J.: Prentice-Hall. **60, 87**

Berry, B. J. L. (ed.). 1972. *City Classification Handbook: Methods and Applications.* New York: Wiley. **87**

Berry, B. J. L. et al. 1976. "Opposition to integration." In B. Schwartz (ed.), *The Changing Face of the Suburbs.* Chicago: University of Chicago Press. **213**

Black, G. S. 1974. "Conflict in the community: A theory of the effects of community size." *American Political Science Review* 68 (September): 1245–1261. **219**

Blau, P. and O. D. Duncan. 1967. *The American Occupational Structure.* New York: Wiley. **77**

Blumenfeld, H. 1971. "Transportation in the modern metropolis." In L. S. Bourne (ed.), *Internal Structure of the City.* New York: Oxford: 231–240. **47**

Blumenthal, M.D., R. L. Kahn, F. M. Andrews, and K. B. Head. 1972. *Justifying Violence: Attitudes of American Men.* Ann Arbor, Mich.: Institute for Social Research, 1972. **193**

Boissevain, J. 1973. *Friends of Friends.* London: Basil Blackwell.

Borhek, J. T. 1970. "Ethnic-group cohesion." *American Journal of Sociology* 76 (July): 33–46. **130, 133**

Booth, A. 1975. "Final report: Urban crowding project." Mimeo. Canadian Ministry of State for Urban Affairs. **58, 162**

Bose, N. K. 1965. "Calcutta: A premature metropolis." In K. Davis (ed.), *Cities.* San Francisco: W. H. Freeman (1973): 251–262. **71**

Bourg, C. J. 1975. "Elderly in a southern metropolitan area." *The Gerontologist* 15 (February): 15–22. **224**

Bourne, L. S. (ed.). 1971. *Internal Structure of the City.* New York: Oxford.

Bradburn, N. M., S. Sudman and G. Glockel. 1970. *Racial Integration in American Neighborhoods.* Chicago: National Opinion Research Center.

Bradfield, S. 1973. "Selectivity in rural-urban migration: The case of Huaylas, Peru." In A. Southall (ed.), *Urban Anthropology.* New York: Oxford: 351–372. **80**

Brail, R. K., and F. S. Chapin, Jr. 1973. "Activity patterns of urban residents." *Environment and Behavior* 5 (June): 163–190. **86, 182**

Breese, G. (ed.). 1969. *The City in Newly Developing Countries.* Englewood Cliffs, N.J.: Prentice-Hall. **247**

Breton, R. 1964. "Institutional completeness of ethnic communities and the personal relations of immigrants." *American Journal of Sociology* 70 (September): 193–205. **65, 131**

Bruce-Briggs, B. 1974. "Gasoline prices and the suburban way of life." *The Public Interest* 37 (Fall): 131–136.

Bruner, E. M. 1961. "Urbanization and ethnic identity in North Sumatra." *American Anthropologist* 63 (1961): 508–521. **130**

Bruner, E. M. 1962. "Medan: The role of kinship in an Indonesian city." In W. Magnin (ed.), *Peasants in Cities.* Boston: Houghton Mifflin (1970): 122–134. **146**

Bruner, E. M. 1973a. "The expression of ethnicity in Indonesia." In A. Cohen (ed.), *Urban Ethnicity.* London: Tavistock: 251–280. **130, 132, 135**

Bruner, E. M. 1973b. "Kin and non-kin." In A. Southhall (ed.), *Urban Anthropology.* New York: Oxford: 373–392. **144, 150, 185**

Bryson, R. A. and J. E. Ross. 1972. "The climate of the city." In T. R. Detwyler and M. G. Marcus (eds.), *Urbanization and the Environment.* Belmont, Cal.: Duxbury: 51–68. **50**

Bultena, G. L. 1969. "Rural-urban differences in familial interaction." *Rural Sociology* 34 (March): 5–15. **146, 147**

Bureau of Labor Statistics. 1969. *Analysis of Work Stoppages, 1968.* Bulletin 164c. U.S. Department of Labor. Washington: U.S. Government Printing Office.

Bureau of the Census. 1968. *Current Population Reports.* Series P-23 No. 25. "Lifetime migration histories of the American people." Washington: U.S. Government Printing Office.

Bureau of the Census. 1969. *Current Population Reports.* Series P-23, Special Studies No. 27. "Trends in social and economic conditions in metropolitan areas." **213**

Bureau of the Census. 1971a. "General demographic trends for metropolitan areas, 1960 to 1970, final report PHC (2)-1 United States." *Census of Population and Housing: 1970.* **48, 72**

Bureau of the Census. 1971b. *Current Population Reports.* Series P-20, No. 218. "Household and family characteristics: March 1970." **143**

Bureau of the Census. 1972. *Census of Population: 1970, General Social and Economic Characteristics.* Final Report PC (1)-C1, United States Summary. **74, 77**

Bureau of the Census. 1973. *We the Americans: Our Cities and Suburbs.* **213**

Bureau of the Census. 1975. *Current Population Reports.* Series P-20, No. 273. "Mobility of the population of the United States: March 1970 to March 1974." **24**

Burgess, A. 1972. "Cucarachas and exiles, potential death and life enhancement." *The New York Times Magazine* (October 29). **18**

Burgess, E. W. and D. J. Bogue (eds.). 1964. *Contributions to Urban Sociology.* Chicago: University of Chicago Press. **29**

Burgess, E. W. and H. J. Locke. 1953. *The Family.* Second edition. New York: American Book Co. **224**

Burnham, D. 1974. "Most call crime worst city ill." *The New York Times* (January 16):1. **94**

Burstein, P. 1972. "Social structure and political participation in five countries." *American Journal of Sociology* 77 (May): 1087–1111.

Butler, E. W. et al. 1968. *Moving Behavior and Residential Choice.* Chapel Hill, N.C.: Center for Urban and Regional Studies. **209, 213**

Butterworth, D. S. 1962. "A study of the urbanization process among Mixtec migrants from Tilantongo to Mexico City." In W. Magnin (ed.), *Peasants in Cities.* Boston: Houghton Mifflin (1970): 98–113. **146, 170**

Calhoun, J. B. 1962. "Population density and social pathology." *Scientific American* 206: 139–148. **154, 159**

Callow, A. B., Jr. (ed.). 1973. *American Urban History.* Second edition. New York: Oxford.

Campbell, A. 1971. *White Attitudes Toward Black People.* Ann Arbor, Mich.: Institute for Social Research.

Campbell, A. K., and J. Dallenmyer. 1975. "Governance in a metropolitan society." In A. Hawley and V. Rock (eds.), *Metropolitan America in Contemporary Perspective.* New York: Halstead Press: 355–396.

Canby, V. 1974. "New York's woes are good box office." *The New York Times* (November 10), Section 2: 1.

Canter, D. 1974. "The menace of suburbia." *The San Francisco Examiner* (December 8): 4. **209**

Cantor, M. H. 1975. "Life space and the social support system of the inner city elderly of New York." *The Gerontologist* 15 (February): 23–26. **224**

Cantril, H. 1965. *The Pattern of Human Concerns.* New Brunswick, N.J.: Rutgers University Press. **77, 174, 175**

Carlos, S. 1970. "Suburban-urban religious participation." *American Journal of Sociology* 75 (March): 742–759.

Carnahan, D., W. Gove, and O. R. Galle. 1974. "Urbanization, population density and overcrowding." *Social Forces* 53 (September): 62–72. **48**

Carp, F. M. 1975. "Life-style and location within the city." *The Gerontologist* 75 (February): 27–33. **224**

Carpenter, D. B. 1960. "Urbanization and social change in Japan." *The Sociological Quarterly* (July): 155–166.

Carr, G. 1975. "Explaining urban form." Paper presented to American Sociological Association (August), San Francisco.

Carrothers, G. A. 1956. "An historical review of the gravity and potential concepts of human interaction." *Journal of the American Institute of Planners* 22 (Spring): 94–102.

Carstairs, G. M. 1969. "Overcrowding and human aggression." In H. D. Graham and T. R. Gurr (eds.), *Violence in America.* New York: Bantam, 751–764.

Cassel, J. 1972. "Health consequences of population density and crowding." In R. Gutman (ed.), *People and Buildings.* New York: Basic Books. **52, 162**

Castells, M. 1968. "Y-a-t-il une sociologie urbaine?" *Sociologie du Travail* 1: 72–90. (Translation by C. G. Pickvance appears in Pickvance [ed.], *Urban Sociology: Critical Essays.* London: Methuen: forthcoming.)

Castells, M. 1969. "Théorie et idéologie en sociologie urbaine." *Sociologie et Sociétés* 1: 171–191. (Translation appears in C. G. Pickvance [ed.], *Urban Sociology: Critical Essays.* London: Methuen: forthcoming.)

Childe, V. G. 1951. *Man Makes Himself.* New York: New American Library.

Chilsom, J. J., Jr. 1971. "Lead Poisoning." *Scientific American* (February); reprinted in K. Davis (ed.), *Cities.* San Francisco: Freeman (1973): 123–131. **52**

Chinoy, E. (ed.). 1973. *The Urban Future.* New York: Lieber-Atherton. **243**

Christian, J. J., J. A. Lloyd, and D. E. Davis. 1960. "Factors in the mass mortality of a herd of Sina deer, *Cervus nippon.*" *Chesapeake Science* 1: 79–95. **159**

Christie, R. and F.L. Geis. 1970. *Studies in Machiavellianism.* New York: Academic Press. **186**

Chudacoff, H. P. 1975. *The Evolution of American Urban Society.* Englewood Cliffs, N.J.: Prentice-Hall. **44**

Clark, S. D. 1966. *The Suburban Society.* Toronto: University of Toronto Press. **216, 220, 225, 232**

Clarke, M. 1974. "On the concept of 'sub-culture.' " *British Journal of Sociology* 25 (December): 428–441.

Clinard, M. B. 1964. "Deviant behavior: Urban-rural contrasts." In C. E. Elias, Jr., J. Gillies and S. Reimer (eds.), *Metropolis: Values in Conflict.* Belmont, Cal.: Wadsworth: 237–244. **166, 171, 195**

Clinard, M. B. and D. J. Abbott. 1973. *Crime in Developing Countries.* New York: Wiley Interscience. **185**

Cloward, R. A., and L. A. Ohlin. 1961. *Delinquency and Opportunity.* Glencoe, Ill.: Free Press. **93**

COFREMCA. 1974. "L'Humeur des Français en Decembre 1973." Multilith. **174, 176, 193**

Cohen, A. 1969. *Custom and Politics in Urban Africa.* Berkeley: University of California Press. **74, 135**

Cohen, S., D. C. Glass, and J. E. Singer. 1973. "Apartment noise, auditory discrimination, and reading ability in children." *Journal of Experimental Social Psychology* 9: 407–422. **50**

Coleman, J. S. 1957. *Community Conflict.* New York: Free Press.

Coleman, J. S. 1971. "Community disorganization and conflict." In R. K. Merton and R. Nisbet (eds.), *Contemporary Social Problems.* Third edition. New York: Harcourt Brace Jovanovich: 657–708. **117**

Commission on Population Growth and the American Future. 1972. *Population and the American Future.* New York: New American Library. **22**

Conzen, K. N. 1975. "Patterns of residence in early Milwaukee." In L. F. Schnore (ed.), *The New Urban History.* Princeton: Princeton University Press: 145–183. **214**

Cooper, C. C. 1972. "Resident dissatisfaction in multi-family housing." In W. M. Smith (ed.), *Behavior, Design, and Policy Aspects.* Green Bay, Wisc.: University of Wisconsin Press: 119–145. **58**

Cornelius, W. A., Jr. 1971. "The political sociology of cityward migration in Latin America: Toward empirical theory." In F. F. Rabinovitz and F. M. Trueblood (eds.), *Latin American Urban Research,* Vol. I. Beverly Hills, Cal.: Sage: 95–147. **82, 116, 130**

Cornelius, Wayne A. 1973. *Political Learning Among the Migrant Poor: The Impact of Residential Context.* Beverly Hills, Cal.: Sage.

Craven, S. and B. Wellman. 1973. "The network city." *Sociological Inquiry* 43: 57–88. **181, 182**

Crowley, R. W. 1973. "Reflection and further evidence on population size and industrial diversification." *Urban Studies* 19: 91–94.

Cuomo, M. 1974. *Forest Hills Diary: The Crisis of Low-Income Housing.* New York: Vintage. **191**

Curtis, J. 1971. "Voluntary association joining: A cross-cultural comparative note." *American Sociological Review* 36 (October): 872–880.

Curtis, J. and S. Hawkins. 1975. "Community size, social status and tolerance." Unpublished paper. University of Waterloo.

Dahl, R. A. 1967. "The city in the future of democracy." *American Political Science Review* 61 (December): 953–970. **250**

Dahl, R. A. and E. R. Tufte. 1973. *Size and Democracy.* Stanford: Stanford University Press. **103**

Danzger, M. H. 1970. "Critical mass and historical process as factors in community conflict." Paper presented to the American Sociological Association, Washington (September). **193**

Danzger, M. H. 1975. "Validating conflict data." *American Sociological Review* 40 (October): 570–584. **133, 193**

Darley, J. M., A. J. Teger, and L. D. Lewis. 1973. "Do groups always inhibit individuals' responses to potential emergencies?" *Journal of Personality and Social Psychology* 26 (June): 395–399. **187**

Davis, D. E. 1971. "The physiological effects of continued crowding." In A. Esser (ed.), *Behavior and Environment.* New York: Plenum Press: 133–148.

Davis, K. A. 1955. "The origin and growth of urbanization in the world." *American Journal of Sociology* 60 (March): 429–437. **5**

Davis, K. A. 1966. "The urbanization of the human population." In Scientific American Cities. New York: Knopf: 3–24. **5, 23, 247**

Davis, K. A. 1972. *World Urbanization 1950–1970*, Vol. II. Berkeley: Institute of International Studies. **5, 243, 247**

Davis, K. A. 1973. "Introduction." In K. Davis (ed.), *Cities.* San Francisco: Freeman: 9–18.

DeGrazia, S. 1962. *Of Time, Work and Leisure.* New York: Twentieth Century Fund. **87**

deJonge, D. 1962. "Images of urban areas." *Journal of American Institute of Planners* 28 (November).

Desor, J. A. 1971. "Toward a psychological theory of crowding." *Journal of Personality and Social Psychology* 33 (December): 444–456.

Deutsch, K. 1961. "On social communication and the metropolis." *Daedalus* 90 (Winter). **30**

Dobriner, W. M. 1963. *Class in Suburbia.* Englewood Cliffs, N.J.: Prentice-Hall: 127–141. **211, 220, 229**

Dohrenwend, Bruce, and Barbara Dohrenwend. 1972. "Psychiatric disorders in urban settings." In *American Handbook of Psychiatry.* New York: Basic Books.

Dollard, J. 1957. *Caste and Class in a Southern Town.* Third edition. New York: Doubleday Anchor. **108**

Donaldson, S. 1969. *The Suburban Myth.* New York: Columbia University Press. **24, 209, 217, 220, 223, 224, 226, 229**

Dotson, F. 1951. "Patterns of voluntary association among working-class families." *American Sociological Review* 16 (October): 687–693.

Doughty, P. L. 1970. "Behind the back of the city: 'Provincial' life in Lima, Peru." In W. Magnin (ed.), *Peasants in Cities.* Boston: Houghton Mifflin: pp. 30–46.

Doughty, P. L. 1972. "Peruvian migrant identity in the urban milieu." In T. Weaver and D. White (eds.), *The Anthropology of Urban Environments.* Monograph 11. Washington: Society for Applied Anthropology: 39–50.

Douvan, E. and Adelson, J. 1966. *The Adolescent Experience.* New York: Wiley. **196**

Downs, A. 1973. *Opening Up the Suburbs.* New Haven: Yale University Press. **209**

Dublin, L. 1963. *Suicide.* New York: Ronald. **167**

Dubos, R. 1970. "The social environment." In H. Proshansky and W. Ittelson (eds.), *Environmental Psychology.* New York: Holt: 202–208.

Duncan, O. D. 1957. "Optimum size of cities." In P. K. Hatt and A. J. Reiss, Jr., (eds.), *Cities and Society.* New York: Free Press: 759–772.

Durkheim, E. 1893. *The Division of Labor in Society* (trans. G. Simpson). New York: Free Press (1933). **113, 171**

Durkheim, E. 1897. *Suicide.* New York: Free Press (1951). **64, 167**

E.P.A. (Environmental Protection Agency). 1971. "The social impact of noise." Washington: U.S. Government Printing Office. **50**

Edel, M., J. R. Harris, and J. Rothenberg. 1975. "Urban concentration and deconcentration." In A. Hawley and V. Rock (eds.), *Metropolitan America in Contemporary Perspective.* New York: Halstead Press: 123–56. **24**

Efros, S. L. 1975. "The allure of Nevada City." *California Living* (January 26): 11. **83**

Einstadter, W. J. 1969. "The social organization of armed robbery." *Social Problems* 17 (Summer): 64–83.

Eisinger, P. K. 1973. "The urban crisis as a failure of 'community.' " Paper presented to the American Political Science Association, New Orleans. **84**

Eldridge, H. W. 1967. "Lessons learned from the British New Towns program." In H. W. Eldridge (ed.), *Taming Megalopolis, Volume II.* New York: Doubleday Anchor: 823–827.

Elgin, D., T. Thomas, T. Logothetti, and S. Cox. 1974. *City Size and the Quality of Life.* National Science Foundation (RANN). Washington: U.S. Government Printing Office. **50, 169, 252, 253**

Elwood, R. (ed.). 1974. *Future City.* New York: Pocket Books. **17**

Ennis, P. H. 1962. "The contextual dimension in voting." In W. M. McPhee and W. A. Glaser (eds.), *Public Opinions and Congressional Elections.* New York: Free Press: 180–211. **108**

Ennis, P. H. 1967. *Criminal Victimization in the United States: A Report of a National Survey.* Chicago: National Opinion Research Center. **91, 92**

Epstein, A. L. 1967. "Urbanization and social change in Africa." *Current Anthropology* 8: 275–296. **136**

Erickson, M. L. 1971. "The group context of delinquent behavior." *Social Problems* 19 (Summer): 114–128.

Erlanger, H. S. 1974. "Social class and corporal punishment in childrearing: A reassessment." *American Sociological Review* 39 (February): 68–85.

Ernst, R. 1949. "The living conditions of the immigrant." In A. M. Wakestein (ed.), *The Urbanization of America.* Boston: Houghton Mifflin (1970): 257–268. **54**

Evans, A. W. 1973. *The Economics of Residential Location.* London: Macmillan. **212**

Evans, G. W. and R. B. Howard. 1973. "Personal space." *Psychological Bulletin* 80 (October): 334–344.

Farley, R. 1976. "Components of suburban population growth." In B. Schwartz (ed.), *Changing Face of the Suburbs.* Chicago: University of Chicago Press. **213, 214, 215**

Fava, S. F. 1959. "Contrasts in neighboring: New York City and a suburban county." In W. M. Dobringer (ed.), *The Suburban Community.* New York: Putnam: 122–130. **219, 220**

Fava, S. F. 1975. "Beyond suburbia." *Annals* 422 (March): 10–24.

Feller, I. 1973. "Determinants of the composition of urban invention." *Economic Geography* 49 (January): 47–58.

Fellin, P. and E. Litwak. 1963. "Neighborhood cohesion under conditions of mobility." *American Sociological Review* 28 (June): 364–376.

Ferdinand, T. N. 1967. "The criminal patterns of Boston since 1849." *American Journal of Sociology* 73 (July): 84–99. **89**

Fine, J., H. D. Glenn, and J. K. Monts. 1971. "The residential segregation of occupational groups in central cities and suburbs." *Demography* 8 (February): 91–101.

Firey, W., C. P. Loomis, and J. A. Beegle. 1957. "The fusion of urban and rural." In P. K. Hatt and A. J. Reiss, Jr. (eds.), *Cities and Society.* New York: Free Press: 214–222.

Fischer, C. S. 1971. "A research note on urbanism and tolerance." *American Journal of Sociology* 76 (March): 847–856.

Fischer, C. S. 1972. " 'Urbanism as a way of life': A review and an agenda." *Sociological Methods and Research* 1 (November): 187–242.

Fischer, C. S. 1973a. "On urban alienation and anomie." *American Sociological Review* 38 (June): 311–326. **143, 170, 173**

Fischer, C. S. 1973b. "Urban malaise." *Social Forces* 52 (December): 221–235. **23, 56, 57, 64, 174, 175, 227**

Fischer, C. S. 1975a. "The study of urban community and personality." *Annual Review of Sociology* 1: 67–89. **6, 28**

Fischer, C. S. 1975b. "Toward a subcultural theory of urbanism." *American Journal of Sociology* 80 (May): 1319–1341. **35**

Fischer, C. S. 1975c. "The effects of urban life on traditional values." *Social Forces* 53 (March): 420–432. **195, 196**

Fischer, C. S. 1975d. "The city and political psychology." *American Political Science Review* 69 (June): 559–571. **218**

Fischer, C. S. 1975e. "The myth of 'territoriality' in van der Berghe's 'Bringing beasts back in.' " *American Sociological Review* 40 (October): 674–676.

Fischer, C. S. 1976. "Alienation: Trying to bridge the chasm." *British Journal of Sociology* 27 (March): 35–49. **169**

Fischer, C. S., M. Baldassare, and R. J. Ofshe. 1975. "Crowding studies and urban life: A critical review." *Journal of American Institute of Planners* 31 (November): 406–418. **155**

Fischer, C. S., M. Baldassare, K. Gerson, R. M. Jackson, L. M. Jones, and C. A. Stueve.

1977. *Networks and Places: Social Relations in the Urban Setting*. New York: Free Press. **137**

Fischer, C. S. and R. M. Jackson. 1976. "Suburbs, networks, and attitudes." In B. Schwartz (ed.), *The Changing Face of the Suburbs*. Chicago: University of Chicago Press: 279–306. **219, 220**

Foley, D. 1975. "Accessibility for residents in the metropolitan environment." In A. Hawley and V. Rock (eds.), *Metropolitan America: Papers on State of Knowledge*. New York: Halstead Press: 157–200. **212**

Foote, M. N., J. Abu-Lughod, M. M. Foley, and L. Winnick. 1960. *Housing Choices and Housing Constraints*. New York: McGraw-Hill.

Forbes, G. B. and H. F. Gromoll. 1971. "The lost-letter technique as a measure of social variables: Some exploratory findings." *Social Forces* 50 (September): 113–115.

Forstall, R. L. 1975. "Trends in metropolitan and nonmetropolitan population growth since 1970." Washington: Population Division, U.S. Bureau of the Census.

Foster, G. M. 1960–61. "Interpersonal relations in peasant society." *Human Organization* 19 (Winter): 174–184. **108, 170**

Foster, G. M. 1961. "The dyadic contact: A model for the social structure of a Mexican peasant village." *American Anthropologist* 63 (December): 1173–1192. **183**

Foster, G. M. 1967. *Tzintzuntzan: Mexican Peasants in a Changing World*. Boston: Little, Brown.

Foster, L. 1974. "Dimensions of 'urban unease' in ten cities." *Urban Affairs Quarterly* 10 (December): 185–196. **84**

Frankenburg, R. 1965. *Communities in Britain: Social Life in Town and Country*. Baltimore: Penguin. **118, 181, 182**

Freedman, J. L. 1973. "The effects of population density on humans." In J. T. Fawcett (ed.), *Psychological Perspectives on Population*. New York: Basic Books: 209–238.

Freedman, J. L. 1975. *Crowding and Behavior*. San Francisco: Freeman. **163**

Freedman, J. L. and P. Erlich. 1971. "The impact of crowding on human behavior." *The New York Times* (September 11): 27. **163**

Freedman, J. L., S. Klevansky, and P. R. Ehrlich. 1971. "The effect of crowding on human task performance." *Journal of Applied Social Psychology* 1 (March): 7–25.

Freedman, J. L., A. Levy, R. Buchanan, and J. Price. 1972. "Crowding and human aggressiveness." *Journal of Experimental Social Psychology* 8: 528–547.

Freeman, H. E. and J. M. Giovannoni. 1969. "Social psychology of mental health." In G. Lindzey and E. Aronson (eds.), *The Handbook of Social Psychology*, Vol. V. Reading, Mass.: Addison-Wesley: 660–719.

Freeman, S. T. 1970. *Neighbors: The Social Contract in a Castilian Hamlet*. Chicago: University of Chicago Press. **119, 183**

Friedl, E. 1964. "Lagging emulation in post-peasant society." *American Anthropologist* 66: 569–586. **197**

Friedmann, J. and J. Miller. 1965. "The urban field." *Journal of the American Institute of Planners* 21 (November): 312–320.

Fuguitt, G. V., and D. R. Field. 1972. "Some population characteristics of villages differentiated by size, location and growth." *Demography* 9 (May): 295–308.

Fuguitt, G. V., and J. J. Zuiches. 1973. "Residential preferences and population distribution: Results of a national survey." Paper presented to Rural Sociological Society, College Park, Md. (August). **24, 226**

Galle, O. R., W. R. Gove, J. M. McPherson. 1972. "Population density and pathology: What are the relationships for man?" *Science* 176 (April): 23–30; reprinted in K. Schirwian (ed.), *Comparative Urban Structure*. Lexington, Mass.: D. C. Heath (1974): 198–214. **157**

Gans, H. J. 1951. "Park Forest: The birth of a Jewish community." *Commentary* 11 (April): 330–339. **215, 222**

Gans, H. J. 1957. "Progress of a suburban Jewish community: Park Forest revisited." *Commentary* 23 (May): 113–122. **222**

Gans, H. J. 1962a. "Urbanism and suburbanism as ways of life: A reevaluation of definitions." In A. M. Rose (ed.), *Human Behavior and Social Processes*. Boston: Houghton Mifflin: 625–648. **34, 210, 230**

Gans, H. J. 1962b. *The Urban Villagers*. New York: Free Press. **34, 114, 133**

Gans, H. J. 1967. *The Levittowners*. New York: Vintage. **34, 210, 211, 212, 215, 216, 220, 221–222, 223, 224, 225, 227, 229, 230**

Gans, H. J. 1969. "Negro-Jewish conflict in New York City." *Midstream* 15 (March): 3–15. **191**

Garigue, P. 1956. "French Canadian kinship and urban life." *American Anthropologist* 58 (December): 1091–1101.

Gates, A. S., H. Stevens, and B. Wellman. 1973. "What makes a good neighbor?" Paper presented to the American Sociological Association. New York (August). **58**

Gelfant, B. H. 1954. *The American City Novel.* Norman: University of Oklahoma Press. **20**

George, M. D. 1964. *London Life in the Eighteenth Century.* New York: Harper Torchbooks. **12**

Gergen, K. J. 1972. "Multiple identity." *Psychology Today* (May): 31ff. **181, 183**

Germani, G. 1966. "Mass immigration and modernization in Argentina." *Studies in Comparative International Development.* St. Louis: Washington University. **74**

Gibbs, J. P. 1971. "Suicide." In R. K. Merton and R. A. Nisbet (eds.), *Contemporary Social Problems.* Third edition. New York: Harcourt Brace Jovanovich: 271–312. **167**

Gillespie, D. L. 1971. "Who has the power? The marital struggle." *Journal of Marriage and the Family* 33 (August): 445–458.

Gillis, A. R. 1974. "Population density and social pathology." *Social Forces* 53 (December): 306–314. **58**

Ginsberg, Y. 1975. *Jews in a Changing Neighborhood.* New York: Free Press. **94, 191**

Girard, A., H. Bastide, and G. Pourcher. 1966. "Geographic mobility and urban concentration in France." In C. J. Jansen (ed.), *Readings in the Sociology of Migration.* Oxford: Pergamon (1970): 179–202. **22**

Girdner, J. H. 1896. "To abate the plague of city noises." *North American Review;* reprinted in A. Cook, M. Gittell, and H. Mack (eds.), *City Life, 1865–1900.* New York: Praeger (1973). **12**

Glaab, C. N. and A. T. Brown, 1967. *A History of Urban America.* New York: Macmillan. **91–92**

Glass, D. C. and J. E. Singer. 1972. *Urban Stress.* New York: Academic Press. **50**

Glazer, N., and D. P. Moynihan. 1970. *Beyond the Melting Pot.* Revised edition. Cambridge: M.I.T. Press. **105, 129**

Glenn, N. K. and J. Alston. 1967. "Rural-urban differences in reported attitudes and behavior." *Southwestern Social Science Quarterly* 47 (March) 1967: 381–406. **197**

Goffman, E. 1971. *Relations in Public.* New York: Basic Books. **190**

Goldsmith, J. R. and E. Jonsson. 1973. "Health effects of community noise." *American Journal of Public Health* 63 (September): 782–793. **50**

Goldsmith, S. and C. Goldscheider. 1968. *Jewish-Americans.* Englewood Cliffs, N.J.: Prentice-Hall. **222**

Goode, W. J. 1963. *World Revolution and Family Patterns.* New York: Free Press. **143, 145, 195**

Gordon, D. N. 1970. "Immigrants and municipal voting turnout." *American Sociological Review* 35 (August): 665–81. **129**

Governor's Commission on the Los Angeles Riots. 1965. *Violence in the City–An End or a Beginning?* Distributed by College Book Store, Los Angeles, Cal. **81**

Graham, F. P. 1969. "A contemporary history of American crime rates." In H. D. Graham and T. R. Gurr (eds.), *The History of Violence in America.* New York: Bantam: 485–504. **89**

Grasmick, H. G. 1974. "Rural culture and the Wallace movement in the South." *Rural Sociology* 39 (Winter): 454–470.

Greer, S. 1956. "Urbanism reconsidered: A comparative study of local areas in a metropolis." *American Sociological Review* 21 (February): 19–25. **145**

Greer, S. 1962. *The Emerging City.* New York: Free Press. **104, 122, 196, 218**

Greer, S. 1963. *Metropolitics.* New York: Wiley.

Greer, S. 1972. *The Urbane View.* New York: Oxford. **232**

Greer, S. and A. L. Greer. 1975. "Suburban politics." In B. Schwartz (ed.), *The Changing Face of the Suburbs.* Chicago: University of Chicago Press.

Greer, S. and P. Orleans. 1962. "The mass society and the parapolitical structure." *American Sociological Review* 27 (October): 643–646.

Griffit, W. and R. Veitch. 1971. "Hot and crowded." *Journal of Personality and Social Psychology* 17: 92–98. **163**

Gruenberg, B. 1974. *How Free Is Time?* Ph. D. dissertation. University of Michigan. **216**

Guest, A. M. 1971. "Retesting the Burgess zonal hypothesis." *American Journal of Sociology* 76 (May): 1094–1108. **213**

Guest, A. M. 1972. "Patterns of family location." *Demography* 9 (February): 159–171.

Guest, A. 1975. "Journey to work, 1960–70." *Social Forces* 54 (September): 220–225. **216**

Gulick, J. 1973. "Urban anthropology." In J. J. Honigman (ed.), *Handbook of Social and Cultural Anthropology.* Chicago: Rand-McNally: 979–1029. **143, 145**

Gurin, G., J. Veroff, and S. Feld. 1960. *Americans View Their Mental Health.* New York: Basic Books. **166**

Gurr, T. R. 1971. *Why Men Rebel.* Princeton: Princeton University Press.

Guterman, S. S. 1969. "In defense of Wirth's 'Urbanism as a way of life.' " *American Journal of Sociology* 74 (March): 492–499.

Gutheim, F. 1967. "Continental Europe offers new town builders experience." In H. W. Eldridge (ed.), *Taming Megalopolis, Volume II.* Garden City, N.Y.: Doubleday Anchor: 823–837.

Gutkind, P. C. W. 1965. "African urbanism, mobility, and social network." In G. Breese (ed.), *The City in Newly Developing Countries.* Englewood Cliffs, N.J.: Prentice-Hall (1969): 389–400. **107**

Hacker, A. 1973. "The city's comings, goings." *The New York Times* (December 2): E-5. **207**

Hall, E. 1966. *The Hidden Dimension.* New York: Doubleday Anchor. **160, 162**

Haller, O. and C. E. Wolff. 1962. "Personality orientations of farm, village, and urban boys." *Rural Sociology* 27 (September): 275–293.

Halpern, J. 1965. "Peasant culture and urbanization in Yugoslavia." *Human Organization* 24: 62–174. **82**

Handlin, O. H. 1951. *The Uprooted.* New York: Grosset and Dunlap.

Handlin, O. H. 1969. *Boston's Immigrants.* Revised edition. New York: Atheneum. **74, 135**

Handlin, O. H., and J. Burchard (eds.). 1961. *The Historian and the City.* Cambridge: M.I.T. Press.

Hanna, W. J. and J. L. Hanna. 1971. *Urban Dynamics in Black Africa.* Chicago: Aldine-Atherton. **22, 24, 71, 74, 80, 135**

Hannerz, U. 1969. *Soulside.* New York: Columbia University Press. **138–139**

Harris, L. 1970. "A *Life* poll." *Life* 68 (January 9): 102. **21**

Hauser, P. H. (ed.). 1957. *Urbanization in Asia and the Far East.* Calcutta: UNESCO.

Hawley, A. 1971. *Urban Society.* New York: Ronald Press. **52, 145, 207, 214, 247, 253**

Hawley, A. and B. Zimmer. 1971. *The Metropolitan Community.* Beverly Hills, Cal.: Sage. **174, 211, 214, 218, 225–226**

Heberle, R. 1960. "The normative element in neighborhood relations." *Pacific Sociological Review* 3 (Spring): 3–11. **117, 118**

Hechter, M. 1974. "The political economy of ethnic change." *American Journal of Sociology* 79 (March): 1151–1178.

Herbert, D. 1972. *Urban Geography.* New York: Praeger. **87, 216**

Heshka, S. and Y. Nelson. 1972. "Interpersonal speaking distance as a function of age, sex and relationship." *Sociometry* 35 (December): 491–499. **160**

Higgs, R. 1975. "Urbanization and inventiveness in the United States, 1870–1920." In L. F. Schnore (ed.), *The New Urban History.* Princeton, N.J.: Princeton University Press: 247–259.

Hirabayashi, J., W. Willard, and L. Kemnitzer. 1972. "Pan-Indianism in the urban setting." In T. Weaver and D. White (eds.), *The Anthropology of Urban Environments.* Monograph 11. Washington: Society for Applied Anthropology: 77–87. **131**

Hobsbawm, E. 1959. *Primitive Rebels.* New York: Norton.

Hoch, I. 1972. "Income and city size." *Urban Studies* 9 (October): 299–328. **24, 77**

Hoffman, M. 1968. *The Gay World.* New York: Basic Books. **111, 195**

Homans, G. C. 1974. *Social Behavior: Its Elementary Forms.* New York: Harcourt Brace Jovanovich. **235**

Hoover, E. M. 1972. "Policy objectives for population redistribution." In S. M. Mazie (ed.), *Population, Distribution, and Policy.* Volume V, Research Reports of U.S. Commission on Population and the American Future. Washington: U.S. Government Printing Office: 649–664.

Hoover, E. M. and R. Vernon. 1959. *Anatomy of a Metropolis.* New York: Doubleday Anchor. **207**

Hoover, J. E. 1971. *Crime in the United States, 1970.* Federal Bureau of Investigation. Washington: U. S. Government Printing Office.

Horowitz, R. and G. Schwartz. 1974. "Honor, normative ambiguity and gang violence." *American Sociological Review* 39 (April): 224–237.

Horton, F. E. and D. R. Reynolds. 1971. "Effects of urban spatial structure on individual behavior." *Economic Geography* 47 (January): 36–48.

Howe, I. 1971. "The city in literature." *Commentary* (May). **16**

Hoyt, H. 1969. "Growth and structure of twenty-one great world cities." In G. Breese (ed.), *The City in Newly Developing Countries.* Englewood Cliffs, N.J.: Prentice-Hall: 205 –218. **46, 207, 214**

Husain, A. F. A. 1956. "Dacca." In R. B. Textor et al. *Social Implications of Industrialization and Urbanization: Five Studies in Asia.* Calcutta: UNESCO: 107–142. **133**

Hynson, L. M., Jr. 1975. "Rural-urban differences in satisfaction among the elderly." *Rural Sociology* 40 (Spring): 64–66. **176**

Inkeles, A. 1969. "Making men modern: On the causes and consequences of individual change in six developing countries." *American Journal of Sociology* 75 (September): 208–225.

Jackson, K. T. 1975. "Urban deconcentration in the nineteenth century." In L. F. Schnore (ed.), *The New Urban History.* Princeton: Princeton University Press: 110–144.

Jacobs, J. 1961. *The Death and Life of Great American Cities.* New York: Vintage. **114**

Jacoby, S. 1974. "49 million singles can't all be right." *New York Times Magazine* (February 17): 13ff. **73**

Janowitz, M. 1967. *The Community Press in an Urban Setting.* Second edition. Chicago: University of Chicago Press. **122**

Jenkins, G. 1968. "Urban violence in Africa." *American Behavioral Scientist* 11 (March-April): 37–39. **108**

Johnston, F. J. 1971. *Urban Residential Patterns.* New York: Praeger.

Jones, E. 1966. *Towns and Cities.* New York: Oxford University Press. **71**

Jones, E. E. and R. E. Nisbett. 1972. "The actor and the observer: Divergent perceptions of the causes of behavior." In E. E. Jones et al. (eds.), *Attribution: Perceiving the Cause of Behavior.* Morriston, N.J.: General Learning Press: 79–94.

Jones, L. M. 1974. *The Labor Force Participation of Married Women.* Master's thesis. Department of City and Regional Planning, University of California, Berkeley.

Juvenal. 1958. *The Satires of Juvenal* (trans. by R. Humphries). Bloomington: Indiana University Press. **16**

Kasarda, J. D. 1972a. "The impact of suburban population growth on central city service functions." *American Journal of Sociology* 77 (May): 1111–1124. **214**

Kasarda, J. D. 1972b. "The theory of ecological expansion." *Social Forces* 51 (December): 166–175. **216**

Kasarda, J. D. 1976. "The changing structure of metropolitan America." In B. Schwartz (ed.), *The Changing Face of the Suburbs.* Chicago: University of Chicago Press: 113–136. **212, 216**

Kasarda, J. D., and M. Janowitz. 1974. "Community attachment in mass society." *American Sociological Review* 39 (June): 328–339.

Kasarda, J. D. and G. V. Redfearn. 1975. "Differential patterns of city and suburban growth." *Journal of Urban History* 2 (November): 43–66. **47**

Keller, S. 1968. *The Urban Neighborhood.* New York: Random House. **114, 118–119, 123**

Kelley, C. M. 1974. *Crime in the United States, 1973.* Federal Bureau of Investigation. Washington: U.S. Government Printing Office. **216**

Kerner Commission. 1968. *Report of the National Advisory Commission on Civil Disorders.* Washington: U.S. Government Printing Office.

Kesselman, M. 1966. "French local politics: A statistical examination of grass roots consensus." *American Political Science Review* 60 (December): 963–974. **104**

Key, W. H. 1968. "Rural-urban social participation." In S. F. Fava (ed.), *Urbanism in World Perspective.* New York: Crowell: 305–312. **146**

Keyes, F. 1958. "The correlation of social phenomena with community size." *Social Forces* 36 (May): 311–315.

Kimball, T. 1965. "The rural community." In C. M. Arensberg and S. T. Kimball, *Culture and Community*. New York: Harcourt Brace Jovanovich: 117–134. **108**

King, S. S. 1971. "Supermarkets hub of suburbs." *The New York Times* (February 7). **212**

Kish, L. 1954. "Differentiation in metropolitan areas." *American Sociological Review* 19 (August): 388–398.

Klatzky, S. R. 1971. *Patterns of Contact with Relatives*. Washington: American Sociological Association. **144, 146**

Kleinfeld, N. R. 1972. "How do you get rid of a dead elephant? Move it to New York: City's offal truck will take expired rhinoceroses, yaks or mules offal your hands." *Wall Street Journal* (October 3): 1.

Komarovsky, M. 1946. "The voluntary associations of urban dwellers." *American Sociological Review* 11 (December): 686–698.

Konig, R. 1968. *Community*. London: Routledge and Kegan Paul.

Kornblum, W. 1974. *Blue Collar Community*. Chicago: University of Chicago Press. **36, 45, 103, 119, 129**

Korte, C. and N. Kerr. 1975. "Response to altruistic opportunities in urban and non-urban settings." *Journal of Social Psychology* 95: 183–184.

Korte, C., I. Ypma, and A. Toppen. 1975. "Helpfulness in Dutch Society as a function of urbanization and environmental input level." *Journal of Personality and Social Psychology* 32 (6): 996–1003.

Koyama, T. 1970. "Rural-urban comparisons of kinship relations in Japan." in R. Hill and R. Konig (eds.), *Families in East and West*. Paris: Mouton: 318–337. **141, 144, 146**

Krapf-Askari, E. 1969. *Yoruba Towns and Cities*. Oxford, England: Clarendon. **78**

Lane, R. E. 1969. "Urbanization and criminal violence in the 19th century: Massachusetts as a test case." In H. D. Graham and T. R. Gurr (eds.), *The History of Violence in America*. New York: Bantam: 468–484. **89**

Langer, W. L. 1964. "The black death." *Scientific American* (February); reprinted in K. Davis (ed.), *Cities*. San Francisco: Freeman (1973): 106–112.

Lansing, J. B. 1966. *Residential Relocation and Urban Mobility*. Ann Arbor, Mich.: Survey Research Center, University of Michigan. **51, 213**

Lansing, J. B. and G. Hendricks. 1967. *Living Patterns and Attitudes in the Detroit Region*. Detroit: Southeast Michigan Council of Governments. **59, 207, 209, 216**

Lantz, H. R. 1971. *Coaltown*. Second edition. Carbondale, Ill.: Southern Illinois University Press. **108, 184**

Lapidus, I. M. 1966. *Muslim Cities in the Later Middle Ages*. Cambridge: Harvard University Press. **11, 12, 116**

Laslett, P. 1973. "The comparative history of household and family." In M. Gordon (ed.), *The American Family in Historical Perspective*. New York: St. Martin's Press: 19–33. **143**

Lasswell, T. E. 1959. "Social class and size of community." *American Journal of Sociology* 64 (March): 505–508.

Latané, B. and J. M. Dabbs, Jr. 1975. "Sex, group size and helping in three cities." *Sociometry* 38 (June): 180–194.

Latané, B. and J. M. Darley. 1969. "Bystander 'apathy.' " *American Scientist* 57: 244–268. **187**

Laumann, E. O. 1966. *Prestige and Association in an Urban Community*. Indianapolis: Bobbs-Merrill. **108**

Laumann, E. O. 1973. *Bonds of Pluralism*. New York: Wiley.

Lawrence, J. E. S. 1974. "Science and sentiment: Overview of research on crowding and human behavior." *Psychological Bulletin* 81 (10): 712–720.

Leeds, A. 1973. "Locality power in relation to supralocal power institutions." In A. Southall (ed.), *Urban Anthropology*. New York: Oxford: 15–42. **116**

Lees, L. H. 1969. "Patterns of lower-class life: Irish slum communities in nineteenth-century London." In S. Thernstrom and R. Sennett (eds.), *Nineteenth-Century Cities*. New Haven: Yale University Press: 359–385.

Leevey, J. R. 1950. "Leisure time of the American housewife." *Sociology and Social Research* 35 (November): 99–105. **86, 144**

Levine, D. N. 1975. "Simmel at a distance: On the history and systematics of the sociology of the stranger." Paper presented to American Sociological Association, San Francisco (August). **83**

Levine, D. N., E. B. Carter, and E. M. Gorman. 1976. "Simmel's influence on American sociology: II." *American Journal of Sociology* 81 (March). **30**

Lewis, O. 1952. "Urbanization without breakdown." *Scientific Monthly* 75 (July): 31–41. **34, 146**

Lewis, O. 1965. "Further observations on the folk-urban continuum and urbanization." In P.H. Hauser and L. Schnore (eds.), *The Study of Urbanization.* New York: Wiley: 491–503. **34, 142, 146**

Leyhausen, P. 1965. "The Communal Organization of Solitary Mammals." *Symposium of the Zoological Society of London* 14: 249–263.

Lieberson, S. 1962. "Suburbs and ethnic residential patterns." *American Journal of Sociology* 67 (May): 673–681. **222**

Lieberson, S., G. Dalto, and M. E. Johnston. 1975. "The course of mother-tongue diversity in nations." *American Journal of Sociology* 81 (July): 34–62.

Liebow, E. 1967. *Tally's Corner.* Boston: Little, Brown. **138**

Lindsey, R. 1975. "Economy mars belief in the American dream." *The New York Times* (October 26): 1. **175**

Lipowski, Z. J. 1975. "Sensory information and inputs overload: Behavior effects." *Comprehensive Psychiatry* 16 (May/June): 199–221.

Lipset, S. M. 1963. *Political Man.* New York: Doubleday Anchor. **193**

Lipset, S. M., M. Trow and J. S. Coleman. 1956. *Union Democracy.* New York: Doubleday Anchor. **110**

Little, K. L. 1965a. "The migrant and the urban community." In S. F. Fava (ed.), *Urbanism in World Perspective.* New York: Crowell (1968): 312–321.

Little, K. L. 1965b. *West African Urbanization: A Study of Voluntary Associations in Social Change.* Cambridge, Eng.: Cambridge University Press.

Little, K. L. 1973. *African Women in Towns.* London: Cambridge University Press. **22, 71, 134**

Litwak, E. 1960. "Geographical mobility and extended family cohesion." *American Sociological Review* 25 (June): 385–394.

Litwak, E. and A. Szelenyi. 1969. "Primary group structures and their functions: Kin, neighbors and friends." *American Sociological Review* 34 (August): 465–481. **144**

Lodhi, A. Q. and C. Tilly. 1973. "Urbanization, crime and collective violence in 19th century France." *American Journal of Sociology* 79 (September): 296–318. **193**

Lofland, L. 1972. "Self-management in public settings: Part I." *Urban Life and Culture* 1 (April): 93–108. **83**

Lofland, L. 1973. *A World of Strangers.* New York: Basic Books. **19, 85, 190**

Long, L. H. and P. C. Glick. 1976. "Family patterns in suburban areas." In B. Schwartz (ed.), *The Changing Face of the Suburbs.* Chicago: University of Chicago Press. **213**

Lopata, H. Z. 1964. "The function of voluntary associations in an ethnic community." In E. W. Burgess and D. J. Bogue (eds.), *Urban Sociology.* Chicago: University of Chicago Press (1967): 117–137. **131**

Lopata, H. Z. 1972. *Occupation: Housewife.* New York: Oxford.

Lorenz, K. 1966. *On Aggression* (trans. by M. K. Wilson). New York: Bantam. **163**

Lorinskas, R. A., B. W. Hawkins, and S. D. Edwards. 1969. "The persistence of ethnic voting in urban and rural areas." *Social Science Quarterly* 49 (March): 891–899. **130**

Lowe, G. D. and C. W. Peek. 1974. "Location and lifestyle." *Rural Sociology* 39 (Fall): 392–420.

Lowry, W. P. 1967. "The climate of cities." *Scientific American* 217 (August): 15–23; reprinted in K. Davis (ed.), *Cities.* Freeman (1973): 141–150. **50**

Lynch, K. 1960. *The Image of the City.* Cambridge: M.I.T. Press.

Malcolm, A. H. 1974. "Crime follows population from cities to suburbs." *The New York Times* (April 21): 49. **216**

Mangin, W. 1967. "Squatter settlements." In K. Davis (ed.), *Cities.* San Francisco: Freeman (1973): 233–240. **80**

Mangin, W. (ed.). 1970. *Peasants in Cities.* Boston: Houghton Mifflin.

Mann, P. H. 1964. *An Approach to Urban Sociology.* London: Routledge and Kegan Paul. **21, 53, 166**

Marans, R. W. and W. Rodgers. 1975. "Toward an understanding of community satisfaction." In A. Hawley and V. Rock (eds.), *Metropolitan America in Contemporary*

Perspective. New York: Halstead Press: 299–354 **23, 57, 59, 95, 174, 175, 211, 217, 227**

Marden, D. G. 1966. "A demographic and ecological analysis of the distribution of physicians in metropolitan America." *American Journal of Sociology* 72 (November): 290–300.

Marshall, H. 1973. "Suburban life styles: A contribution to the debate." In C. H. Masotti and J. K. Hadden (eds.), *The Urbanization of the Suburbs.* Urban Affairs Annual Review, No. 7. Beverly Hills, Cal.: Sage: 123–148. **220**

Martin, R. D. 1972. "Concepts of human territoriality." In P. J. Veko, R. Tringham and G. W. Dimbelby (eds.), *Man, Settlement and Urbanism.* Cambridge, Mass.: Schenkman: 427–445.

Martin, W. T. 1959. "The structuring of social relationships engendered by suburban residence." In W. M. Dobriner (ed.), *The Suburban Community.* New York: Putnam: 95–103. **218**

Mathiasson, C. J. 1974. "Coping in a new urban environment: Mexican-Americans in Milwaukee." *Urban Anthropology* 3 (Fall): 262–277. **131**

Mazie, S. M. and S. Rawlings. 1972. "Public attitude towards population distribution." In S. M. Mazie (ed.), *Population, Distribution and Policy.* Research Report V, Commission on Population Growth. Washington: U.S. Government Printing Office: 599–616. **252**

McCarthy, J. D., O. R. Galle, and W. Zimmern. 1975. "Population density, social structure, and interpersonal violence." *American Behavioral Scientist* 18 (July/August): 771–791. **91**

McCausland, J. L. 1972. "Crime in the suburbs." In C. M. Haar (ed.), *The End of Innocence: A Suburban Reader.* Glenview, Ill.: Scott, Foresman: 61–64. **216**

McDermott, W. 1961. "Air pollution and public health." *Scientific American* (October); reprinted in K. Davis (ed.), *Cities.* San Francisco: Freeman (1973): 132–140. **52**

McDonald, J. S. and L. D. McDonald. 1964. "Chain migration, ethnic neighborhood formation, and social networks." In C. Tilly (ed.), *An Urban World.* Boston: Little, Brown (1974): 226–235.

McGahan, P. 1972. "The neighbor role and neighboring in a highly urban area." *Sociological Quarterly* 13 (Summer): 397–408.

McGee, T. G. 1975. "An aspect of urbanization in South-East Asia." In E. Jones (ed.), *Readings in Social Geography.* London: Oxford University Press: 224–239. **71**

McPherson, J. M. 1975. "Population density and social pathology: A reexamination." *Sociological Symposium* 14 (Fall): 77–92.

Mead, G. H. 1934. *Mind, Self, and Society.* Chicago: University of Chicago Press. **181**

Meier, R. L. 1962. *A Communications Theory of Urban Growth.* Cambridge: M.I.T. Press. **30, 64, 181**

Merton, R. K. 1938a. "Social structure and anomie." In *Social Theory and Social Structure.* Revised and expanded edition. New York: Free Press (1968): 185–214. **64, 93, 171**

Merton, R. K. 1938b. *Science, Technology and Society in Seventeenth Century England.* New York: Howard Fertig (1970).

Merton, R. K. 1964. "Anomie, anomia, and social interaction: Contexts of deviant behavior." In M. B. Clinard (ed.), *Anomie and Deviant Behavior.* New York: Free Press: 213–242. **34**

Michelson, W. 1970. *Man and His Urban Environment.* Reading, Mass.: Addison-Wesley. **57, 58, 162**

Michelson, W. 1973a. "Environmental change." Research Paper No. 60, Centre for Urban and Community Studies, University of Toronto. **58, 59, 212, 216, 220, 224, 225, 226, 228, 229, 232**

Michelson, W. 1973b. "The reconciliation of 'subjective' and 'objective' data on physical environment in the community." *Sociological Inquiry* 43: 147–173. **58**

Michelson, W., D. Belgue, and J. Stewart. 1973. "Intentions and expectations in differential residential selection." *Journal of Marriage and the Family* 35 (July): 189–196. **209, 220**

Mileski, M. and D. Black. 1972. "The social organization of homosexuality." *Urban Life and Culture* 1 (July): 187–202. **111**

Milgram, S. 1970. "The experience of living in cities." *Science* 167 (March): 1461–1468. **30, 64, 187**

Milgram, S. et al. 1972. "A psychological map of New York City." *American Scientist* 60 (March-April): 194–200. **154**

Millon, R. 1967. "Teotihuacan." *Scientific American* (June); reprinted in K. Davis (ed.), *Cities.* San Francisco: Freeman (1973): 82–92.

Miner, H. and G. DeVos. 1960. *Oasis and Casbah.* Ann Arbor: University of Michigan Museum of Anthropology.

Mitchell, J. C. (ed.). 1969. *Social Networks in Urban Situations.* Manchester, Eng.: Manchester University Press.

Mitchell, J. C. 1970. "Africans in industrial towns in Northern Rhodesia." In W. Mangin (ed.), *Peasants in Cities.* Boston: Houghton Mifflin: 160–169.

Mitchell, R. E. 1971. "Some social implications of high density housing." *American Sociological Review* 36 (February): 18–29. **58, 162**

Mitchell, R. E. 1974. "Misperceptions about man-made space." *The Family Coordinator* (January): 51–56. **58, 155**

Mitchell, R. E. 1975. "Ethnographic and historical perspectives on relationships between physical and socio-spatial environments." *Sociological Symposium* 14 (August): 25-42. **158**

Mogey, J. M. 1956. *Family and Neighborhood.* London: Oxford University Press.

Molotch, H. 1969. "Racial integration in a transition community." *American Sociological Review* 34 (December): 878–893. **85, 185**

Montagu, A. (ed.). 1973. *Man and Aggression.* Second edition. New York: Oxford.

Morgan, N. R. and T. N. Clark. 1973. "The causes of racial disorders: A grievance-level explanation." *American Sociological Review* 38 (October): 611–624. **75, 133, 193**

Morris, D. 1968. *The Naked Ape.* New York: McGraw-Hill.

Morris, D. 1969. *The Human Zoo.* New York: McGraw-Hill.

Morris, R. N. 1968. *Urban Sociology.* New York: Praeger.

Morton, J. 1972. "Urban entrapment." Unpublished undergraduate paper. New York: Hunter College.

Muller, P. O. 1974. "Toward a geography of the suburbs." *Proceedings of the Association of American Geographers* 6: 36–40. **212, 213**

Mulvihill, D. J. and M. M. Tumin (co-directors). 1969. *Crimes of Violence: A Staff Report to the National Commission on the Causes and Prevention of Violence,* Vol. 12. Washington: U.S. Government Printing Office. **91, 92**

Mumford, L. 1961. *The City in History.* New York: Harcourt Brace Jovanovich. **77, 79, 170**

Murphy, R. 1954. "The city as a center of change: Western Europe and China." *Annals of the American Association of Geographers* 44 (December): 349–362.

Murray, E. and N. Hege. 1972. "Growth center population redistribution 1980–2000." In S. M. Mazie (ed.), *Population, Distribution, and Policy.* Vol. V, Research Reports, U.S. Commission on Population growth and the American Future. Washington: U.S. Government Printing Office: 183–227. **253**

National Center for Health Statistics (N.C.H.S.). 1967a. "Health characteristics . . . July 1963–June 1965." *Vital and Health Statistics.* Series 10, No. 36. Public Health Service. Washington: U.S. Government Printing Office. **53**

N.C.H.S. 1967b. "Suicide in the United States 1950-1964." *Vital and Health Statistics.* Series 20, No. 5.

N.C.H.S. 1968. "Trends in illegitimacy. United States—1940–1965." *Vital and Health Statistics.* Series 21, No. 15. **195**

N.C.H.S 1969a. "Chronic conditions causing activity limitations, United States—July 1963–June 1965." *Vital and Health Statistics.* Series 10, No. 51: Tables 2 and 14. **51, 53**

N.C.H.S. 1969b. "Family use of health services, United States—July 1963–June 1964." *Vital and Health Statistics.* Series 10, No. 55. **62**

N.C.H.S. 1969c. "Divorce statistics analysis." *Vital and Health Statistics.* Series 21, No. 17.

N.C.H.S. 1971. "Health characteristics . . . 1969–1970." *Vital and Health Statistics.* Series 10, No. 86. **53**

N.C.H.S. 1972. "Hearing levels of children by demographic and socioeconomic characteristics." *Vital and Health Statistics.* Series 11, No. 111. **51**

N.C.H.S. 1973. "Hypertension and hypertensive heart disease in adults." *Vital and Health Statistics.* Series 11, No. 13. **166**

Nayacakalov, R. R. and A. Southall. 1973. "Urbanization and Fijian cultural traditions in the context of Pacific port cities." In A. Southall (ed.), *Urban Anthropology*. New York: Oxford: 393–406.

Nelli, H. M. 1970. *The Italians in Chicago 1880–1930*. New York: Oxford. **130, 133**

Nelsen, H. M. and S. E. Storey. 1969. "Personality and adjustment of rural and urban youth." *Rural Sociology* 35 (June): 43–55.

Nelsen, H. M., R. L. Yokley, and T. W. Madron. 1971. "Rural-urban differences in religiosity." *Rural Sociology* 36 (September): 389–396.

Nelson, J. 1973. "Participation and college aspirations: Complex effects of community size." *Rural Sociology* 38 (Spring): 7–16.

Nelson, J. M. 1969. *Migrants, Urban Poverty, and Instability in Developing Nations*. Cambridge, Mass.: Harvard University Center for International Affairs Occasional Paper No. 22.

Nelson, S. D. 1974. "Nature/nurture revisited I: A review of the biological bases of conflict." *Journal of Conflict Resolution* 18 (June): 285–335.

Newman, O. 1973. *Defensible Space*. New York: Collier. **58**

Newman, W. 1976. "Religion in suburbia." In B. Schwartz (ed.), *The Changing Face of the Suburbs*. Chicago: University of Chicago Press.

Nie, N. H., G. G. Powell, and K. Prewitt. 1969. "Social structure and political participation: Developmental relationships, Part I." *American Political Science Review* 63 (June): 361–378.

Nisbet, R. 1967. *Community and Power* (original title: *The Quest for Community*). New York: Oxford. **113, 123**

Oelsner, L. 1971. "The world of the city prostitute is a tough and lonely one." *The New York Times* (August 9): 31–33. **110**

Ogburn, W. F. 1937. *Social Characteristics of Cities*. Chicago: International City Managers' Association. **211**

Ogburn, W. F. 1954. "Why the family is changing." In O. D. Duncan (ed.), *William F. Ogburn on Culture and Social Change*. Chicago: University of Chicago Press (1964): 174–186. **144**

Ogburn, W. F., and O. D. Duncan. 1964. "City size as a sociological variable." In E. W. Burgess and D. F. Bogue (eds.), *Urban Sociology*. Chicago: University of Chicago Press: 58–76.

Oi, N. Y., and P. W. Shuldiner. 1962. *An Analysis of Urban Travel Demands*. Evanston, Ill.: Northwestern University Press.

Pahl, R. E. 1970. *Patterns of Urban Life*. London: Longmans, Green. **226**

Palmore, J. A., R. E. Klein, and A. Bin Marzuki. 1970. "Class and family in a modernizing society." *American Journal of Sociology* 76 (November): 375–396. **146, 147**

Park, R. E. 1916. "The city: Suggestions for investigation of human behavior in the urban environment." In R. Sennet (ed.), *Classic Essays on the Culture of Cities*. New York: Appleton-Century-Crofts (1969): 91–130. **29, 108, 109, 112, 113, 138, 181, 184, 199**

Park, R. E. 1952. "The city as a natural phenomenon." In *Human Communities*. Glencoe, Ill.: Free Press: 118–127.

Park, R. E. and H. A. Miller. 1921. *Old World Traits Transplanted*. New York: Harper. **127**

Parsons, T. 1951. *The Social System*. New York: Free Press.

Pedersen, D. M. and L. M. Shears. 1973. "A review of personal space research in the framework of general systems theory." *Psychological Bulletin* 80 (November): 367–388.

Perlman, J. E. 1975. *Myths of Marginality*. Berkeley: University of California Press. **24, 80, 82**

Petersen, K. K. 1971. "Villagers in Cairo: Hypotheses versus data." *American Journal of Sociology* 77 (November): 560–573.

Petersen, W. 1961. *Population*. New York: Macmillan.

Pettigrew, T. F. 1967. "Social comparison theory." *Nebraska Symposium on Motivation*. Lincoln: University of Nebraska Press: 241–315. **64**

Photiadis, J. D. 1967. "Social integration of businessmen in varied size communities." *Social Forces* 46 (December): 229–236. **170**

Pickard, J. P. 1972. "U. S. metropolitan growth and expansion, 1970–2000." In S. M. Mazie (ed.), *Population, Distribution, and Policy*. Vol. V, Research Reports, U.S. Commi sion on Population Growth and the American Future. Washington: Government Printing Office: 127–182. **243**

Pickvance, C. G. 1974. "On a materialist critique of urban sociology." *The Sociological Review* 22 (May): 203–220.

Pilcher, W. W. 1972. *The Portland Longshoremen: A Dispersed Urban Community.* New York: Holt. **110**

Piliavin, J., J. Rodin, and J. A. Piliavin. 1969. "Good Samaritanism: An underground phenomenon?" *Journal of Personality and Social Psychology* 13 (December): 289–330. **187**

Pirenne, H. 1956. *Medieval Cities.* New York: Doubleday.

Plotnicov, L. 1967. *Strangers to the City.* Pittsburgh: University of Pittsburgh Press. **183**

Polanyi, K. 1944. *The Great Transformation.* Boston: Beacon. **27**

Polls. 1967. 2 (Summer). **21**

Pons, V. 1969. *Stanleyville.* London: Oxford University Press. **183**

Prabhu, P. N. 1956. "Bombay." In R. B. Textor et al., *The Social Implications of Industrialization and Urbanization: Five Studies of Asia.* Calcutta: UNESCO: 49–106. **133**

Prewitt, K. and H. Eulau. 1969. "Political matrix and political representation." *American Political Science Review* 63: 427–461. **103, 219**

Price, J. A. 1975. "U. S. and Canadian Indian urban ethnic institutions." *Urban Anthropology* 4 (Spring): 35–52. **135**

Provencher, R. 1972. "Comparisons of social interaction styles: Urban and rural Malay culture." In T. Weaver and D. White (eds.), *The Anthropology of Urban Environments.* Monograph 11. Washington: Society for Applied Anthropology: 69–76. **190**

Ramsøy, N.R. 1966. "Assortative mating and the structure of cities." *American Sociological Review* 31 (December): 773–786. **120**

Redfield, R. and M. Singer. 1954. "The cultural role of cities." *Economic Development and Cultural Change* 3 (October): 53–77.

Reed, R. 1975a. "Rural areas' population gains outpacing urban regions." *The New York Times* (May 18).

Reed, R. 1975b. "Influx of retired people to Ozarks a mixed blessing." *The New York Times* (May 19).

Rees, P. H. 1972. "Problems of classifying subareas within cities." In B. J. L. Berry (ed.), *City Classification Handbook.* New York: Wiley: 265–330. **46**

Riemer, S. and J. McNamara. 1957. "Contact patterns in the city." *Social Forces* 36 (December): 137–140.

Reiss, A. J., Jr. 1955. "An analysis of urban phenomena." In R. M. Fisher (ed.), *The Metropolis in Modern Life.* New York: Doubleday: 41–51. **34, 63, 100**

Reiss, A. J. 1959a "The sociological study of community." *Rural Sociology* 24 (June): 118–130. **6**

Reiss, A. J. 1959b. "Rural-urban and status differences in interpersonal contacts." *American Journal of Sociology* 65 (September): 182–195. **86, 139, 147, 182**

Reiss, I. 1967. *The Social Context of Premarital Sexual Permissiveness.* New York: Holt. **195**

Reissman, L. 1964. *The Urban Process.* New York: Free Press.

Reskin, B. and F. L. Campbell. 1974. "Physician distribution across metropolitan areas." *American Journal of Sociology* 79 (January): 981–998.

Revelle, R. 1970. "Pollution and cities." In J. Q. Wilson (ed.), *The Metropolitan Enigma.* New York: Doubleday Anchor: 96–143. **52**

Reynolds, P. D. and D. A. Blyth. 1974. "Sources of variation affecting the relationship between ˌlice and survey based estimates of crime rates." Paper presented to American ˌ ˌical Association, Montreal (August). **92**

B. M. 1973. "Urbanization and political participation: The case of Japan." ˌal Science Review 67 (June): 433–452. **104**

L. 1973. *The Economics of City Size.* London: Saxon House. **60,**

The Lonely Crowd. New Haven: Yale University Press. **172**

"The suburban sadness." In W. M. Dobriner (ed.), *The Suburban* Putnam: 375–408. **209, 229**

ˌer. 1968. *Aging and Society.* New York: Russell Sage. **62**

Roberts, B. 1973. *Organizing Strangers*. Austin: University of Texas Press. **144, 183**

Robinson, W. C. 1963. "Urbanization and fertility: The non-western experience." *Milbank Memorial Fund Quarterly* 41 (July): 291–308. **72**

Rogers, E. M. 1962. *Diffusion of Innovations*. New York: Free Press.

Roof, W. C., and R. L. van Valey. 1972. "Residential segregation and social differentiation in American urban areas." *Social Forces* 51 (September): 87–91.

Rosenthal, E. 1967. "Jewish inter-marriage in Indiana." *American Jewish Yearbook* 68: 243–264. **131**

Ross, M. et al. 1973. "Affect, facial regard and reactions to crowding." *Journal of Personality and Social Psychology* 28: 69–76.

Rossi, P. H. 1955. *Why Families Move*. Glencoe, Ill.: Free Press.

Rossi, P. H. et al. 1974. "The seriousness of crimes: Normative structure and individual differences." *American Sociological Review* 39 (April): 224–237.

Rotondo, H. 1962. "Problems psychologiques et de santé mentale resultant de l'urbanisation d'après des cas études au Perou." In P. H. Hauser (ed.), *L'urbanisation en Amerique Latine*. Liege, Belgium: UNESCO: 249–257.

Rotter, J. B. 1966. "Generalized expectancies for internal versus external control of reinforcements." *Psychological Monographs*. Whole No. 609. **170**

Rourke, F. E. 1964. "Urbanism and American democracy." *Ethics* 74 (July): 251–268. **16**

Rowe, W. L. 1973. "Caste, kinship and association in urban India." In A. Southall (ed.), *Urban Anthropology*. New York: Oxford: 211–250. **78**

Royal Commission on Local Government in England. 1969. *Report, Volume III: Research Appendices*. London: H.M.S.O. **102**

Schact, R. 1971. *Alienation*. New York: Doubleday Anchor.

Scherer, K. R., R. P. Abeles, and C. S. Fischer. 1975. *Human Aggression and Conflict*. Englewood Cliffs, N.J.: Prentice-Hall.

Schildkrout, E. 1974. "Ethnicity and generational differences among urban immigrants." In A. Cohen (ed.), *Urban Ethnicity*. London: Tavistock: 187–222.

Schiltz, T. and W. Moffitt. 1971. "Inner-city/outer-city relationships in metropolitan areas: A bibliographic essay." *Urban Affairs Quarterly* 7 (September): 75–108. **214**

Schnaiberg, A. 1970. "Rural-urban residence and modernism: A study of Ankara province, Turkey." *Demography* 7 (February): 7–85. **144, 146, 147**

Schnaiberg, A. 1971. "The modernizing impact of urbanization: A causal analysis." *Economic Development and Cultural Change* 20 (October): 80–104.

Schnore, L. F. 1957. "Satellites and suburbs." *Social Forces* 36 (December): 121–127. **211**

Schnore, L. F. 1963. "Some correlates of urban size." *American Journal of Sociology* 69 (September): 185–193. **47**

Schnore, L. F. 1965. "On the spatial structure of cities in the two Americas." In P. H. Hauser and L. F. Schnore (eds.), *The Study of Urbanization*. New York: Wiley: 347–398. **46, 214**

Schnore, L. F. 1967. "Community." in N. Smelser (ed.), *Sociology*. New York: Wiley: 100–102. **87**

Schnore, L. F. 1972. *Class and Race in Cities and Suburbs*. Chicago: Markham. **214**

Schnore, L. F., and H. H. Winsborough. 1972. "Functional classification and the residential location of social class." In B. J. L. Berry (ed.), *City Classification Handbook*. New York: Wiley: 124–151.

Schooler, C. 1972. "Social antecedents of adult psychological functioning." *American Journal of Sociology* 78 (September): 299–322. **170**

Schorr, A. L. n.d. *Slums and Social Insecurity*. Social Security Administration, Division of Research and Statistics, Report No. 1. Washington: U.S. Government Printing Office. **57**

Schorske, C. E. 1963. "The idea of the city in European thought: Voltaire to Spengler." In O. Handlin and J. Burchard (eds.), *The Historian and the City*. Cambridge: M.I.T. Press: 95–115. **16**

Schwab, J. J., G. J. Warheit, and C. E. Holzer III. 1972. "Mental health: Rural-urban comparisons." Paper presented to the Fourth International Congress of Social Psychiatry, Jerusalem (May). **168**

Schwab, W. A. 1968. "Oshogbo: An urban community?" In H. Kuper (ed.), *Urbanization and Migration in West Africa*. Berkeley: University of California Press: 85–109.

Schwartz, B. (ed.). 1976. *The Changing Face of the Suburbs.* Chicago: University of Chicago Press. **207**

Seeman, M. 1959. "On the meaning of alienation." *American Sociological Review* 24: 783–791.

Seeman, M. 1971. "The urban alienations: Some dubious theses from Marx to Marcuse." *Journal of Personality and Social Psychology* 19 (August): 135–143. **169**

Seeman, M. 1972. "Alienation and engagement." In A. Campbell and P. Converse (eds.), *The Human Meaning of Social Change.* New York: Russell Sage: 441–466. **170**

Seeman, M. 1975. "Alienation studies." *Annual Review of Sociology* 1: 91–124.

Seligson, M. A. 1972. "The 'dual society' thesis in Latin America: A reexamination of the Costa Rican case." *Social Forces* 51 (September): 91–98.

Selznik, G. J. and S. Steinberg. 1969. *The Tenacity of Prejudice.* New York: Harper.

Sengstock, M. C. 1969. "Differential rates of assimilation in an ethnic group: In ritual, social interaction, and normative culture." *International Migration Review* 3 (Spring): 18–32.

Sewell, W. H. and E. E. Amend. 1943. "The influence of size of home community on attitudes and personality traits." *American Sociological Review* 8 (April): 180–184.

Shack, W. A. 1973. "Urban ethnicity and the cultural process of urbanization in Ethiopia." In A. Southall (ed.), *Urban Anthropology.* New York: Oxford: 251–287. **146**

Sherrod, D. R. and R. Downs. 1974. "Environmental determinants of altruism." *Journal of Experimental Social Psychology* 10 (September): 468–479. **163**

Shils, E. 1962. "The theory of mass society." *Diogenes* 39 (Fall).

Short, J. F., Jr. 1971. "Introduction." In Short (ed.), *The Social Fabric of the Metropolis.* Chicago: University of Chicago Press. **29**

Shorter, E. 1971. "Illegitimacy, sexual revolution and social change in modern Europe." *Journal of Interdisciplinary History* 2 (August): 237–272. **195**

Shulman, N. 1972. *Urban Social Networks.* Ph.D. dissertation. University of Toronto. **137**

Sieber, S. D. 1974. "Toward a theory of role accumulation." *American Sociological Review* 39 (August): 567–578. **183**

Simic, A. 1973. "Kinship reciprocity and rural-urban integration in Serbia." *Urban Anthropology* 2 (Fall): 205–213.

Simmel, G. 1905. "The metropolis and mental life." In R. Sennet (ed.), *Classic Essays on the Culture of Cities.* New York: Appleton-Century-Crofts (1969): 47–60. **30, 138, 184, 187**

Simmel, G. 1950. "The stranger." In *The Sociology of Georg Simmel* (trans. by K. Wolff). New York: Free Press: 402–408. **83**

Sjoberg, G. 1960. *The Preindustrial City.* New York: Free Press. **42**

Sjoberg, G. 1964. "The rural-urban dimension in preindustrial, transitional and industrial societies." In R. E. L. Faris (ed.), *The Handbook of Modern Sociology.* Chicago: Rand McNally: 127–160. **196**

Sjoberg, G. 1965a. "Cities in developing and in industrialized societies: A cross-cultural analysis." In P. H. Hauser and L. F. Schnore (eds.), *The Study of Urbanization.* New York: Wiley: 213–263. **196**

Sjoberg, G. 1965b. "Theory and research in urban sociology." In P. H. Hauser and L. F. Schnore (eds.), *The Study of Urbanization.* New York: Wiley: 157–190.

Sklare, M., and J. Greenblum. 1967. *Jewish Identity on the Suburban Frontier.* New York: Basic Books. **222**

Slesinger, D. P. 1974. "The relationship of fertility to measures of metropolitan dominance: A new look." *Rural Sociology* 39 (Fall): 350–361. **72**

Smith, J., W. H. Form, and G. P. Stone. 1954. "Local intimacy in a middle-sized city." *American Journal of Sociology* 60 (November): 276–284. **139**

Smith, P. 1968. *As a City Upon a Hill: The Town in American History.* New York: Knopf.

Smith, R. J. 1973. "Town and city in pre-modern Japan: Small families, small households, and residential instability." In A. Southall, *Urban Anthropology.* New York: Oxford: 163–210.

Snyder, P. Z. 1971. "The social environment of the urban Indian." In J. O. Waddell and O. M. Watson (eds.), *The American Indian in Urban Society.* Boston: Little, Brown: 206–243.

Somer, R. 1969. *Personal Space.* Englewood Cliffs, N.J.: Prentice-Hall Spectrum. **157, 160**

Sorokin, P. A., C. C. Zimmerman, and C. J. Galpin. 1930. *A Systematic Source Book in Rural Sociology.* Minneapolis: University of Minnesota.

Southall, A. (ed.) 1973a. *Urban Anthropology.* New York: Oxford.

Southall, A. 1973b. "The density of role-relationships as a universal index of urbanization." In A. Southall (ed.), *Urban Anthropology.* New York: Oxford: 71–106. **182**

Spengler, J. J. 1967. "Africa and the theory of optimum city size." In H. Miner (ed.), *The City in Modern Africa.* New York: Praeger: 55–90. **250**

Spiegel, I. 1973. "Jews assay life in small towns." *The New York Times* (November 25): 53.

Spilerman, S. 1971. "The causes of racial disturbances: Tests of an explanation." *American Sociological Review* 36 (June): 427–442. **133, 193**

Srole, L. 1972. "Urbanization and mental health: Some reformulations." *American Scientist* 60 (September/October): 576–583. **166, 168**

Statistics Canada. 1973. *Crime Statistics 1971.* Ottawa: Information Canada. **89**

Stegman, M. A. 1969. "Accessibility models and residential location." *Journal of American Institute of Planners* 35 (January): 22–29.

Stein, M. R., 1960. *The Eclipse of Community.* New York: Harper. **102, 196, 226**

Stevenson, G. M., Jr. 1972. "Noise and the urban environment." In T. R. Detwyler and M. G. Marcus (eds.), *Urbanization and Environment.* Belmont, Cal.: Duxbury: 195–228. **50**

Stinchcombe, A. L. 1963. "Institutions of privacy in the determination of police administrative practice." *American Journal of Sociology* 69: 150–160.

Stokols, D. 1972a. "A social-psychological model of human crowding phenomena." *Journal of the American Institute of Planners* 38 (March): 72–83. **158**

Stokols, D. 1972b. "On the distinction between density and crowding." *Psychological Review* 79 (May): 275–278.

Stokols, D. 1974. "The experience of crowding in primary and secondary environments." Paper presented to American Psychological Association, New Orleans (September). **155**

Stokols, D. 1977. *Human Crowding.* Monterey, Cal.: Brooks-Cole.

Stokols, D. et al. 1973. "Physical, social, and personal determinants of the perception of crowding." *Environment and Behavior* 5 (March): 87–116.

Storr, A. 1968. *Human Aggression.* New York: Atheneum. **155**

Strauss, A. L. 1961. *Images of the American City.* New York: Free Press. **17**

Stueve, C. A., K. Gerson, and C. S. Fischer. 1975. "The structure and determinants of attachment to place." Paper presented to the American Sociological Association, San Francisco (August). **212**

Sundquist, J. L. 1975. *Dispersing Population.* Washington: The Brookings Institution. **155, 251, 252, 253**

Sutcliffe, J. P. and B. D. Crabbe. 1963. "Incidence and degrees of friendship in urban and rural areas." *Social Forces* 42 (October): 60–67.

Suttles, D. 1968. *The Social Order of the Slum: Ethnicity and Territory in the Inner City.* Chicago: University of Chicago Press. **85, 114, 132, 185**

Suttles, G. D. 1972. *The Social Construction of Communities.* Chicago: University of Chicago Press.

Swedner, H. 1960. *Ecological Differentiation of Habits and Attitudes.* Lund, Sweden: GWK Gleerup. **87, 144, 146, 175**

Szabo, D. 1960. *Crimes et Villes.* Paris: Cujas. **166, 167**

Taeuber, I. B. 1972. "The changing distribution of the population of the United States in the twentieth century." In S. M. Mazie (ed.), *Population, Distribution and Policy.* Vol. V, Research Reports, U.S. Commission on Population Growth and the American Future. Washington: U.S. Government Printing Office: 31–108. **73**

Tallman, I. 1969. "Working-class wives in suburbia: Fulfillment or crisis?" *Journal of Marriage and the Family* 31 (February): 65–72. **225**

Tallman, I. and R. Morgner. 1970. "Life-style differences among urban and suburban blue collar families." *Social Forces* 48 (March): 334–348. **219**

Tarr, J. A. 1973. "From city to suburb: The 'moral' influence of transportation and technology." In A. B. Callow, Jr. (ed.), *American Urban History.* Second edition. New York: Oxford: 202–212. **24, 209**

Tarrow, S. 1971. "Political involvement in rural France." *American Political Science Review* 65 (June): 341–357.

Tedesco, J. F., and D. K. Fromme. 1974. "Cooperation, competition, and personal space." *Sociometry* 37 (March): 116–121. **160**

Thernstrom, S. 1968. "Urbanization, migration and social mobility in the late nineteenth-century America." In B. J. Bernstein (ed.), *Towards a New Past: Dissenting Essays in American History.* New York: Pantheon: 158–175. **80**

Thernstrom, S. 1973. *The Other Bostonians: Poverty and Progress in the American Metropolis, 1880–1970.* Cambridge: Harvard University Press. **80**

Thomas, J. L. 1951. "The factor of religion in the selection of marriage mates." *American Sociological Review* 16 (August): 487–491. **131**

Thomas, R. 1969. *London's New Towns.* PEP Vol. 35, Broadsheet S10. London: Political and Economic Planning.

Thomas, W. I. and F. Znaniecki. 1918. *The Polish Peasant in Europe and America.* New York: Knopf (1927). **133**

Thompson, R. W. 1974. "Rural-urban differences in individual modernization in Buganda." *Urban Anthropology* 3 (Spring): 64–78.

Thompson, S. I. 1974. "The survival of ethnicity in the Japanese community of Lima, Peru." *Urban Anthropology* 3 (Fall): 243–261.

Thompson, W. R. 1965. *A Preface to Urban Economics.* Baltimore: Johns Hopkins University Press. **87**

Thompson, W. R. 1973. "A preface to suburban economics." In L. H. Masotti and J. K. Hadden (eds.), *The Urbanization of the Suburbs.* Urban Affairs Annual Review 7. Beverly Hills: Sage: 410–30. **216**

Thrupp, S. L. 1963. "The city as the idea of social order." In O. Handlin and J. Burchard (eds.), *The Historian and the City.* Cambridge: M.I.T. Press: 121–132. **18**

Tilly, C. 1965. *Migration to an American City.* Wilmington: University of Delaware Press.

Tilly, C. 1969. "Collective violence in European perspective." In H. Graham and H. Gurr (eds.), *The History of Violence in America.* New York: Bantam: 4–44.

Tilly, C. 1970a. "Migration to American cities." In D. P. Moynihan (ed.), *Urban America: The Expert Looks at the City.* Washington: Voice of America Forum Lectures: 171–186.

Tilly, C. 1970b. "Race and migration to the American city." In J. Q. Wilson, Jr. (ed.), *The Metropolitan Enigma.* New York: Doubleday Anchor: 144–169. **80**

Tilly, C. 1973. "Do communities act?" *Sociological Inquiry* 43: 209–240.

Tilly, C. 1974. "The chaos of the living city." In C. Tilly (ed.), *An Urban World.* Boston: Little, Brown: 86–107. **108, 193**

Tilly, C., L. Tilly, and R. Tilly. 1975. *The Rebellious Century.* Cambridge: Harvard University Press. **108, 109**

Tisdale, H. 1942. "The process of urbanization." *Social Forces* 20 (March): 311–316. **26**

Tobias, J. J. 1972. *Urban Crime in Victorian England.* New York: Schocken. **12, 89, 93**

Tomeh, A. K. 1964. "Informal group participation and residential pattern." *American Journal of Sociology* 70 (July): 28–35. **219, 223**

Tomeh, A. K. 1967. "Informal participation in a metropolitan community." *Sociological Quarterly* 8 (Winter): 85–102.

Tonnies, F. 1887. *Community and Society.* Translated by C. P. Loomis. New York: Harper (1963).

Treadway, R. 1969. "Social components of metropolitan population densities." *Demography* 6 (February): 55–74. **212**

Trice, H. M. 1966. *Alcoholism in America.* New York: McGraw-Hill. **167**

Turner, R. E. 1940. "The industrial city: Center of cultural change." In C. F. Ware (ed.), *The Cultural Approach to History.* New York: Columbia University Press: 228–242.

Useem, R. H., J. Useem, and D. L. Gibson. 1960. "The function of neighboring for the middle-class male." *Human Organization* 19: 69.

Valentine, C. A. 1968. *Culture and Poverty.* Chicago: University of Chicago Press.

van den Berghe, P. 1974. "Bringing beasts back in: Toward a biosocial theory of aggression." *American Sociological Review* 39 (December): 777–788. **156, 163**

van Es, J. C., and J. E. Brown, Jr. 1974. "The rural-urban variable once more." *Rural Sociology* 39 (Fall): 373–391.

Vatuk, S. 1972. *Kinship and Urbanization*. Berkeley: University of California Press.

Verba, S. and N. H. Nie. 1972. *Participation in American Life: Political Democracy and Social Equality*. New York: Harper. **218**

Verbrugge, L. 1973. *Adult Friendship Contact*. Ph.D. dissertation. University of Michigan.

von Rosenbladt, B. 1972. "The outdoor activity system in an urban environment." In A. Szalai (ed.), *The Use of Time*. The Hague: Mouton: 335–355. **216**

Walker, R. H. 1962. "The poet and the rise of the city." In A. B. Callow, Jr. (ed.), *American Urban History*. New York: Oxford (1969): 363–372. **17**

Wallace, K. 1975. "A fond look at the No. 30." *San Francisco Examiner Sunday Punch* (June 29). **86**

Wallden, M. 1975. "Activity patterns of urban residents: Part 2: The frequence of activities outside the home." *National Swedish Building Research Summaries* R9:1975. **216**

Walter, B., and F. M. Wirt. 1972. "Social and political dimensions of American suburbs." In B. J. L. Berry (ed.), *City Classification Handbook*. New York: Wiley: 97–123. **211**

Ward, D. 1971. *Cities and Immigrants*. New York: Oxford. **214**

Ward, J. 1972. "Peter Goldmark and the electronic rural society." *Intellectual Digest* (June): 82–84.

Ward, S. K. 1974. "Overcrowding and social pathology: A re-examination of the implications for the human population." Paper presented at the Annual Meeting of the Population Association of America, New York.

Warner, S. B. 1962. *Streetcar Suburbs*. Cambridge: Harvard University Press. **24, 44, 207, 209, 211**

Warner, W. L. et al. 1963. *Yankee City*. Abridged edition. New Haven: Yale University Press. **108**

Watson, O. M. 1972. "Symbolic and expressive uses of space: An introduction to proxemic behavior." *McCaleb Module in Anthropology* No. 20. Reading, Mass.: Addison-Wesley. **158**

Wattel, H. L. 1958. "Levittown: A suburban community." In W. M. Dobriner (ed.), *The Suburban Community*. New York: Putnam: 287–313. **229**

Webber, M. M. 1963. "The urban place and the nonplace urban realm." In *Explorations into Urban Structure*. Philadelphia: University of Pennsylvania Press.

Webber, M. M. 1968a. "Planning in an environment of change, I." *The Town Planning Review* 39 (October): 179–195. **123**

Webber, M. M. 1968b. "The post-city age." *Daedalus* 97 (Fall): 1091–1110. **244**

Webber, M. M. 1970. "Order in diversity: Community without propinquity." In R. Gutman and D. Popenoe (eds.), *Neighborhood, City and Metropolis*. New York: Random House: 792–811.

Webber, M. M. 1973. "Urbanization and communications." In G. Gardner, L. P. Gross, and W. H. Melody (eds.), *Communications Technology and Social Policy*. New York: Wiley: 293–304.

Wellman, B. 1972. "Who needs neighborhoods?" In A. Powell (ed.), *The City: Attacking Modern Myths*. Toronto: McClelland and Stewart: 94–100. **121**

Wellman, B. et al. 1973. "Community ties and support systems." In L. S. Bourne, R. D. MacKinnon, and J. W. Simmons (eds.), *The Form of Cities in Central Canada*. Toronto: University of Toronto Press. **121, 145**

Westergaard, J. H. 1966. *Scandinavian Urbanism*. London: Centre for Urban Studies.

White, E. B. 1949. "Here is New York." In O. Shoenfeld and H. MacLean (eds.), *City Life*. New York: Grossman (1969). **19**

White, J. W. 1973. *Political Implications of Cityward Migration: Japan as an Exploratory Case*. Sage Professional Paper in Comparative Politics 01–038. Beverly Hills Cal.: Sage.

White, M. and L. White. 1962. *The Intellectual Versus the City*. New York: Mentor. **16, 169**

Whitt, H. P. and H. M. Nelsen. 1975. "Residence, moral traditionalism, and tolerance of atheists." *Social Forces* 54 (December): 328–340.

Whyte, W. F. 1955. *Street Corner Society*. Enlarged edition. Chicago: University of Chicago Press. **114**

Whyte, W. H. 1956. *The Organization Man*. New York: Simon and Schuster. **209, 210, 229**

Whyte, W. H. 1968. "The case for crowding." In *The Last Landscape*. New York: Doubleday Anchor. **209, 253**

Wicker, A. W. 1968. "Undermanning, performance, and students' subjective experiences. . . ." *Journal of Personality and Social Psychology* 10: 255–261.

Wicker, A. W. 1969. "Size of church membership and members' support of church behavior settings." *Journal of Personality and Social Psychology* 13: 278–288.

Wicker, A. W. 1973. "Undermanning theory and research." *Representative Research in Social Psychology* 4 (January): 185–206. **155, 182**

Wilensky, H. 1964. "Mass society and mass culture." *American Sociological Review* 29 (April): 173–197.

Wilks, J. A. 1967. "Ecological correlates of crime and delinquency." In *Crime and its Impact—An Assessment*. Task Force Report of the President's Commission on Law Enforcement and Administration of Justice. Washington: U.S. Government Printing Office: 138–156.

Willbern, Y. 1964. *The Withering Away of the City*. Tuscaloosa: University of Alabama Press.

Willems, E. 1970. "Peasantry and city: Cultural persistence and change in historical perspective, a European case." *American Anthropologist* 72 (June): 528–544.

Willitis, F. K., R. C. Bealer, and D. M. Crider. 1973. "Leveling of attitudes in mass society: Rurality and traditional morality in America." *Rural Sociology* 38 (Spring): 36–45. **197**

Willitis, F. K., R. C. Bealer, and D. M. Crider. 1974. "The ecology of social traditionalism in a rural hinterland." *Rural Sociology* 39 (Fall): 334–349.

Willmott, P. 1963. *The Evolution of a Community*. London: Routledge and Kegan Paul. **225**

Willmott, P. 1967. "Social research and new communities." *Journal of American Institute of Planners* (November).

Wilson, J. Q. 1968. "The urban unease." *The Public Interest* 12 (Summer): 1125–1139. **84**

Winch, R. F. and S. A. Greer. 1968. "Urbanism, ethnicity and extended familism." *Journal of Marriage and Family* 30 (February): 40–45. **146, 147**

Wirt, F. M., B. Walter, E. F. Rabinovitz and D. R. Heusler. 1972. *On the City's Rim: Politics and Policy in Suburbia*. Lexington, Mass.: D. C. Heath. **229**

Wirth, Louis, 1928. *The Ghetto*. Chicago: University of Chicago Press (1956). **34, 127**

Wirth, L. 1938. "Urbanism as a way of life." *American Journal of Sociology* 44 (July): 3–24; Reprinted in R. Sennett (ed.), *Classic Essays on the Culture of Cities*. New York: Appleton-Century-Crofts (1969): 143–164. **27, 29, 100, 142, 164, 165, 170, 181, 185, 235**

Wirth, L. 1956. "Rural-urban differences." In R. Sennett (ed.), *Classic Essays on the Culture of Cities*. New York: Appleton-Century-Crofts (1969): 165–169. **7, 8**

Wolfgang, M. E. 1970. "Urban crime." In J. Q. Wilson (ed.), *The Metropolitan Enigma*. New York: Doubleday Anchor: 270–311. **92**

Wolfgang, M. E. and F. Ferracuti. 1967. *The Subculture of Violence*. London: Tavistock.

Wolfinger, R. E. 1965. "The development and persistence of ethnic voting." *American Political Science Review* 59: 896–908. **129**

Wood, R. C. 1958. *Suburbia: Its People and Their Politics*. Boston: Houghton Mifflin.

Wright, R. A. 1970. "Apartment living gaining favor in U.S." *The New York Times* (July 12): 1.

Wurster, C. B. 1963. "The form and structure of the future urban complex." In L. Wingo, Jr. (ed.), *Cities and Space*. Baltimore: Johns Hopkins Press: 73–101. **243, 245**

Wylie, L. 1964. *Village in the Vaucluse*. New York: Harper. **172**

Wylie, L. 1973. "The new French village, *helas*." *The New York Times Magazine* (November 25).

Wynne-Edwards, V. C. 1964. "Population control in animals." *Scientific American* (August); offprint No. 192.

Yazaki, T. 1973. "The history of urbanization in Japan." In A. Southall (ed.), *Urban Anthropology*. New York: Oxford: 139–162.

Yeates, M. H. and B. J. Garner. 1971. *The North American City*. New York: Harper. **62**

Young, M. and P. Willmott. 1957. *Family and Kinship in East London*. Baltimore: Penguin. **114, 145, 225**

Zelan, J. 1968. "Does suburbia make a difference?" In S. F. Fava (ed.), *Urbanism in World Perspective*. New York: Oxford: 401–408. **216, 220, 226, 229**

Zikmund, J., II. 1971. "Do suburbanites use the central city?" *Journal of American Institute of Planners* 37 (May): 192–195. **207, 216**

Zimbardo, P. G. 1969. "The human choice: Individuation, reason and order vs. deindividuation, impulse and chaos." In J. Helmer and N. A. Eddington (eds.), *Urbanman*. New York: Free Press (1973): 196–238.

Zimmer, B. G. 1975. "Urban centrifugal drift." In A. Hawley and V. Rock (eds.), *Metropolitan America in Contemporary Perspective*. New York: Halstead Press: 23–92. **24, 47, 207, 212**

Zimmer, B. G. and A. H. Hawley. 1959. "Suburbanization and church participation." *Social Forces* 37 (May): 348–354.

Zuiches, J. J. and G. V. Fuguitt. 1972. "Residential preferences." In S. M. Mazie (ed.), *Population, Distribution, and Policy*. Vol. V., Research Reports U.S. Commission on Population Growth and the American Future. Washington: U.S. Government Printing Office: 617–631.

INDEX

This is primarily a subject index, with a minimum of names. Readers can locate the page where a particular study is discussed by checking the bold-face page numbers at the end of the relevant entry in the References section beginning on page 276.